THE ROBERT KINSMAN
GUIDE TO
TAX HAVENS

THE ROBERT KINSMAN GUIDE TO TAX HAVENS

Robert Kinsman

Dow Jones-Irwin
Homewood, Illinois 60430

ISBN 0-87094-150-X
Library of Congress Catalog Card No. 77–90481

Printed in the United States of America

2 3 4 5 6 7 8 9 0 K 5 4 3 2 1 0

PREFACE

THIS BOOK was written to provide an explanation of the advantages and disadvantages of investing your money in countries where the tax laws appear to be more favorable than the tax laws of the United States.

The least you'll get out of this book is a secure knowledge that hiding money just is not for you, plus a number of interesting stories about how Big Dollars have been hidden (usually illegally and unsuccessfully), along with some delightful ideas for vacation spots. The most you will gain will be several concrete steps to take on the road to protecting your money from inflation, disregard of privacy, and fiscal mismanagement.

This book is not intended as a substitute for legal or investment counsel. It was written to help you discover what might be done to realize greater tax savings. It should give you enough background to better evaluate the tax counseling you receive. What you learn in this book should be applied to an actual situation in your real world only with the assistance of a qualified expert in federal taxation. Competent counsel will always be required in both the United States and the haven under consideration. Legal rulings must be verified and appropriate documents must be prepared. This book does not discuss specific investment opportunities, because the merits of any specific property, business, or security change too rapidly to be accurately described in a book.

I am most grateful to all of the people who assisted me in researching this subject, both in the United States and in each of the havens about which I have written. They are legion and to identify them would be impossible. However, special appreciation is acknowledged to Marshall Langer of the firm of Bittel, Langer and Blass who wrote the pioneering book on this subject (*How to Use Foreign Tax Havens,* 1975). Without that book and his advice, I would have floundered in a job similar to that of sweeping up smoke! My appreciation is also given to the many other tax attorneys who gave prompt and authoritative answers to many detailed queries. The time they gave me shortened my time on this project notably. To all,my sincerest thanks.

December 1977 ROBERT KINSMAN

CONTENTS

chapter 1

YOU CAN STILL HIDE MONEY

Over and over again courts have said that there is nothing sinister in so arranging one's affairs as to keep taxes as low as possible. Everybody does so, rich or poor, and all do right, for nobody owes any public duty to pay more than the law demands: taxes are enforced exactions, not voluntary contributions. To demand more in the name of morals is mere cant.

JUDGE LEARNED HAND

WHAT DO I MEAN by "hiding money?" Simply protecting it from anyone who covets it while it is *legally* yours, so that you may use it later or pass it to chosen beneficiaries. Hiding money is also the search for *legal* investment methods and locales that maximize money protection and privacy. It is a broad concept which is becoming increasingly important to all of us.

Writing about how to hide money is difficult for two reasons. On one hand it is a highly subjective matter, while on the other it can become breathtakingly complex. In the first case, how much money one has or realistically expects to have, where it is or will be located, the owner's level of investment sophistication, and his/her financial needs or problems are personal points difficult to generalize upon. In the second case, once the personal profile of a potential money hider is decided upon, the subject rapidly attracts an invisible hand: the United States Internal Revenue Service. It becomes a full partner to all considerations about legal money burying. To ignore it is folly. To invoke it bogs one down in a myriad of regulations, interpretations, and legal scrambles sufficient to glass over the eyes and fog the clearest of brains.

The man in the street hears little about this Scylla and Charibydis. Tons of paper are used to explain various aspects of money hiding tricks to tax professionals and practitioners, which they eke out to the rest of us at a price. Occasionally, whenever the number of persons affected by a given law or regulation reaches the millions, bits of information dribble out through various media and reporting services. This book will tell you in the plainest language possible what you'll need to know about legally hiding money outside the United States from anyone who has designs on it—*before* you start running up big legal, accounting, or psychiatric fees. I attempt to do so in a way which will not only reveal whether you should bother with this undertaking, but will also tell you what to do next if you should.

In short, this book is a full-flavor taste of what is involved with certain important methods of money hiding. It is emphatically not a comprehensive A–Z guide to all ways, means, places, and motives for money placement. It is also not a quick two-step guide that promises simple solutions to saving or gaining a fortune. As readers of those books have learned, there is no such thing. "If it's too good to be true, it isn't."[1]

---

[1] Ray Sommerfeld, *The Dow Jones-Irwin Guide to Tax Planning*, rev. ed. (Homewood, Illinois: Dow Jones-Irwin, 1978).

REASONS FOR HIDING MONEY

There is a dramatically increasing need to find secure and private means of money placement. Over the past decade three pressures have, in separate ways, made the search for secure money caches vitally important. Inflation is the most obvious of these and one which we will likely have to deal with for some time to come. Aside from an occasional "win" in the inflation battle, most of us have dealt with it by default: we've owned homes which have inflated through no shrewd selection, canny financing, or other indication of investment acumen. What's more, only rarely could equity in our homes be considered a part of our investable funds. True, some have found inflation protection in income property or collectibles such as stamps, coins, art, or antiques. But, if the well-publicized poor results of the nation's professional money managers are any indication, it appears that the best we can count on in dealing with this pressure in the future will be, as in the past, to receive part of inflation's bite back through modest investment returns and reduce a net loss in purchasing power. Whatever our success or lack of it, the inflation pressure is a key reason for locating secure, private, and viable money placements, especially if tax advantages are obtainable.

The second pressure is more insidious, but nevertheless steadily increasing. The trend in this country and most other industrial societies is to regard the accumulation of wealth as somehow sinful, as something done only by the oppressors of the masses. "Share the wealth" is the popular motto of those who hold this opinion. "Equality in poverty" has not yet become their catch phrase, but the trend in its direction is real. This pressure has generated an equal and opposite drive to find legal and secure ways to accumulate the capital that others want to see more "equitably" distributed.

Closely tied to this is a third pressure: an unmistakable diminishing of privacy in the use of our funds. The argument runs that if we are to share the wealth and the tax burden more fairly, we won't require secrecy in our financial dealings. Secrecy is only for those doing illegal things with their funds. (The ultimate end of this reasoning must be that, having accumulated little or no wealth, we will have nothing to deal secretly with.) We can observe how public our financial dealings in this country have become, when for ostensible reasons of tracking down underworld money and tax evaders (1) all of our checks in the amount of $100 or more are copied by our banks for possible use by federal agencies, (2) all personal and corporate transactions of $10,000 or more are reported automatically by the banks to the U.S. Treasury, (3) all movements of $5,000 or more out of the country are required to be reported, and (4) all foreign bank accounts and trusts are required to be reported to the IRS. If Representative Vannick, Chairman of the House Ways and Means Committee's Oversight Subcommittee, has his way with a bill before Congress, the taxpayer will face a civil penalty for simply not answering any question about foreign holdings on tax form 1040. Finally, the Treasury has the power to impose direct foreign exchange controls in the "national interest" to prevent outflows of capital to attractive foreign caches.

It is with these three pressures in mind that we begin a search for methods, means, and locales that are still available for secure money hiding. Now that the dust has settled from the Tax Reform Act of 1976, we can see that the legitimate use of foreign tax havens is one such method. Tax havens can be used to ease two of the pressures noted above, the social trend against capital accumulation and the reduction in financial privacy. And through their tax advantages, they mitigate the bite of inflation.

TAX SHELTERS AND TAX HAVENS

Some confusion exists between the definitions of tax "shelters" and tax "havens." Tax shelters are generally defined as tax loophole vehicles that provide opportunities for tax-advantage investments, anywhere, most often within the United States. Pure tax havens are countries having tax laws that exact little or no local tax and thereby permit accumulation of capital until it is returned to a high tax nation.

As Marshall Langer pointed out in his comprehensive but now regrettably dated book on tax havens, ". . . loopholes exist because governments, as a matter of tax policy, want them to exist to encourage one type of activity over another. . . . unintended loopholes sometimes arise, but these generally do not last very long unless there is some policy reason permitting them to continue."[2]

The Tax Reform Act of 1976 closed numerous loopholes in both the shelters and havens areas. Still, some large areas were left either unchanged or only slightly modified. Real estate in general and oil/gas were left least changed as investment vehicles with tax advantages (tax shelters). Tax haven use via foreign trusts and foreign corporations, narrowed in their usefulness to the general public, were harmed the least in concept. In fact, as we shall see, certain aspects of foreign trusts in tax havens were actually clarified and made more usable than before. The areas that came under strongest attack and got curbed most were the more "gimmicky" forms of tax *shelters*. Films, sports franchises, and equipment leasing loopholes were each notably changed. New specialized shelters such as these carry with them a high probability for future modification as well. However, unless further widespread abuse is found in the foreign trust and haven areas, it is the opinion of experts that these "loopholes" will continue to exist in largely their present form over the longer term.

---

2 Marshall J. Langer, *How to Use Foreign Tax Havens* (New York: Practising Law Institute, 1975).

THREE REASONS FOR TAX HAVENS

There are three principal reasons why tax havens exist; we will expand upon them in Chapter 3. First, every country is a tax haven to some degree, depending on whose taxes are being considered. This includes the United States. Foreigners leaving money on deposit in the United States are not required to pay any tax here on the interest earned, either by withholding or by direct levy. As public policy, this encourages foreigners to hold deposits in U.S. banks, and with our efficient capital markets provides an immense source of capital for this country. To change this condition would be highly disruptive to these major markets.

Second, tax havens exist because not every country has the same taxing ability or needs. The lack of natural resources, typical of most island tax havens, is a strong reason for offering foreigners tax incentives to invest, incorporate, or otherwise do business there. On the other side of the coin, to levy high personal tax rates on haven citizens would make no sense because it would raise virtually no revenue. The populations are too small in the first place, and would soon depart, in the second.

Third, large developed countries tolerate tax havens. They permit their citizens to utilize them, so long as the revenue runoff is not considered excessive and they are not used to evade domestic taxes. This tolerance often involves some form of quid pro quo. The examples usually cited in this regard are Liberia and Panama. U.S. shipping firms can substantially reduce their labor costs by registering ships there, without upsetting the labor situation for U.S.-registered ships. Moreover, the governments of both countries have agreed to make the U.S.-owned, foreign-registered ships available to the United States in event of national emergency.

These are the three strongest reasons why tax havens will continue to exist, and bode well for the likelihood (never a certainty) that U.S. citizens will be permitted to use them. However, U.S. tax law enforcement people have a great concern. That concern was put lucidly by the counsel to a congressional tax oversight subcommittee: "If you could establish havens in a fish bowl for legitimate tax avoidance, that would be fine. But now it's just as easy to evade taxes. Given human nature, the latter gets more emphasis." That is the reason, valid or not, why the government is scrutinizing tax haven use both through special projects and normal enforcement procedures. It is also the reason why we must become familiar with the complex rules of the Great Tax Game and their applicability to tax havens. To utilize tax havens in accordance with tax laws is a legitimate method of hiding money from the government. To use them to evade our tax laws is not.

chapter 2

THE GREAT TAX GAME

THE GREAT UNITED STATES TAX GAME has the world's largest playing team, 87.5 million of us. Its rules have been enshrined in virtually every American institution, including every church, corporation, foundation, union, and partnership. Its fundamentals are more or less understood by a majority of those who work for a living, and it has functioned, albeit somewhat haltingly, for over 70 years. Yet it is still one of the most mystifying, big-stakes, status-altering games we will ever be involved with in this life. What is more, none of us really plays it of his or her own free will, despite the fact that it operates under a "voluntary assessment" compliance system.

The Game's great battles are fought in terrain abundant with chasms, set with land mines of rulings ready to explode at the most critical moments, and covered with shifting mists of obscure language that seemingly blur every objective. The Game is presided over by a 535-member national Rule Making Body and 50 other lesser bodies, which change the rules at will and with frequency, usually giving relatively little notice to the players. Even the mere announcement that the Body is deliberating a point can constitute an effective rule change. Important arguments over the rules are continually going on among the leading players, usually dealing with what certain rules mean or were intended to mean. The outcome of the skirmishes will legally affect anywhere from one to 87.5 million other players, though they may not be directly aware of it.

The leading contenders in the nonstop debates form roughly two groups, one thought to be underpaid and overworked (on the government's side), the other allegedly well paid, sometimes enormously so (in the private sector) and, if not always overworked, certainly ready to be compensated as if it were. The groups generally oppose each other under our adversary system of law for immense stakes, on the order of $500 billion per year. Quite frequently smaller groups within the groups directly mistrust or oppose each other to such a degree that they carry on a whole series of internecine battles, usually to the detriment of most rank and filers.

Small wonder that the Great Tax Game is increasingly frustrating to its huge player armies, and that its changes of rules contribute mightily to the increasing complexity of our lives. Yet we play on with a modicum of grumbling, and only a small part of the complexity captures our collective consciousness.

In a very real sense, the Game has become legally so "appallingly complex" that the most proficient experts in the nation cannot fully grasp it.[1] The Committee on Taxation of the Bar of the City of New York observed in 1969 that "the U.S. Tax) Code is already far beyond the capacity of the great majority of tax experts . . . to understand sufficiently to allow accurate and forwardlooking tax planning." And that was *before* the Tax Reform Act of 1969, before DISC in 1971, ERISA in 1974, and the Tax Reform Act of 1976, the latter of which was understatedly referred to by a New York University law professor as "truly lovely in its baroque com-

[1] Remarks of Judge Tannewald, Ninth Seminar for Attorneys and Accountants, Jewish Community Federation of Cleveland, December 5, 1968.

plexity."[2] Each of these marvels of legislative genius has also quite accurately been described as "The Lawyers' and Accountants' Relief Act of—(year)." With a certainty equal to that of the sun's rising tomorrow, this same appellation will serve the next decade's tax "reform" legislation equally well.

Few persons would dispute the appalling complexity of our tax laws. That it required a document of over 1,000 pages to alter a small proportion of the Tax Code in 1976 should make the point abundantly clear. In fact, it has been abundantly clear for decades. Referring to the 1939 Code, Judge Learned Hand wrote:

> The words of such an act as the Income Tax merely dance before my eyes in a meaningless procession: cross-reference to cross-reference, exception upon exception—couched in abstract terms that offer no handle to seize hold of—leave in my mind only a confused sense of some vitally important, but successfully concealed, purport, which it is my duty to extract, but which is within my power, if at all, only after the most inordinate expenditure of time. I know that these monsters are the result of fabulous industry and ingenuity, plugging up this hole and casting out that net against all possible evasion; yet at times I cannot help recalling a saying of William James about certain passages of Hegel: that they were no doubt written with a passion of rationality; but that one cannot help wondering whether to the reader they have any significance save that the words are strung together with syntactical correctness.[3]

And *that* Code has not yet had foisted upon it the famous sentence of Sec. 341 (e) (1) added in 1958, which ran several times the length of the Gettysburg Address, let alone Subpart F of 1962, nor the ludicrous "reform" acts of 1969–76. Indeed, the experts have been increasingly admitting recently a

[2] James Eustice, "Tax Complexity and the Tax Practitioner," *The Tax Adviser,* January 1977, as reprinted from *The California CPA Quarterly,* September 1976.

[3] Quoted in Eustice, "Tax Complexity."

fact that we lower Game players have been feeling for some time. It was put most deftly in the academic manner by Professor Eustice: "Whole new courses in the tax curriculum may well be unteachable in a meaningful way, and I am omitting vast segments of the law that I can no longer stand, understand, or certainly communicate to my increasingly befuddled students."[4] He went on to say:

> . . . the day is not far away when a "master's" degree in tax law may require 10 or 15 years of concentrated study of the Code, regulations, rulings, and decisions (and by the end of such period, the law will have changed so much that the true tax student will have to start all over again to refresh his competence).

And only a handful of the great Tax Game players are willing students.

WHOSE OX IS BEING GORED?

For some deviously obscure reason, this matter of Tax Code complexity is now widely recognized by the great majority of Tax Game players, well noted by the experts, but remains unchanged.

The New York State Bar Association addressed itself to this problem in 1972, in "A Report on Complexity and the Income Tax,"[5] The 50-page study was widely acclaimed, and also widely ignored. It documented the very problem of social change through tax legislation that we noted in Chapter One, and delineated many of the causes and effects of tax law complexity about which we need a passing familiarity before plunging into the problems of foreign money placement. The Report dealt specifically with the taxpaying minority who receive income which is largely not subject to withholding (except those with their own corporations), who do not prepare their own returns, and who often require the advice

---

[4] Ibid.

[5] "A Report on Complexity and the Income Tax," New York State Bar Association, *Tax Law Review*, 1971–72, pp. 327–77.

of lawyers and accountants in tax matters. In short, the primary audience for this book.

The Report addressed the matter of complexity as having two elements: (1) those areas of the tax law where a reasonably certain conclusion cannot be determined despite diligent and expert research, and (2) the areas where a reasonably certain conclusion can be determined only after an excessive cost in time and money.

The first question the Report asked was whether it was important that only a minority number of taxpayers would, with an exception section of the Report, be affected by changes in areas addressed by the study. The answer went to the heart of the Tax Game: the morality of the system of tax collection and the wide public perception of how fairly it functions. "The self-assessment system demands that the majority of taxpayers retain some degree of confidence that they are paying no more than their fair share of the burden. We cannot accept with equanimity a breakdown in compliance by the minority, which *we believe may occur*." (Italics mine.) "Some assert," it went on, "that the public forms its views of our system of justice more from their direct contact with traffic court and negligence cases than from the decisions of the Supreme Court of the United States. In the same way, the tax system affects a wider swath of the public at a sensitive and very personal point for each of them. Their impression of the tax system results not only from its impact on them personally, but from what they hear and read about its impact on others. Thus, the integrity and fairness of the tax system is more significant than the substantial revenues it collects; any weakening of the fabric affects the attitude of the public toward the entire system of government."

In this regard, we might well wonder whether the rhetoric and publicity given to "reform" actions taken against "loopholes of the wealthy" may not be as pertinent to achieving apparent reform as the actual changes made. To portray loophole closing as a means of controlling the affluent may have as its primary objective the controlling of public perception of the fairness of the system as a whole. This may be one of the means of social pressure against wealth accumulation to which I referred in Chapter 1.

But does it matter in any case, since wealthier taxpayers have the means to hire expert tax help? The previous observations that the tax system is too complex for even sophisticated tax advisors provide an important answer.

For one thing, there is a cumulative effect of ambiguous tax laws whereby each new one compounds the degree of complexity of the overall Code. For another, development of the law after enactment, especially through Treasury Department regulations, does not serve to transform an ambiguous and complex law into a reasonably clear one. Cited in the Report in support of these points are Code sections dealing with collapsible corporations, section 341 (1950); mitigation of the statute of limitations, section 1311 (1938); small business corporations, subchapter S (1958); and subpart F, controlled foreign corporations (1962). All of these are still ambiguous today: "Neither regulations, nor litigation, nor age has ripened these provisions into readily ascertainable rules," observes the Report. What good does it do, in certain tax areas, to hire experts to read the unreadable?

Probably more significant are what the Report calls the "tax lottery" and "Gresham's Law of Tax Practice."

The tax lottery

The Report cites several factors which tend to work together to turn the wealthier taxpayer's tax return into something of a lottery: the complexity of the law itself, the manpower of the IRS devoted to the complexity, the inadequacy of audits, the impracticality of teaching revenue agents a largely unlearnable law, and the ability of the taxpayer to resolve in his favor a doubt arising from the complexity. In practice, the lottery proceeds as follows: "Will (my) return be selected for audit; if so, will the agent be sufficiently skilled to discover the doubtful issue; if so, can the issue be resolved by compromise on the basis of trial hazards; if not, will the government counsel make the telling contentions to the court; if so, will the court understand the issue?" The Report continues, "Thus, in numerous doubtful areas, the practice of tax law tends to descend to a level, not of what the law provides, equally applicable to all like taxpayers, but of what will be discovered in a particular return." The better-off taxpayer requires little expert assistance to proceed with his own lottery; the less conscionable among them run even better odds.

IRS Commissioner Jerome Kurtz has addressed himself to this lottery problem, identifying it as a major obstacle to making the IRS run more efficiently. Noting that the Service can only audit about 2.5 percent of the tax returns it receives, and about 10 percent of wealthier persons' returns, Kurtz has reportedly formulated a plan to get at the lottery. He would require "wealthy, sophisticated" taxpayers to disclose on their returns any disputed legal positions upon which their deductions and credits are based, thus allowing the IRS to challenge them. "If there's a legal dispute, then let's dispute it legally," he offers. "Let's not have a lottery first and then decide that we want to dispute it legally."

Kurtz admits the plan, if carried through, would likely provoke "screaming and yelling." It did, even on proposal, and six months later no formal implementation step had been taken. However, it did raise two important questions: what will be the definition of "wealthy, sophisticated" taxpayers? Recalling the controversy Mr. Carter stirred during the 1976 campaign in suggesting that wealthier persons were those with income above the median for the country, around $14,000 per year (later clarified to mean those well above that level), let us not call "wealthy" those persons with income in the $15,000 to $20,000 range. If this is the area with which the IRS wishes to deal, so be it; a term such as "upper middle income" would be more accurate and would get us away from the psychological attack on wealth accumulation referred to in Chapter 1.

Another query: what would constitute a "legal dispute" within the Commissioner's meaning—any tax issue before any court or only one on appeal? Would legal disputes include all Treasury regulations, IRS procedures, or rulings being disputed outside of court? A broad definition here might do much for the income levels of tax practitioners who would be hired to do more research, but would leave their clients less than enchanted, and in the process would delay or complicate further the mess we are presently dealing with. Another and even greater difficulty with such a definition is that it would virtually halt the use of any deduction or credit while it is in any form of dispute. The IRS could thus effectively stop the use of any part of the Code simply by disputing it; the legal process to resolution, unless specified to be via the Tax Court on a priority basis, could take a decade. One may readily doubt whether the IRS requires, or should be allowed, a power source of that magnitude.

Finally, would such a plan promote better tax advice or poorer? Here we come to Gresham's Law of Tax Practice, mentioned above.

Gresham's Law

Gresham's Law allows for the probability that "bad" tax advice tends to drive out the "good." "Where conscientious practitioners can advise on adverse tax consequences of a transaction with some degree of certainty," the Report states, "they can discourage clients from undertaking a transaction that is not based on a sound interpretation of the law. . . . If the law is uncertain in application, the conscientious practitioner is denied the opportunity of advising, with a reasonable degree of certainty, on the tax consequences. . . .

Simple economics must cause the 'bad' to drive out the 'good'; if the 'good' practitioner cannot achieve a reasonably certain conclusion, why pay the fees that are required to arrive at that uncertainty? The 'bad' practitioner can often reach the same conclusion at a lower cost. . . ." Indeed.

We will deal with the causes of Tax Game complexity and its implications for hiding money shortly. Before we do so, however, two other matters demand attention. What about the idea of tax law simplification for middle- or lower-income taxpayers? First of all, some progress has been made in this area since the 1972 Report. Such devices as the modest increase in both percentage and limit in the standard deduction with the attendant increased usability of Short Form 1040A have moved in this direction. This is one area where the Report's recommendations were partially heeded. However, a fundamental problem remains: simplification for middle-income taxpayers is largely concerned with returns and record keeping requirements, and with the frequency of IRS audits. Housekeeping chores, if you will. It is doubtful that much can be accomplished in these areas without a major overhaul of the whole system: substantial changes in standard deductions, as simple as they may appear to enact, raise substantial problems in revenue loss/recovery; record keeping affects both wealthier and middle-income taxpayers; return form changes and auditing requirements are largely a function of the other two. Room for change seems narrow.

In sum, it strikes me that the Report made a rather impelling case for action to deal with tax law complexity as applicable to better-off taxpayers. Since this group comprises over 65 percent of the Tax Game players (using as a measure those who itemized deductions on their 1976 returns), and certainly the more powerful and probably leading segment of our economy, the relevance of the Report's target is heightened. Simplification must attack the most complex areas of the law, and in so doing address itself to the stronger public opinion setters.

Reasons for the complexity

Thus far, in dealing with this tax complexity issue, I've ignored a second important problem: is the Great Tax Game so complex because our country and its systems are so complex? And, if that is true, can it ever be reasonably expected to change? A good case can be made in favor of the near impossibility of true simplification. Professor Eustice set the case quite well, in referring to the "built-in factors that are going to practically ensure a complicated tax system no matter what we do."

The sheer size of our country and the complexity of our society and economy may make a simple tax system out of the question. (Here we come across the chicken-egg problem: which first contributed to the growth of the complexity, society or the tax system? Probably both, alternately feeding upon each other.) The large sums at stake are inherently complicating. "The income tax system is composed of a multitude of 'debatable judgments' and compromises," Eustice observes, "arrived at within the matrix of a democratic form of government, which is *per se* a complicating process (or, stated differently, democracy is inherently one of the messier forms of government). Moreover, because of this 'largeness' of the general subject matter of our taxing system, and the breadth of its coverage, it is probably inherent in this process that there will always be a fundamental lack of national consensus as to who is going to be taxed and how much they are going to be taxed, and for that matter, how the money is going to be spent."

Eustice further identifies what he calls the structural or other unavoidable causes of tax complexity. "Our system has, for good or ill, chosen the income tax as its primary instrument of fiscal policy. It is a mass tax of extraordinarily broad coverage, applying to practically every person and to almost every conceivable transaction. That *per se* is going to create a complicated system because such an approach must answer the following questions (and must answer those questions repeatedly, on at least an annual basis):

"What is going to be taxed . . . when will the tax be levied . . . who is going to be taxed . . . and, how will the tax be levied, namely what is the rate of tax?"

Given this rather grim state of affairs, one can quite logically wonder whether there can be any escape. Eustice suggests facetiously that a moratorium on Congress, and if not that, at least "a truce or cease fire, for Congressional tax 'tinkering,' is both do-able and eminently desirable." But, alas, we now have the Carter Administration's efforts to save us from complexity. That should insure congressional tinkering until circa the election of 1980.

Fortunately, both Eustice and the New York Bar Association Report make significant suggestions for easing the complexity morass. To view these properly, we need to look a bit more closely at the perpetrators of the Tax Game complexity.

WHO CAUSED THE MESS?

Perhaps the solution to tax law complexity lies in identifying who or what caused it, and proceeding to attack the perpetrators. Certainly there is little doubt that anything as mired in complexity as the rules of the Great Tax Game was caused by more than one party. The Bar Association Report lays the blame at the feet of each group that determines the application of the tax law, which is to say, Congress, the private tax bar, the Treasury Department and IRS, and the courts. Regrettably, each of these groups has made its own special contribution, but a view of certain of their donations will be useful, as we'll see.

Battles within battles

The Leading Players in our Great Tax Game are undoubtedly the Rule-Making Body, otherwise known as Congress, and the Treasury Department with its subarmy, the Internal Revenue Service. (An army it is: 82,000 toilers and still increasing.) Anyone who has spent time in Washington dealing with any of these bodies cannot help but feel the aura of mistrust which pervades the dealings between Congress and the Treasury. Congressional committees, especially their staffs, worry that the Treasury and IRS will not interpret their laws in precisely the way intended. Result: add greater details and specifics to the law. Second result: complexity. On the other side, the Treasury has the job of proposing legislation sought by the administration in the tax area, to wit, the Carter Administration's tax "reform" package which seems most likely to introduce another new set of complexities. While the Congress slogs through this package, the Treasury people will hold some reasonable doubt about the passage of specific provisions. They will, if history is any guide, attempt to work their way in the direction of their proposals via new rulings, regulations, etc.[6] The inevitable result of this will be the opening of new litigation over the new regulations.

In other instances, the Treasury will push Congress for changes when the law is already too complicated for understanding. The Complexity Report notes that it was widely recognized that the law involving trusts was generally ignored because of auditing difficulties arising out of its complexity. But, through Treasury pressure in part, the 1969 Reform Act and the 1971 Revenue Act *added* complexities while trying to achieve substance.

Inexperience

Then there is the problem of inexperience. Not inexperience within a given profession, but inexperience with a pertinent problem in writing or enforcing a tax law. "Congress enacts laws with little regard to the necessity of the Service (IRS) to produce a comprehensible income tax return," the

[6] New York State Bar Association, "Report," p. 338.

Report observes, "and of the Treasury to issue regulations within the relatively short time before the law becomes effective." Not to mention the retroactive provisions in recent laws, notably the 1976 Reform Act. And the Report goes on to note the inexperience of both the Treasury and the tax bar in dealing with unsophisticated taxpayers and their advisors; their contacts are almost invariably with the most sophisticated. (It appears to me that they don't have time for the unsophisticated, largely because the unsophisticated don't have the money.)

Taxation as a social lever

Another important cause of complexity has been the use of the tax law by congresses and administrations for decades as a solution to nearly every social and economic blight imaginable. To note a few: income redistribution; subsidies for the blind, for the aging, and for homeowners; presidential campaign financing; low-cost housing; pollution control; and garden tool usage (H.R. 10612). Even more blatant are the anti-wealth measures of the minimum tax, preference income, and tax shelter curbs. "Surely there must be some limits to what this structure can carry," says Eustice. "It seems clear that these peripheral uses of the tax system have gone too far afield. . . ."

The limitations of Congress

Of course, it is Congress that is the greatest engine for change in tax laws. A first specific blame for Code complexity must reside on Capitol Hill. The initial problem with Congress and the tax laws, according to Eustice, is that few Congressional leaders understand the technical implications of the provisions they're writing. If the tax experts can't, how can a person in Congress who deals with energy problems one day, foreign policy the next, and health care another? Even long-standing members of the tax writing committees must have very limited knowledge of the interrelationships of one Code section, with which they have not tampered in several years, and one they are amending this week. Even if a given set of interrelationships could be firmly grasped, there is still the problem of Treasury housekeeping—i.e., that of drafting regulations designing a form, and setting audit standards. These, the experts say, are rarely on the congressional conscience.

But this is only part of the picture. Congress is not an initiator of tax legislation, except in rare instances. Its role is more like that of a referee in a public free-for-all. "Thus," notes Eustice, "the legislative process often degenerates into a wild, wide open free-for-all between sharply contending forces with Congress trapped in the middle. Sometimes they go this way, sometimes they go that way, and sometimes they even go their own way, which, of course, creates its own special difficulties."

A further congressional problem is a lack of time. While the average person may believe that laws proceeding through Congress move at just under a snail's pace, the fact is that tax laws, given their complexity, move with the speed of lightning. The required research can't be done. "It is easy," observes the New York Bar Association Report, "under such pressure, to fail to anticipate the need for more simplicity, to fail to anticipate the abuses to which a proposed provision is susceptible, and to fail to recognize the interrelationship of the section to the law as a whole." Add to this the oft-quoted chestnut that Congress legislates in haste and repents in leisure, and we have a tax law legislative condition which approaches the worst of all worlds.[7] There may be solutions, but no pragmatist would dare long dwell on them. Even Eustice's "cease fire" has been unarrangeable. Congressional tinkering with the Tax Code has been virtually nonstop for a decade, with a major new law every two years or so.

---

[7] Ibid., pp. 342–44.

Pressures on the Treasury

But there are other large hands in the pie. We have touched upon the Treasury's pressure role on both Congress and the Code itself, and must now provide for them an excuse, which in itself is a force for complexity: its battlefront is constantly being bombarded from several different directions. At any given moment, the Treasury is apt to be in combat with Congress, lobbyists, the tax bar, and even taxpayers (not counting internecine battles). Its subarmy, the IRS, tends to have it even worse because some administrations regard the Service as a handy source of manpower/womanpower trained in accomplishing unpleasant tasks. The IRS has been used as a *force majeur* against crime, against famous people (as in the White House "enemies list" of Watergate fame), and in enforcement of the wage-price freeze of 1971—all duties somewhat tangential to the administration of the tax system. "All of which," Eustice notes, "stretches even thinner what is already, to borrow a British phrase, 'a thin red line' between chaos and absolute confusion. Consequently," he goes on, "the administrators, even when they try to administer the system, do not always do so with the sensitivity to complexity problems that ought to be present."

An added problem here is what, for lack of a better name, may be called the "self-breeding" aspect of complexity. The IRS is caught between pressure for speedy decisions and promulgations of private rulings on one hand, and the need for clarity and soundness of these rulings on the other. Given the present state of affairs in which a private ruling may take anywhere from several months to several years, the IRS appears to have opted for clarity over speed. Yet the ruling history in some code areas has shown that clarity and certainty are not always gained by slowing down. A good example was the ambiguity stemming from a number of private rulings on the subject of "swap funds," which travelled a rocky road from 1962 to 1966 and ultimately had to be resolved by legislation.[8] In that case, a dawning recognition by the IRS of the importance and impact of the questions begat delay in a final ruling on the issues. This created both confusion and complexity for several years ultimately clarified only by Congress. No doubt the matter absorbed much IRS staff time in the interim, to the detrimental delay of other private ruling requests. The New York Bar Association Report suggests establishment of an IRS interim ruling procedure as one method of dealing with this problem: a small step to be sure, but at least one in the simple direction of self-assistance by the IRS.

The complexity/time problem has occasionally become ludicrous. A case in point is a dispute between the IRS and a Milwaukee man over his wife's estate. The argument went before the Tax Court.[9] At issue was a Tax Code life insurance marital deduction clause which could reduce the tax on monies paid to the surviving spouse. The IRS contended that $2,486 tax was due on $5,000 proceeds paid to the husband because of a provision in the law requiring insurance benefits to be payable within 13 months after the insured's death. The husband had waited 20 months to tell the insurance company how he wanted the proceeds paid, but contended the delay was necessary. The story concluded, "The (Tax) Court reminded the IRS that its regulations say the 13 month rule is met if the surviving spouse 'has the right to require payment' within 13 months of a spouse's death. The husband had this right when his wife died; he merely waited to exercise it. *The IRS's own regulation supports our conclusion and undermines the (IRS's) position, the court declared.*"

In sum, the Treasury and IRS additions to complexity fall principally in a time vs. clarity syndrome, one which seems unbreakable as Congress and the courts constantly pile more work in front of their staffs.

8 Ibid., p. 364.

9 *The Wall Street Journal,* November 22, 1976, p. 1.

AND WE'VE BEEN COURTED

Both the Report and Professor Eustice deal with the problem of the courts in creating complexity for players of the Great Tax Game, an area of specialized competence which I believe is best left to them, except to note that it is immense: one can easily spend eight to ten years and a virtually infinite number of dollars in pursuit of a final court decision in an important tax case. When superimposed upon the regulation, ruling, and procedure efforts of the Treasury and the IRS, which it must be, and seen as brought about partially by the existence of three tax trial courts and appeals to eleven different circuit courts, which have on occasion ruled differently on virtually the same set of circumstances, there can be little doubt that the judicial process in tax matters does much to foster mistrust and disbelief in the Tax Game. Eustice is blunt about it. "If you were to conceive of a judicial system more designed to create confusion, it would be hard to come up with a better one." He concludes, ". . . it is not surprising that the vast outpouring of tax law cases in certain areas tends eventually to become overwhelming to the point of near meaninglessness."

Mercifully, there is one court in the tax procedure which works to speed up the tax process, both for average persons and for giant corporations. Called simply the U.S. Tax Court, it will hear cases for only a $10 filing fee, frequently in one day's time, doesn't require that only attorneys present cases before it, and either directly or via its small tax division, will hear cases involving any sum. The only requirement is that a taxpayer must have gone through the full IRS appeals process and wish to postpone payment of the disputed tax before litigation. Since some 97 percent of the disputes with the IRS are settled before litigation, however, the Tax Court doesn't become involved as often as one might expect from its simple, quick procedure. Nevertheless, the Tax Court is handling a rapidly increasing volume of business: 11,000 cases were filed there in 1976, a 30 percent increase in two years.

Cases handled by this court can become bizarre.[10] A restaurateur claimed the care and feeding of two Russian wolfhounds as a business expense for adding chic to his place of business. A young man disputed an IRS requirement for a self-employment tax while earning his entire income of $9,000 per year betting at race tracks five days a week. And a lawyer claimed depreciation on his cocktail table, maintaining it was crucial to his business. All of these cases were heard by the Tax Court and ultimately upheld there or on appeal to a Circuit Court of Appeals.

It seems, in fact, that there is only one problem with this court. In fiscal year 1976, taxpayers won their disputes in only 11 percent of the cases heard. The other 89 percent were either compromises or outright IRS victories. That problem notwithstanding, at least the Tax Court is a force operating against the complexity process in our courts. It appears to stand alone in the otherwise ever-deepening Tax Game whirlpool.

A GROWTH INDUSTRY?

A final generator of Tax Game complexity is what has become the "tax industry," the apparently steadily expanding number of persons who make their living from interpreting, advising, representing, and arguing the complexities of the Code for the "uninformed" taxpayer in any of the forums previously noted. This industry includes the tax bar (attorneys involved in tax practice), accountants, CPAs, and other para-professional tax advisers. It is hard to estimate precisely the number of persons working in this industry, or the sums they earn for their services. While most CPAs, accountants and H & R Block category strivers fit clearly within the

[10] *Newsweek,* April 4, 1977, p. 82.

tax industry, attorneys and general advisers have a tendency to moonlight in other endeavors, or deal in tax matters part time. Only a portion are truly tax specialists, although with the likes of ERISA and the 1976 Tax Reform Act, it would certainly appear that the temptation to increase income from tax-related matters could grow exponentially. However, the mere existence of this growing industry is *prima facie* evidence of one of the larger problems in the Tax Game: the more complex the law becomes, the more people and time required to deal with it, and the more people who will find it rewarding to do so. Because these are generally bright persons, they will discover loopholes and means of getting through them, which in turn requires still more effort by the Treasury/IRS, the courts, and all too often, Congress. The tax industry is the private side of the expanding battlefront noted earlier.

A second aspect of the industry problem is the "perverse joy" many practitioners find in mastering some obscure and detailed aspect of the Code, and then pursuing it to great heights of gamesmanship with administrators, other practitioners, and the courts.[11] While this may eventually result in serving a client well, it effectively keeps the practitioner away from concerns of overall Game complexity. In fact, the adversary legal system is designed quite well never to question the system *in toto,* but rather to focus entirely on the skirmish at hand, on winning as the only worthwhile objective, both financially and egotistically. In fact, it could be well argued that to concern a tax lawyer with the public problem of legal complexity overall is bad for business. (Unless someone pays for it, *per se.*) That this process contributes neatly to the burgeoning complexity of tax laws through neglect of the broad problem by those most capable of solving it, is almost a self-evident truth.

Other perversions follow. Professor Eustice: "To some extent, I think it (Code complexity) at least makes the legal

[11] New York State Bar Association, "Report," p. 367.

and accounting profession virtually malpractice proof; you cannot be guilty of malpractice here if you, or anyone else, cannot understand what it is you did, or failed to do." A marvelous plus for the industry, obviously.

All of this leads to two conclusions about the tax industry. First, that there is an increasing tendency for the tax practitioner to give up intellectually on some provisions of the law, and make a go/no-go decision based on fear or a client's lack of patience and/or funds ("We just won't try this tricky transaction"), or based on the lottery approach ("Let's try it and see what happens"). Either course is lamentable. They both aid the operation of Gresham's Law.

Secondly, with "Lawyers' and Accountants' Relief Acts" cascading out of Congress biennially, and the Great Tax Game already fiendishly snarled, it is difficult to imagine the tax industry undertaking a major public interest stance for simplicity at the risk of losing significant business. It is the private industry equivalent of Parkinson's Law of expanding bureaucracy. To appeal to a broad public interest as an alternative to more income, however modest, is not a course to which capitalistically oriented humans are inclined.

CHANGING THE RULES

Now that we have got a moderate grip on the facts of how and why the Great Tax Game exists, I would be remiss, as somewhat of a student of the subject, if I didn't suggest a few methods for improvement in the Game rules. My proposals are culled from and expand upon those of the New York Bar Association and Eustice, but they reflect what a Small Player believes might actually work. In setting them down, I establish myself as an expert in the mode suggested by Eustice: "a person who avoids the small errors as he sweeps on to the grand fallacy."

For Congress: While likely to be resisted, perhaps mightily, by the Administration, it seems the time is long overdue for a formally established agency under the direct control of Congress to deal with both tax revision and new proposals, plus congressional education.[12] If set up similarly to the recent Office of Economics, such an entity, if properly staffed, would do fundamental tax simplification research, research on new tax proposals, and periodic review of existing statutes for substantive change. This "Office of Tax Control" should be advised by a panel of leading tax practitioners and academicians to bring the tax industry's public interest capability to bear on both current law complexity and future law proposals. To give the Office adequate stature, Congress should not permit passage of any new tax legislation until a thorough review of the most complex areas of the current law is completed and recommendations are made for simplification. A similar process should be completed for any new proposals. Current efforts in this area by the Joint Committee on Taxation and the Treasury have certainly not been fruitful to date.

One idea to be considered early-on by such an Office should be a "split-tier" tax system.[13] It would provide a simple tax computation for a solid majority of taxpayers on either a mandatory or an optional basis. This would take the form of a more flexible standard deduction, with a specified floor under certain deductions. Those persons unwilling or unable to use the split-tier system would be left to play the Great Tax Game. To be meaningful, this simple tax would need to be made attractive to the widest possible number of taxpayers, including those who now significantly rely on itemized deductions. A phasing in of the system might be necessary to allay concern over revenue loss, but it could go far in giving an increasingly irritated public a better tax concept to live with. The attendant decrease in need or inclination to play tax lottery, and with it a decrease in IRS audit workload could measurably ease the Tax Game's cur-

[12] Ibid., p. 349.

[13] New York State Bar Association, "Report," p. 33.

rent complexity. In any case, it would make much sense if carried forward under a banner other than preventing the wealthy from playing "tax lottery." It should be far broader based than that.

For the IRS: Eustice's suggestion for development of a series of IRS-approved forms for taxpayers to utilize with given transactions, makes sense. The IRS has clearly developed a great many forms, but they are all *reporting* forms, those used with returns. Would it not also be appropriate for the Service to develop a series of (hopefully) simplified record-keeping and transaction forms which taxpayers could rely on, when fully filled out, as being acceptable proof of the given transaction? They need not even be government printed; a master form for each transaction would be grabbed by the publishing industry as a nifty new source of revenue, even at relatively low cost to the taxpayer. Such transactions as business entertainment, sick pay and medical expenses, and, pertinent to our area of discussion, proper record-keeping forms for foreign bank accounts and trusts are high on the list. I have yet to understand why the latter must be reported in detail and sent to the IRS. Would it not involve less IRS paper handling and be just as effective if a simple box could be checked on a Form 1040 return and the taxpayer required, if audited, to produce the master record form? This would, additionally, place the burden of honesty on the taxpayer. If he or she wanted to be in full compliance and safe in case of audit, the form would be filled out and even authenticated, if necessary, and held with other records. If the detailed form was not available on audit, the taxpayer would be in trouble; if presented, properly completed, the person would be in the clear.

I suspect the IRS has not done this in the past out of the belief that taxpayers would not fill out the record forms at time of the transaction. But, since it is quite permissible for a taxpayer to reconstruct records, so long as they are properly verifiable, *when* it was done is irrelevant.

I believe that in trade for the certainty that a given transaction was proper, taxpayers would be less inclined to play lottery. Why attempt deviousness when, by obtaining the required information, one can be certain of compliance? It is the lack of certainty that one is complying that is a major cause of lottery playing. When one doesn't know what will be accepted as adequate proof of a given transaction, as in many areas of the complex Code which we have previously noted, then one is tempted to play lottery. When increased certainty can be obtained, the only reason remaining for lottery gamesmanship must be that the transaction was improper in the first place. This could be discovered quite quickly on audit.

Indeed, the audit process itself could be simplified by the use of standard, approved record forms. Take, for example, the long-embattled child support verification needed to determine which parent gets the child's tax exemption. If a simple form were required to be signed by both parents verifying which received the exemption, a single query on the tax return would establish a basis for audit: "Is Reporting Form XYZ available: Yes–No–. Name and Address of Parent Not Claiming Exemption———." Those checked "No" could be flagged for audit. Those checked "Yes" could be sample-audited with a simple letter to *both* parents requiring presentation of their copies of the form. Upon signature verification, the sample audit would be completed. Without doubt, the IRS could audit far more returns on this question than it can through the present method of either personal interview or more complicated record submission. The added certainty offered the taxpayer, for both the positive and negative responses, would decrease the interest in playing lottery. True, it might increase the temptation for outright lying, but that's perjury. More importantly, the IRS could sample-audit many more returns by mail than it can presently. With thorough publicity of a change to the suggested form well in advance of the actual requirement, both added compliance and greater certainty would result. And that's what the issue of Tax Code simplification is all about.

A naïve suggestion

Of course, it may be said that our total discussion about the need for Tax Code simplification, and especially the recommendations for change, addressing as they must many details, begs the question. One might wonder whether we shouldn't start with a whole new system. There must be days when literally thousands of persons in this country wish that it were possible. Venturing for a moment into the realm of the impossible, we might consider the Swiss tax system as a replacement for our own.

On the surface, the two systems are not greatly dissimilar. Both require annual declarations of income, both have specified deductions, both have progressive rates of tax, and both have federal and local taxes. But the systems differ mightily in practice. The Swiss system presumes taxpayer honesty. Ours presumes, or at least mightily suspects, dishonesty. As the counsel to a House of Representatives subcommittee frequently dealing with the tax laws put it, "Our tax system is based on voluntary compliance. The only way to make that more effective is through increased *fear.*"

Contrast that with the Swiss tax system which does *not* require that verification of earnings be submitted with the tax declaration if one is self-employed. In practice, many persons do submit verification, since Swiss tax authorities are well aware that all corporations must prepare wage statements similar to our W-2 forms, and self-employed persons submit supporting verification to avoid an inquiry. The point is that the individual's signed declaration is the legal requirement, similar to a customs declaration. Thus, when a Swiss taxpayer submits a declaration, the Swiss tax bureau will accept it if it is at about the level or above that normal for a person of his position or type of work. Each Swiss taxpayer earning over

SFr. 3,000 annually, or about $1,200, submits such a declaration. "The main difference between the U.S. and Swiss tax systems," points out Alfred Matter, Central Manager of Swiss Credit Bank's Zurich main office, "is that the Swiss government cannot ask a bank or any other third party for proof of income." A tax situation which accepts self-declaration with some evidence supporting it, but which is unverifiable through third parties, offers the strongest form of support to honesty. It might even end Kurtz's lottery problems. Moreover, the top combined tax bracket, including federal, cantonal, and church taxes is 40 percent, and that is reached at the SFr. 250,000 level ($100,000 a $.40 per franc).

The obvious advantages of the Swiss tax system to the government are relatively low administrative costs and a high degree of certainty of income. It may well be argued that in a country the size of Switzerland with a population about that of Los Angeles County, such a system is workable, whereas in the United States with 35 times as many people it is not. Clearly, the job of categorizing millions of occupations by locale to determine proper earning levels would be staggering. But one wonders whether its cost in time and money wouldn't be made up very rapidly in reduced enforcement and haggling expenses every year. Not counting the multitude of benefits flowing from the attendantly simplified tax return preparation process. But then, it is all a naive idea. The resistance to such a change would be altogether stupefying. Still, one wonders.

THE HAVEN CONNECTION

As I observed earlier in this chapter, our discussion of Tax Game complexity is a way of gaining perspective on the Code sections affecting tax havens. From this perspective we will be able to understand what has happened to them: their misuses, legal uses, and future use potential. Without knowing, for example, that Tax Code Subpart F, the one dealing with controlled foreign corporations, is still one of the most ambiguous in the whole Code, one will be dangerously unaware of the potential problems in this area. At the same time, to view the Code portions affecting havens from a purely technical standpoint is to become involved in a discussion that is so involuted and caveated as to be only of use to tax industry experts, and then probably only on the occasion when a client demands an explanation while in some form of catatonic tax collapse.

What most of us need to know is whether tax havens are still usable, still legal, still acceptable. Or are we headed for an audit, jail, or purgatory in using one? In short, are they still OK? (They are, but not for the broad population.) In sum, we must look at havens in sufficient detail to gain an awareness of the problems in dealing with them, but not so deeply as to make this a tax attorney's handbook. Another example: It is sufficient for you to know that lawyers are still arguing about the tax angles involved with a grantor trust (one of the important devices in tax haven use), rather than to understand fully the merits of each legal position. What you need to know is whether you should ask your attorney about grantor trusts. We will generalize sufficiently about them to give you guidelines. And we'll give your attorney a few points to ponder as well. It is between the precipice of too deep involvement on one hand, and the rocks of too little knowledge on the other, that our investigation must proceed. This chapter has provided an aerial view of the rock and chasm road ahead. We now need to walk the edge of the precipice to view tax havens in general.

chapter 3

BEHIND IT ALL

ANY TAXPAYER'S interest in finding a safe haven for capital must be motivated, at least in part, by the facts behind the chart in Figure 3–1.[1] Those diagonal lines, much resembling a driven rain, specify the twin effects of those great destroyers of capital, taxes and inflation. Following the captioned instructions, you will discover just how devastating they truly are. For example, if you invest in a security or deposit yielding a *money* return (cash) of 10 percent per year in an inflationary climate of 6 percent per year, when your federal and state combined top tax bracket is 40 percent, your real return is *zero*. Increase the inflation rate to 8 percent *or* your top bracket to 50 percent and you'll be *losing* money on a 10 percent yield investment. For lower initial yields, both the inflation rate and top tax bracket can be lower and you'll still lose money.

For most investors in the 70s, this twin-barreled affect has been accepted to the point of trying to minimize the loss or taking lower tax-exempt yields. One exception seems to have been real estate, but often the true after-tax effect less inflation is not fully considered. The chart is the simplest reminder of the magnitude of the need to shelter income from taxes.

---

[1] Marcia Stigum, *How to Turn Your Money into More Money* (Homewood, Illinois: Dow Jones-Irwin, 1976), p. 13.

FIGURE 3–1

Real after-tax rates of return (r) on a security paying a 10 percent money rate of return. To find your real return, draw a line upward from your marginal tax rate, then draw a line across the page from the current inflation rate. Where these lines intersect is your real return (r) on a 10 percent cash yield.

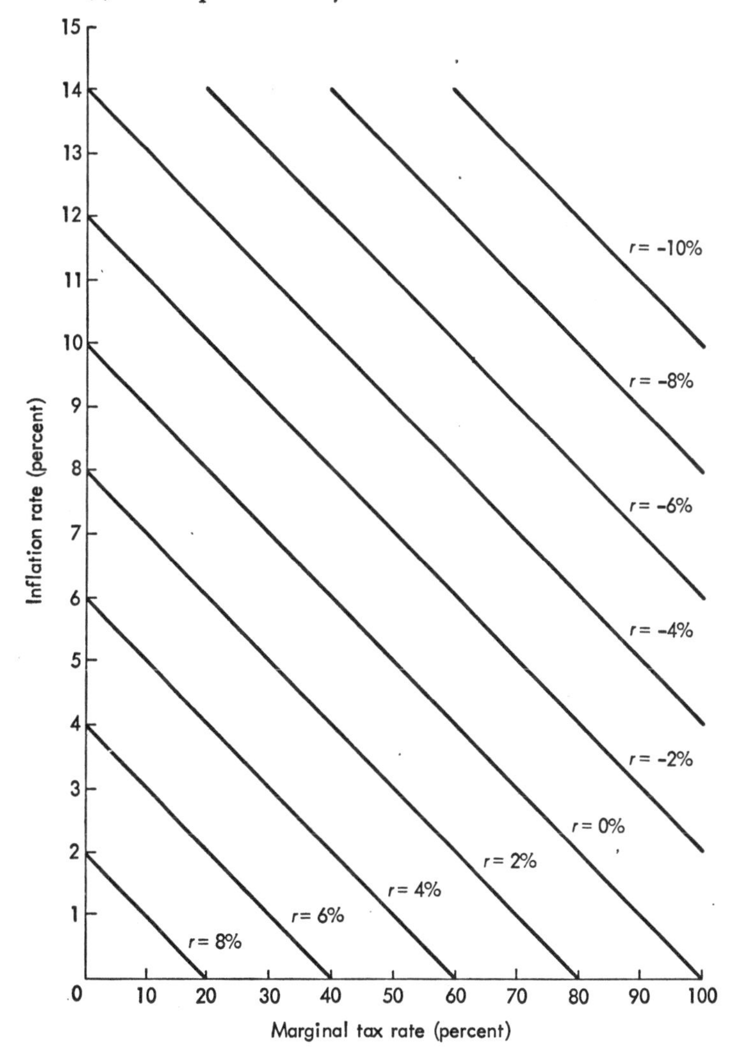

As it has with domestic tax shelters, the Tax Reform Act of 1976 has done much to make a positive investment return difficult via tax havens. Difficult, but by no means impossible. What we witnessed in the passing of that Act was a change in U.S. congressional/governmental tolerance of tax havens, allegedly because of their widespread abuse. The stories of abuses are legion; we'll look at a few of them. But parenthetically, it is also possible to wonder whether the government's measures against this tax loss have been worth the effort.

Some estimates have put the amount of illegal U.S. funds hidden through tax havens at a size sufficient to have deprived the government of some $2 billion in income taxes. And yet efforts to collect this through numerous means, most prominent of which is the IRS Project Haven, have produced a very small bang for the buck. In the ten-year history of that project through November 24, 1975, some $50.1 million was recommended for collection or actually assessed, but only $14.4 million had been collected. IRS resources and costs: $1.5 million. Net gain: an average of about $1.3 million for each year of the project. At that rate it would take 154 years to collect the full estimated loss.

The IRS has persuasively argued insufficient personnel and inadequate laws as reasons for not accomplishing the task. In any case, the 1976 Reform Act did strengthen the Service's hand against haven users. But perhaps the problem calls for more than putting new strictures in the law. In the last chapter we dealt with what may also be the fundamental difficulty here: the tax law's complexity itself. One assessment of the situation was made by a source close to the Miami Grand Jury investigation of the alleged misuse of the Castle Bank of the Bahamas, who reportedly observed that the 18-month probe may wind up with no one being indicted because of the complexity and confusion of the U.S. tax laws.[2] Small wonder that the line between the outright

[2] *The Miami Herald,* March 10, 1977, p. 2–B. (Author's note: In September 1977, the U.S. Department of Justice confirmed that one indictment had been made by that grand jury.)

tax evader and the honest taxpayer legitimately trying to beat the devastation portrayed in Figure 3–1 is deeply blurred. This chapter will attempt to define the edges of that fuzzy line as it applies to tax havens.

First, we need to know why tax havens exist and what they really are. For example, when many nations are able to levy income taxes at confiscatory rates above 50 percent, why should any country wish to forego this marvelous revenue source and consider itself a tax haven, or more gently, an "offshore financial center?" Simply because high tax rates may not work effectively in smaller, resource-deficient areas. The citizenry might well consider doing what the Mayans are said to have done, and wander off into the jungle to avoid payment. Second, a resource-deficient nation needs to promote industrial development, or at least commercial/tourist growth to provide adequate jobs and incomes for its citizens. (One characteristic of tax havens is that they are almost always small in area, often island-states.) Offering tax incentives to foreign residents to establish companies is one natural solution to the problem. In addition, the direct need for capital to establish a viable "financial intermediary" industry, which in turn can lend or invest in new enterprises in the haven nation, is a primary force. Capital is attracted through banking and trust services, sometimes insurance companies, and smaller investment firms. It shouldn't be surprising, therefore, that most havens have a relatively large financial intermediary community. It is a prime source of internal funding, attracted from external sources. Each of these reasons and often a long tradition of tax-free development work in favor of the tax haven concept. Directly offsetting these apparent advantages is the prevalent mundane need to impose a substantial revenue-raising apparatus of some kind. Most often this has taken the form of high import duties on goods/services brought into the tax haven. The average import duty in the Bahamas is now about 35 percent, for example.

If a smaller, resource-limited nation can find advantages in offering a tax haven status, the next question follows: why do industrialized neighboring countries permit the haven to attract capital from their shores if they must chase it later? Again, there are sensible reasons, despite the rather clear trend in many industrialized nations to diminish haven attractiveness through anti-avoidance tax legislation. Britain, the United States, and France are generally considered the leaders in this dubious distinction.

If we observe the fact that every country is a tax haven to some degree or another, we come to the first answer to this toleration query. The United States, probably the least frequently thought of as a tax haven, does indeed attract capital through a tax-free incentive: it does not impose an income withholding tax on the interest paid to foreigners on their U.S. bank accounts. Whatever foreigners do about reporting this nontaxed income to their governments is their business. But the policy amounts to a tax incentive to leave funds in the U.S. With this imported capital figure now in the range of $100 billion, if we include the foreign branches of U.S. banks,[3] one can conceive of certain significant damage to capital availability from foreign sources if a direct tax were imposed on such funds. The outflow could be monumental. Thus the condition of the capital market is one important consideration in large industrialized nations' tolerance of tax havens. Then too, if the United States offers tax advantages to attract capital, it cannot logically (although that may be irrelevant) attempt to deny the same methods to small offshore neighbors.

A more persuasive argument in the capital market reasoning comes from the need of large corporations in the industrialized nations to raise funds in foreign markets. Clearly, if this can be done by offering some sort of tax incentive, foreign lenders will be less chary of offering their funds than if the reverse were true. Yet, if the borrowing company's country does not permit tax-free payment of interest or dividends,

---

[3] *Federal Reserve Bulletin,* December 1976, pp. A63, A71.

(the United States has a 30 percent withholding rate), a different method of accomplishing this purpose could gain much for the borrower. Many firms have found the means through an offshore subsidiary which issues debt instruments from a tax haven. The haven permits the company to pay tax-free interest, or at worst, provides for its recapture through a double taxation treaty. The industrialized nation tolerates this rather modest loss of revenues instead of altering its existing withholding rate or tax structure. So, altogether, capital market considerations have become a major justification for tax havens.

We have additionally noted in Chapter 1 a third reason for the existence of tax havens, the mutual accommodation between larger nations and the havens, as for example that enjoyed by U.S. shipping companies in Panama and Liberia as a *quid pro quo* for a U.S. merchant marine fleet-in-being in event of a U.S. national emergency.

If the havens have reasons for existence interrelated with large nations, however convoluted they may be, we must wonder why governments are concerned with the havens at all? An obvious answer lies in that $2 billion allegedly missing from U.S. tax revenues. The theory is that abuse follows quickly in the footsteps of use. This concept flies under a more or less patriotic flag. Its banner argument was put to me directly by a House of Representatives subcommittee counsel with many years of experience on the Hill. "We have a very dangerous thing here in the misuse of tax havens," he observed. "Once we have a mass movement in this direction, then we have a mass ripoff of the U.S. Treasury."

One might question just how "mass" the movement might ever become, but nevertheless that's the popular argument for the long reach of Uncle Sam's arm. (There are other legal arguments for the case, as we'll see.) Bolstering his point, counsel added, "once you're dealing with human nature and the door is open to do something illegal, chances are that once people know someone else is doing it, they'll do it too." That concept, of course, leaves us with the fascinating task of legislating morality by Tax Code, or, at a minimum, enforcing some perception thereof.

The fact of the matter is that the United States is one of only two nations which tax their citizens wherever they are and however they earn their income, simply for the privilege of being citizens. (The other, the Philippines, learned this handy gambit from us.) Tax experts call this "taxation on all jurisdictional bases." The United States taxes both domestic and foreign income of its citizens, no matter where they reside. It taxes resident and nonresident aliens on their U.S. income, and even goes so far as to tax nonresident aliens on their foreign income if it is directly connected with running a U.S. trade or business. That must be considered the longest of long reaches. And it gives the government a perfectly marvelous reason for caring about what goes on in tax havens used by U.S. citizens. What is more, this "all bases" taxation principle has been long established in law. Marshall Langer, in his book *How to Use Foreign Tax Havens* (1975), offers an intriguing insight into the court case establishing the principle.

> The Supreme Court has held that the United States has the power to tax its citizens on their worldwide income solely by reason of their citizenship. (*Cook* v. *Tait,* 265 U.S. 47, 1924). . . . The amount in controversy was less than $300 which Cook had paid out of a total assessment of less than $1,200. The tax involved was levied at rates between 4 percent and 8 percent under the Revenue Act of 1921. One must wonder whether the Supreme Court would have reached the same decision had the tax rate been 50 percent or more.[4]

Apparently no enterprising attorney has been willing to test that decision with the larger tax rate numbers of recent

---

[4] Marshall Langer, *How to Use Foreign Tax Havens* (New York: Practicing Law Institute, 1975), p. 78.

decades. At least, none has taken a case back to the final judicial jurisdiction.

CHOOSING THE HAVEN

The next tax haven facet we must address is a very fundamental one: how to usefully categorize them for selection purposes. In the broadest sense, a tax haven is any nation that offers tax incentives to its own or foreign citizens to do business within its borders. Unfortunately, that parameter leaves us with a list of most nations of the world. Such smaller countries as Ireland and Sri Lanka have tax incentives for writers and artists. Puerto Rico, Thailand, and a dozen other countries have incentives for promotion of industrial plants. The United States has its bank deposit interest lure for foreign capital. Countries as large as Canada and Venezuela were good corporate tax havens a couple of decades ago, but are no longer. We need a narrower definition.

Going to the other end of the scale, we can begin with nations which now have no income or capital taxes of any kind, and proceed up the scale to the lowest levels of taxation. This provides a more manageable list of about a dozen and a half countries.

No-tax countries	*Low-tax countries*
Bahamas	Bermuda
Cayman Islands	Netherlands Antilles
Turks and Caicos islands	Channel Islands
New Hebrides	British Virgin Islands
Nauru	Monserrat
	Panama
	Liechtenstein
	Monaco
	Bahrain
	Hong Kong

It is with this grouping that we can deal most effectively, keeping in mind that under one's personal or corporate circumstances, the use of other national jurisdictions might become appropriate. Indeed, tax status itself is a sometime thing. While certain countries guarantee tax-free status to certain entities, that is, Cayman Islands for nonexempt companies and Bermuda for exempt firms, even long-standing policies are subject to change. Bermuda, for many years considered one of the best no-tax jurisdictions, enacted a hospital tax based on company employee income in 1976. The 1.5 percent rate was barely enough to notice, but it applies to exempt firms' employees as well as to local firms'. The intriguing method: assignment of a *national* salary resulting in a tax of $270 per year per employee for exempt firms. This is a sufficient problem in tax status planning to technically remove the island from the no-tax group. However, as this tax is not a tax on the *company's* income, Bermuda's no-tax guarantee for exempt firms stands until the year 2006. Technically speaking.

TABLE 3–1
Tax haven comparison table (ideal = 5.0)

	Bahamas	*Bermuda*	*Cayman Islands*	*Channel Islands*	*Liechtenstein*	*Nauru*	*New Hebrides*	*Turks and Caicos*
Accessibility (from U.S.)	5.0	5.0	4.0	5.0	3.5	2.0	2.0	3.0
Communications	5.0	5.0	4.5	4.5	4.5	2.0	3.0	4.0
Foreign exchange freedom	4.5	4.5	4.5	4.0	4.5	4.5	4.5	5.0
Government stability	4.5	4.5	5.0	5.0	5.0	4.5	4.5	4.5
Government attitude	4.5	4.0	5.0	5.0	4.0	3.5	5.0	5.0
Language	5.0	5.0	5.0	5.0	4.0	4.5	4.5	5.0
Laws	4.5	4.0	5.0	4.0	4.0	4.0	4.5	4.5
Professionals	5.0	5.0	5.0	5.0	5.0	2.0	3.0	3.0
Operating conditions	4.0	4.5	4.5	5.0	4.5	3.0	4.0	4.0
Racial matters	4.0	3.5	5.0	5.0	5.0	4.0	4.0	4.0
Disclosure	4.5	4.5	5.0	4.5	5.0	4.5	4.5	4.5
Special factors	4.5	4.0	5.0	4.5	4.0	4.0	4.5	4.5
Totals (60.0 possible)	55.0	53.5	57.5	56.5	53.0	42.5	48.0	51.0

BROAD CRITERIA

The tax haven table compares a number of the most important general criteria in tax haven selection for several of the most widely used havens. It does not attempt to rank the criteria themselves in order of importance, but rather the relative strength of each haven per criterion. Precise differentials between any of the havens must be relative to your personal circumstnces and what you wish to accomplish in their use. To attempt to erect a fence around all of these considerations without knowing what you might require would be a waste of time. This must be left to you and your attorneys, who are familiar with your means and goals, with the applicable U.S. tax laws, and with the laws of the havens under consideration. Moreover, it is frequently wise tax planning to make use of more than one haven for a given transaction or series of them. Thus the table can be considered no more than a broad guide. We make no implied or definitive recommendations for any of the havens. In Chapter 7 we'll deal in broader brush strokes with the specific advantages of several other important jurisdictions.

The selection criteria require only brief comment.

Accessibility refers to the ease with which one can travel to and from the haven from the United States. Frequency and comfort of transportation schedules are primary.

Communications are a vital consideration for any jurisdiction, and takes into account telephone, telegraph, telex, and mail service.

Professionals deals with the availability and number of serious professional persons and institutions in the haven, including lawyers, accountants, and financial intermediaries.

Racial considerations are important in many of the havens. Several have widely mixed racial make-ups, a potential factor in the stability of the country. This is closely related to the criteria of *Government Stability* and *Government Attitude* toward the tax-haven function. No truly attractive haven can include a significant measure of instability or negative government posture toward tax matters. Tax haven planning is a long-term process which becomes considerably more expensive and time consuming if the haven user must face long-term problems with the local government. Certain havens are better programmed in this respect.

Language is of obvious assistance if the primary or secondary means of communication is English. The same applies to *Laws:* Where based on English common law, certain entities such as trusts will be far more workable than if based on European civil codes. The companies' laws of each nation can add to complexities where they are archaic or involuted. Most are, even when based on British systems.

Foreign Exchange Freedom refers to ease of capital entry and exit. Exchange controls make life more difficult in certain nations, although they are subject to change and can be adequately dealt with where they have existed for a period of time.

Operating Conditions refers to the business climate in the haven especially as it affects ease of entry, size of market, and profit potential.

Trusts refers to the availability of the trust form of tax entity, a concept unknown in civil law but most useful under certain circumstances in English law.

Disclosure is an important privacy consideration, and refers to requirements for public disclosure of companies' financial statements and records. Lack of a substantial disclosure requirement is an advantage in privacy.

Special Factors is a catch-all category covering such diverse legal requirements as pre-incorporation screening, the existence of special exempted entities, banking secrecy laws, and availability of bearer shares.

A brief perusal of the table reveals the relative attractiveness of the Bahamas and Cayman to the other havens listed, despite certain Bahamian weaknesses in government attitude, exchange control, tax guarantees, and racial matters. Both havens share a notable weakness in business operating conditions, Cayman because of its lack of domestic market and the Bahamas because of its business operating restrictions on foreigners. Note that this latter criterion is ranked generally low for all havens, however.

The Turks and Caicos, Nauru, and New Hebrides are not strong in most categories due largely to their remoteness and size. Only the government attitude is truly strong in two of these islands.

We have arbitrarily selected four havens, two each from the no-tax and low-tax groups, for a more detailed discussion of laws, advantages and disadvantages, and specific comparisons. Our concentration will be on the Bahamas, Cayman and Channel Islands, and Liechtenstein as representative types. The table's cumulative totals for the four havens reveal the principal reason for our focus: relatively good rankings in each criterion under consideration.

Further exploration of the correct haven or havens for your particular goals now must be expanded to a discussion of the most usable tax haven vehicles, and of what has occurred to their viability as a result of the Tax Reform Act of 1976.

CONSIDERING A VEHICLE

A wide range of vehicles exist that can be used to obtain the tax benefits of the havens noted above. Again, they will become relatively attractive or unattractive depending upon your personal circumstances and goals. Their review should be undertaken with counsel; we can note here only the broad types of vehicles and general considerations for their use in the various havens.

Among the more esoteric of these vehicles are the international finance subsidiaries of U.S. corporations; banks and trust companies; shipping companies; captive insurance companies; finance companies; and various types of holding companies including special investment companies. As these are highly specialized, they will be useful under circumstances peculiar to a limited number of persons or U.S. corporations. Trusts, general businesses, and trading companies will find wider usefulness and be treated in more detail.

International finance subsidiaries (IFS) of U.S. corporations are those which are principally engaged in the business of raising capital for the U.S. corporations' foreign subsidiaries and affiliates. An IFS is usually an arm of a large multinational corporation and arranges debt financing abroad, often through Eurodollar bond issues. Countries usually considered for establishment of these entities are the Netherlands Antilles (due to its favorable tax treaty with the United States), Bermuda, the Channel Islands, and Luxembourg.

Banks and trust companies have been the most prolific in taking advantage of haven tax breaks in recent years, with the result that many havens are overflowing with offshore banking subsidiaries or locally incorporated entities. Their advantages are in their ability to pay tax-free deposit interest, their direct participation in international corporate financing and their use to establish trusts and companies in the haven for external customers.

Shipping companies, long given substantial tax and nontax advantages through registry in shipping havens such as Panama and Liberia, have come under significantly penetrating new restrictions in the Tax Reduction Acts of 1975 and 1976. Highly complicated tax considerations now apply in this area, which has never been straightforward. Despite this, the Bahamas, Cayman, and Bermuda are attempting to increase business in this specialized area.[4]

Captive insurance companies are well known to persons

---

[4] For a more detailed discussion, see Roy A. Povell's articles "New Developments in Foreign Flag Shipping" and "Tax Planning for a Foreign Flag Shipping Company" in *Foreign Tax Planning, 1977,* Course Handbook Number 106, Practicing Law Institute, New York, pp. 379–402 and 443–488, respectively.

involved in large corporate self-insurance programs and the insurance industry generally, but are little known outside. Their concept is simple: Why pay an outside insurance company substantial premiums to insure certain risks of a corporation's subsidiaries and affiliates, when that corporation has large amounts of cash flow and can calculate its risk experience and statistical potential as well as an insurance company can? Add in the fact that establishment of a self-insurance reserve is not usually tax deductible in any country, while a fair premium paid even to a related company has been a deductible expense, and we see why captive insurance companies became highly attractive to major corporations. However, in recent years the IRS has attempted a crackdown under IRC para. 162 over the deductibility of the premiums paid to captives. Attorney Marshall Langer advises in his excellent book on havens that "anyone setting up a pure captive to insure its foreign affiliates must now do so with the expectation of probable litigation on the subject with the IRS." Also, captive insurance of U.S. risks runs afoul of IRC Subpart F convoluted language. When captives have been found useful, Bermuda has been the most important haven used.

Holding companies are among the most popular general-use vehicles in tax havens, but it is important to distinguish among the various types since different laws apply. Also, foreign holding companies lose tax benefits for U.S. companies if they receive income from a personal holding company or income which qualifies the foreign company as a personal holding company. (Any other "tainted" income specified in Subpart F is equally destructive of tax advantages. But personal holding company considerations are more likely here.) The no-tax havens will generally provide the most advantageous situations for use of holding companies, as will those nations involved in double taxation treaties, which also have low taxes on domestic holding companies, such as the Netherlands Antilles, the British Virgin Islands, and Montserrat.

Finance companies in general, as distinguished from the international finance subsidiaries noted above, are usually a form of holding company established within a multinational company group to hold debt instruments, and occasionally stocks of other companies. A differentiation between interest and dividend income is usually important. Double taxation treaties again offer the primary advantages here, with the Netherlands Antilles a prime candidate haven.

Investment companies are usually differentiated from holding companies in an important way as far as many national laws and treaties are concerned. The distinction is one of passive versus active voice in operation of the companies in which investments are made. The passive role, that of a portfolio investor, is generally descriptive of an investment company, in contrast to the active participation in management made by typical holding companies. This distinction will cause disqualification of investment companies under the otherwise liberal holding company law of the Netherlands Antilles. Investment companies privately owned by individuals or families may be taxed as foreign personal holding companies under Subpart F. Those publicly held usually fall into the category of open-end mutual funds where shares are redeemable, or in jurisdictions where this is not permissible, such as those following British companies laws, they are in some form of unit trust arrangement. Real estate holding companies form a special category, often dependent on treaty potentials.

As can be readily determined from the foregoing, these forms of tax haven vehicles have innate requirements which cannot be met by most persons, or even most companies, considering tax haven use. Sizable capital blocks are required for nearly all of them, plus either a good deal of expertise in day-to-day operation, or a direct involvement with a large corporate group.

One other type of vehicle is also specialized, but may be more appropriate in that both capital and expertise requirements are diminished. When patents, copyrights, trademarks, and royalties are involved, such as in films, video programs, records, and the like, establishment of companies to receive the funds generally makes sense in havens where tax treaties exist. The three Caribbean havens, the Netherlands Antilles, British Virgin Islands and Montserrat are interesting in this regard.

It is important to note, as we have stressed, that several of the foregoing tax vehicles, as well as other considerations we will discuss shortly, involve the use of tax treaties to gain tax benefits. As in the case of patents, copyrights, and royalties, these treaties can offer significant tax advantages when properly used. However, this whole area is in the process of major change, both favorably and unfavorably for the tax vehicle user, as a result of the Treasury Department's stated intention to begin negotiations with nearly all of its tax treaty partners based on the U.S. Model Income Tax Treaty released by the Treasury on May 18, 1976.[5] A half dozen new treaties were pending before the Senate Foreign Relations Committee in the spring of 1977, including those with the U.K., Philippines, Egypt, Israel, and South Korea. Under negotiation were treaties with France, West Germany, Italy, Spain and several developing countries.

An additional word of caution is appropriate here. The IRS position on "shopping" for a country in which to establish a treaty advantage corporation appears negative. As one attorney put it, "this is a cutting edge of new efforts by the IRS." At least one court case has bolstered this opinion. However, in one recent IRS ruling, Revenue Ruling 75–23 regarding the Netherlands Antilles treaty, the IRS appears to take a position favorable to "shopping." *Caveat emptor.*

U.S. tax laws are reasonably favorable to investors engaging directly in business abroad such as trading, providing services, manufacturing, or mining, where permitted

---

[5] See the copy of the Model Treaty with comments by Perry A. Lerner in *Foreign Tax Planning, 1977,* pp. 495–561.

by local laws, and even when the three-country or triangle approach is being used. (The triangle business, involving the so-called vector theory, begins with Country X, the place of residence/citizenship of the investor, proceeds to Country Y, where the investment is actually made, and then to Country Z, the tax haven where a corporation is established to make the investment.)

In general, the U.S. taxes domestic companies on their worldwide income, but not on their foreign-source income, except in certain cases arising out of the five sources of "tainted income" described by Professor Harvey Dale of New York University as the "pentapus" of IRC Subpart F or as specified in TRA 1976.

The pentapus will cause U.S. tax liabilities to the U.S. company or investor if the foreign corporation can be considered any of the following:

1. A foreign investment company as defined by Internal Revenue Code pars. 1246–47.
2. A personal holding company as defined by IRC pars. 541–47.
3. A foreign personal holding company as specified in IRC pars. 551–58.
4. A controlled foreign corporation as detailed in IRC pars. 951–64, or
5. The foreign corporation falls into the definitions contained in IRC pars. 531–37 when it is subject to an accumulated earnings tax.

The Tax Reform Act of 1976 made a number of detailed changes in Code provisions affecting businesses abroad, but they were largely of a technical nature. In summary, they include:[6]

---

[6] *Tax Reform Act, 1976, Provisions Affecting Business* (New York: Price Waterhouse & Co., 1976), p. 8, and *Provisions Affecting Income Earned Abroad,* pp. 19–22.

1. A controlled foreign corporation was given two new exemptions from investments it may make in U.S. property without subjecting its U.S. shareholders to U.S. tax: (1) stocks or obligations of domestic corporations where that company is not a shareholder in the foreign corporation nor owned nor controlled over 25 percent by the foreign corporation's U.S. shareholders, and (2) certain resource development equipment used in waters above the U.S. continental shelf.
2. Credits against U.S. income tax for company taxes paid in foreign countries and losses incurred there continue deductible, but the U.S. owner must use the overall method of computing the amount, not the country-by-country method.
3. Earnings of U.S. corporations operating in Puerto Rico and U.S. possessions can be repatriated tax free.
4. Two special forms of overseas companies, Domestic International Sales Corporations and Western Hemisphere Trade Corporations, were made substantially less attractive through lessening of tax deferral and increased tax rate, respectively.
5. Corporations are now taxed on foreign bribes paid by controlled foreign corporations and related DISCs. Participation or cooperation in international boycotts results in loss of tax deferral and denial of foreign tax credits on income attributed to the boycott activity.
6. Technical changes were made affecting: gains from disposition of shares in foreign corporations, foreign insurance company dividends, interest and capital gains, foreign shipping companies, and "third-tier" foreign subsidiaries of U.S. corporations.

While the foregoing tax restrictions on foreign business operations clearly constrain and complicate life for U.S. investors wishing to do business abroad, we can see emerging the outline of the tax chasm which must be avoided. The pentapus-type restrictions are generally to be shunned (although special cases may warrant diving into that pit), and capital-intensive or detailed expertise-intensive businesses will probably not be useful except to those already involved in them domestically. This latter group would include not only the shipping, banking, insurance, finance, and portfolio investment companies, but probably also heavy manufacturing and extractive industries.

This leaves us with a number of potential businesses into which an investor may go, with the normal beginning constraints of gaining required expertise, adequate capital, market knowledge, etc. Certainly the patent, copyright, trademark, and royalty area should be interesting to those having such income potential, as it permits revenue earned in the United States to be transmitted without U.S. withholding tax to the haven, which, if correctly selected in turn, should levy a low tax on the haven company's net income. Thus a Netherlands Antilles permanent company, not engaged in U.S. business or associated with a U.S. company, may receive royalty income from U.S. sources free from U.S. tax.

Clearly the trading or sales company concept, where it can avoid the commonly found restrictions on foreigners doing business *within* a tax haven, is viable and interesting. This might take the form of establishing a tax haven company which buys its product from an unrelated company, perhaps in the United States, and sells to an unrelated company outside the United States. As long as the offshore sales office contributes materially to the actual sales, this is probably a workable idea. Selling services within the tax haven, where not prohibited by local law, is a simple means of doing business abroad under tax protection, as long as the market is sufficiently sizable to receive those services at a profit to the investor.

Another type of offshore business relates to treaty advantages for real estate holdings in certain jurisdictions. Accomplished most often through an offshore holding company, investments in unimproved land, even in the United States, are relatively clear of U.S. tax complications. Investments in improved property cannot be made in the United States by U.S. citizens without incurring a tax liability on their income, except in special cases, but can be made in other countries permitting property acquisition by foreigners, on a U.S. tax-free basis and from an offshore base. Real estate holdings through an offshore trust may also have interesting tax advantages under provisions of TRA 1976. See the following section "In Trusts We Trust."

With any of these legitimate U.S. tax-exempt foreign businesses to which your circumstances and goals may lead you, it is important to note that their U.S. tax liability is only *deferred indefinitely,* not obliterated or forgiven. If the foreign company is eventually sold or liquidated, a full U.S. tax liability may be incurred, depending upon the status of profits and assets. It will be similar to disposition of a U.S. company. And it will probably be at ordinary income rates.

If any of these types of entities appears potentially useful to you, a few words about incorporating in foreign jurisdictions are apropos.

The establishment of any entity in a foreign jurisdiction must be considered from the standpoint of what type of entity it will be designated as for tax purposes, both in the foreign country and in the United States. A corporation formed in Liberia, Panama, or any other nation which has patterned its corporate law on U.S. corporate law, will undoubtedly be considered a corporation for U.S. tax purposes. The same has been usually true of a company limited by shares under the British-type companies laws operative in several important havens, including the Bahamas, Cayman, and Channel Islands. Other foreign companies have also generally been considered corporations for U.S. tax purposes if they fall into the categories of the French/Spanish *SA,* the German *AG,* or the Dutch *NV.* However, these civil-law nations have other entities which possess characteristics of the partnership as well as the corporation. The German *GmbH,* for example, may not be recognized as a corporation for U.S. tax purposes, depending on the laws of the country in which it is formed and the local equivalent of its articles of incorporation. Even more difficult are the Liechtenstein entities which will be discussed in Chapter Six, the *anstalt* and *stiftung,* which combine characteristics of trusts, foundations, and corporations as they are known in the United States. These entities' U.S. tax status is indeterminate at present, and may, after litigation, be determined to be the equivalent of whichever U.S. entity would yield the greatest amount of taxes—an uncommonly unsatisfactory state of affairs.

Even the establishment of a foreign trust runs afoul of these same "what would it be in the United States" problems. To wit, Treasury Regulation 301.7701-1 (c) :

> Although it is the Internal Revenue Code rather than local law which establishes the tests or standards which will be applied in determining the classification (i.e., as a trust or an association taxable as a corporation) in which an organization belongs, local law governs in determining whether the legal relationships which have been established in the formation of an organization are such that the standards are met.

The entity doesn't even have to be foreign to run into that problem.

Further specific incorporation methods will be discussed in the chapters for each locale.

IN TRUSTS WE TRUST

The creation of a foreign trust for your selected beneficiaries, despite the truly significant changes made in their use by TRA 1976, and the increased potential for harassment by the IRS (they must be reported on Information Returns), is still a viable means of utilizing tax havens. The number of persons who will find them useful has been reduced, while the amount of capital required has been increased by TRA 1976. But this by no means prevents their use, nor diminishes their attractiveness where a trust is appropriate. What, then, exactly is a foreign trust? Attorney Langer explains it thus:[7]

> A foreign trust is a trust created by an individual in a country other than his country of residence, normally in a common law jurisdiction because the law governing trusts developed in England over the centuries. This case law became a part of the English common law not only in the United Kingdom, but also in most present and former British overseas territories. Thus, there is a recognized body of trusts law in most common law countries. . . . [A foreign trust] is an equitable obligation which binds a person (the trustee) to deal with the property over which he has control (the trust property) for the benefit of designated persons (the beneficiaries). The trust is generally created by a written document which sets forth the manner in which the trustee must deal with the trust property. Any one of the beneficiaries may enforce the obligation. Any act or neglect on the part of the trustee which is not authorized or excused by the terms of the trust instrument, or by law, is a breach of trust. . . . The grantor of the trust creates the trust either by a transfer during his lifetime (living trust) or by a transfer after his death in accordance with his last will (testamentary trust). . . . The common law trust is not a contract. Generally, only a person who is a party to a contract can sue on it. The beneficiaries of a common law trust are not parties to the document creating the trust. Yet they can sue to enforce the obligation. The grantor cannot sue to enforce the trust unless he is a beneficiary or he reserves the power to revoke.

In the preceding section we noted one condition for determining that an entity is not a proper trust—i.e., when

---

[7] *How to Use Foreign Tax Havens,* pp. 80–81.

it is an association taxable as a corporation. Tax experts generally believe that a trust will not meet that condition if the trustee is responsible for conserving the trust property for beneficiaries who cannot share this responsibility. Where a manager of an entity carries on business and divides any gains among persons who have a voice in the business, that entity will likely be taxed as a corporation, or possibly a partnership. Additional considerations which determine a trust's tax status include: (1) it cannot have as its primary purpose the avoidance of tax, (2) it cannot have personal income assigned to it, and (3) the creator of the trust cannot usually be a beneficiary or have access to trust assets. These rules apply to all trusts, domestic or foreign.

This brings us to a problem arising from what one would think is a simple question: how can one make the trust foreign? At least five conditions appear necessary:[8] (1) the trust must be administered outside the United States; (2) the trustee must be foreign, preferably a corporation with no branches in the United States; (3) trust assets should be kept outside the United States; (4) the trust must be formed in and governed by the law of a foreign country; and (5) the trust should not have a discretionary U.S. investment advisor. All these conditions should exist for the trust to be "foreign."

Prior to TRA 1976, U.S. persons were permitted to establish foreign trusts under the above criteria, which could then accumulate income tax-free for designated U.S. beneficiaries. The United States would only tax the income of such a trust upon its distribution to the beneficiaries. Now, and in certain cases retroactively to May 21, 1974, if the creator (grantor) of a foreign trust and a beneficiary of a foreign trust are U.S. persons, the U.S. grantor is treated as the owner of the portion of the trust attributable to the property transferred. The U.S. grantor is then subject to U.S. tax on income earned by the trust, even though not receiving that income. However,

[8] See *Foreign Tax Planning, 1977*, p. 15.

these provisions only apply to *inter vivos* (living) foreign trusts.[9] More on what happens to testamentary and other non-grantor trusts in a moment.

Regarding beneficiaries, a foreign trust is now considered to have a U.S. beneficiary *unless:* (1) the trust does not permit the distribution of accumulated income or corpus of the turst to or for the benefit of a U.S. person; and (2) if the trust were terminated during a given year, no part of the income or corpus could be paid to or for the benefit of a U.S. person. This is a year-by-year test, and apparently means that if a U.S. beneficiary does exist in some year after formation of the trust; i.e., if a nonresident alien beneficiary becomes a U.S. citizen, the U.S. grantor will be taxed in that year, not only on that year's income, but all prior years' undistributed net income as well. Certain other characteristics of foreign trusts will cause them to have U.S. beneficiaries.[10] These include circumstances where: (1) the trust has a foreign corporation as a beneficiary which is more than 50 percent owned, or considered owned, by U.S. shareholders; (2) the trust has a foreign partnership as beneficiary when the partnership has a U.S. person, either directly or indirectly, as a partner; and (3) the trust has another foreign trust or estate as a beneficiary that has a U.S. beneficiary itself. Quite clearly, TRA 1976 took dead aim on the use of foreign living trusts to benefit any U.S. taxpayer. Thus in order to have a foreign trust considered a non-grantor type, it must be testamentary or have no U.S. beneficiaries or a non-U.S. grantor.

However, it should be noted that grantor trust rules apply only to income tax considerations, not to estate or gift tax rules. Any transfer made by reason of death of a U.S. person is not covered, nor is a living trust owned by a U.S. person treated as owned by his/her estate upon death.

---

[9] *Tax Reform Act, 1976, Provisions Affecting Income Earned Abroad,* p. 16.

[10] See U.S. Internal Revenue Service, *Tax Reform Act, 1976, Explanation,* pp. 222–23.

Another important point about grantor trusts: Just to make sure no one was skipped over lightly, TRA 1976 also taxes any gain existing in *all* property transferred to a foreign trust at an excise tax rate of 35 percent of the appreciation, compared to the previous 27½ percent for securities transfers only. This also applies to transfers to foreign corporations and partnerships. Transfers which either recognize a gain in transferred property for tax purposes, or which have no gain, are not affected by this excise tax. If the trust passes these tests, the new law now gets at the beneficiaries in another way. Foreign trust income distributions to U.S. beneficiaries from non-grantor trusts, including testamentary trusts, are now subject both to the beneficiaries' regular tax rate and to a nondeductible interest tax of 6 percent per years the income is earned, on the U.S. tax payable on the income which is distributed. This appears to mean, for example, that if a foreign testamentary trust beneficiary receives income which has an average "age" of being earned in the trust of five years, he or she will pay 30 percent more than the taxes otherwise payable from this income source.

Add to these blasts at foreign trust usefulness the requirements for an information tax return from a U.S. grantor 90 days after the creation of a foreign trust or the transfer of money or property to a foreign trust, plus an annual tax return from the grantor (with a penalty for failure to file of 5 percent of the value of the trust corpus), and it's clear that foreign trusts aren't the handy devices they once were. They can hardly now be termed a "tax scam."

But not to worry. Despite this destruction of the foreign trust terrain, there is still a viable path on which one may walk, depending upon an investor's needs.

Certainly the testamentary transfer of property or cash to a foreign trust with U.S. beneficiaries is viable if one wishes to hold funds outside the United States over the long term. Our discussion in Chapter One about U.S. social trends may provide a reason, as could potential U.S. foreign exchange controls. The 6 percent per annum interest charge based on the tax due from distributions to beneficiaries is significant only if the annual distribution is sizable and/or the beneficiaries are in a high tax bracket. Moreover, transferring property without a gain at fair market value to the trust, or recognizing the gain at time of transfer, in either case as part of a testamentary transfer, will not have any effect on whether the trust is to be considered a grantor type, and the above distribution rules will apply for U.S. beneficiaries.

And there are other possibilities. One tax expert told me that it might well be possible for a nonresident alien person, such as a foreign resident grandfather, to establish a living trust for his grandchildren who are U.S. citizens. As he is not a U.S. grantor, he would allegedly have no current U.S. taxable income, and the trust could therefore accumulate income free of tax. The grandchildren could receive distributions under the 6 percent interest charge rule. And the law clearly specifies that if the beneficiaries of a foreign trust established by any person are not now, and don't become, U.S. citizens, they can receive benefits without the 6 percent additional tax penalty.

Another tax attorney raised with me the probability (later confirmed by a tax law professor), that since the grantor trust requires that income it receives be taxable to the grantor annually, it is likely that if the trust generated legitimate losses these would be deductible by the grantor as well. A depreciable asset or income property might be considered in this case, he said. A variation on this could be a life insurance trust, utilizing the so-called minimum pay plans, so that loan interest deductions could flow through to the grantor.

If a foreign trust was established under U.S. grantor rules to make investments offshore in non–dividend-paying companies which grow in value, the trust, and therefore the grantor, will have no income to be taxed, and U.S. beneficiaries could later receive income from the presumably increased corpus. However, no capital gain treatment of any foreign trust assets is possible upon distribution.

A potentially significant variation on this theme comes through the use of a U.S. domestic corporation. If a corporation is established with two classes of stock, one a dividend-paying preferred, the other a non–dividend-paying common, the founder, a person holding a substantial amount of securities, could effect a swap of those securities for the preferred shares, continuing to receive income essentially as before the swap. The company, of course, would be a nonoperating company, and likely be classed as a personal holding company for tax purposes, which makes little difference to the person making the swap and receiving income since he was receiving it previously on a taxable basis. However, a potentially significant next step is taken. The new corporation's non–dividend common stock is placed in a foreign testamentary trust with named U.S. beneficiaries. Upon death of the corporate founder, the corporation could be liquidated, the original securities sold, and the proceeds invested offshore through the foreign trust until distribution to the U.S. beneficiaries. Their distributions would be taxable with the 6 percent interest penalty.

In an area as new as the foreign trust treatment resulting from TRA 1976, it is quite likely that new methods of handling them will be found, and that some tightening of presently-considered permissible methods will occur. No foreign trust should be undertaken without full consultation with a U.S. attorney who is well versed in the field, especially in the current case law and Treasury department/IRS promulgations.

As Chicago-based tax attorney Burton Kanter put the matter in a recent article on grantor trusts, "The use of grantor trusts involves a high degree of sophistication about their terms and the circumstances in which they should be utilized. Consequently, considerable care should be exercised on the part of advisors in recommending the use of grantor trusts in any circumstances."[11]

While our discussion in this chapter has clearly dwelt upon tax considerations in use of foreign corporations and trusts, there may well be important nontax considerations, too. In the same article, Kanter enumerates a number of nontax uses of grantor trusts which deserve summary mention here. These considerations will be appropriate in both foreign and domestic grantor trusts. They include the fact that trust assets are not usually a part of the trust creator's estate for federal tax purposes, the fact that alterations in beneficiaries may be provided for in the trust agreement under trustee supervision, and the point that trust assets are not considered, whether domestic or foreign, a part of the grantor's assets in the event of claims by creditors on the grantor.

One example noted by Kanter is the use of a grantor trust in conjunction with a premarital agreement. Here the intended spouse is established as a beneficiary by effecting an agreed property settlement in the event of separation or divorce. This would assure her of an effective income (penalized in the case of a foreign trust) though the grantor husband remains owner of the trust. It also gains psychological stability for her, and may better protect him from possible challenge to the agreement. This trust could also, if domestic, have tax advantages for him in that while he would bear the tax on the income paid her from the trust, it might be less than a compounded tax burden if he were to later provide her a tax-free income.

We have already noted the potential tax advantages to a grantor in the use of minimum pay insurance plans involving a foreign trust. This use also should provide benefits from a specific transfer of cash to the trust by way of a taxable gift; exclusion of the proceeds of insurance from anyone's estate, especially that of the grantor; and security of the funds

[11] Burton W. Kanter, "Supplementary Comment on the 'Defective Trust Gambit'," in *Taxes—The Tax Magazine*, November 1976, p. 730.

apart from the estate for such purposes as the family might wish, including possible loan to the estate for settlement of other estate tax liabilities.[12]

A third nontax use of grantor trusts is to achieve the general investment advantages of a limited partnership in cases where it might not qualify under Treasury IRS rulings or where the principal requirement is an effective limitation on liability. Here a general partnership may be used to make a given investment or series of them through a grantor trust, which will limit the partners' liability to the amount invested and permit flow-through of tax considerations to the partners/grantors. Expanding the limitation of liability concept further, Kanter notes that grantor trusts have been increasingly used by physicians concerned about the rising cost of malpractice insurance and the enormous impact any excess liability may have on their families.

Kanter also points out a situation where a foreign grantor trust may be used by a domestic corporation for both tax and nontax purposes. "A U.S. corporation may wish to engage in an offshore activity which requires that the ownership entity be a local entity. For example, the development of property on certain islands requires that the developer and owner of the property be a locally established entity." He went on, "Ordinarily, one would consider the establishment of a local corporation. However, because the nature of the business enterprise will involve significant start-up losses, the U.S. corporate entity, which files a consolidated income tax return, wishes to take these losses into account to offset its risk in the venture and to do so currently rather than on a deferred basis. It is not possible to achieve both these objectives through the use of a foreign corporation as a subsidiary of the domestic company because the foreign corporation cannot become a member of the consolidated group." Kanter concluded, "Accordingly, the use of a grantor trust as the local

---

12 Kanter, "Supplementary Comment," p. 727.

entity holding title to the property and developing the property can be a means whereby that condition can be satisfied, while at the same time having its operations attributed to the domestic corporate grantor as the deemed owner. On this basis, losses from the venture can be taken into account in the consolidated return (subject only to other problems in the case of the consolidated return)."[13]

This chapter, after a brief look at the nature of tax havens, has of necessity dealt with the least personal, coldest, and most complicated aspects of placing funds abroad—the domestic legal, tax, and nontax considerations. These are the most critical, yet sometimes slighted, criteria in the whole issue of tax haven use. The laws and tax considerations of the United States must be understood by Americans first and foremost above any other facet of capital placement outside this country. Unless one wishes to become a full citizen of another country, one will be governed by U.S. tax laws wherever one resides and blanketed by them whatever entities may be assembled. To ignore or gloss over these laws is folly. We have attempted an overview of the most important of them for laymen and professional advisors unfamiliar with the subject. There are certainly other detailed aspects that we have not explored, because of their complexity, their limited interest, or perhaps just plain oversight. They are, however, properly raised by and developed with your attorney in light of your personal circumstances.

At this point we will liven our discussion by making a short trip to each of the four havens chosen for closer examination. We will meet three special persons through whose eyes we will observe the havens close-up. Each of these travel-

---

[13] Ibid., p. 728. The following footnotes were included in the article: "The only foreign corporations that may be part of a consolidated group are Canadian and Mexican corporations and only under most limited circumstances. Also, a Sec. 931 corporation is inapplicable except in case of qualifying activity in a U.S. possession."

"Whether more complex and sophisticated planning is desirable in any given situation to permit the ultimate recipients of profits and growth from the venture to be other than the corporation is an issue not pertinent here."

ers has certain financial and personal characteristics that we will find useful in our exploration. They were selected as traveling companions because they typify broad categories of persons who might readily consider the use of a haven. We'll find all three aboard an Eastern Airlines plane departing Miami for Nassau in the Bahamas Islands.

chapter 4

THE BAHAMAS

The two principal airlines serving Nassau, the key city and capital of the Bahamas Islands, arrive and depart for Miami almost every morning, afternoon, or night. Jet trips of 45 minutes via Eastern Airlines or Bahamasair rarely leave even a two-hour time gap in their combined schedules. And frequent direct flights from New York, Boston, Chicago, several Florida cities, Montreal, Toronto, London, Frankfurt plus Caribbean islands, and Mexico City, make access to this archipelago, scattered over some 100,000 square miles of ocean, a simple project for upwards of 1.4 million visitors per year.

Three of those visitors are aboard our Eastern 727, preparing to depart Miami toward the end of the tourist season in March. Each has a general goal for the trip: to discover what is financially possible under his/her own circumstances in this best-known Western Hemisphere tax haven. We'll find that they each represent a broad category of potential haven user, those with whom you might identify in the most common needs for a foreign tax haven.

Take Dr. Fred, for example. At age 58 he is considering retiring after a long and successful practice somewhere in the

South. He has amassed a net worth in the middle six figures and a family of three grown children and five grandchildren. He is looking forward to traveling and teaching in retirement, accompanied by his 56-year-old wife. Dr. Fred is certainly well off by any measure but is not atypical of many professional persons or senior executives approaching retirement. His net worth could be in the low six figures and still be appropriate to our discussion, given one more fact. Dr. Fred belongs to that somewhat mysterious, often suspect group of individuals known euphemistically as "gold bugs." He has followed the trials and tribulations of the gold market, made a good deal of money from it, and lost some. He has been for years a subscriber to the Harry Schultz International Letter and the Dines Letter, among others. He has held a Swiss bank account for ten years without any sizable sum in it, and has continually instructed his accountant and attorney to "do things right by the law." Dr. Fred is a conservative by every standard and attributes most of his well-being to it. He shares with most persons of this persuasion a dislike of the liberal social trends in the United States, and most importantly, believes that exchange controls on the dollar are a predictable coming event. He is surprised that they have been this long delayed. He rationalizes this by recalling his knowledge that the dollar had to be devalued a half dozen years before it was.

Sitting down the aisle from Dr. Fred and his wife is our second inquirer of tax haven potential, Aunt Audrey, presently of Rossmoor Leisure World in Laguna Hills, California. A youthful-looking 53, she is just two years a widow. Fortunately, her husband's 30 years as a California real estate broker, commanding a string of six offices and 40 salespersons when he died, have left Aunt Audrey with not only a most comfortable home but also three pieces of income property and the proceeds of a substantial insurance policy. At the height of the California home price boom in 1977, she sold their house for $174,000, $5,000 more than she had asked, and bought a modest two-bedroom townhouse in Leisure World for $79,000 cash. A bright and active lady, Aunt Audrey is taking her fourth trip abroad in the past three years, this time to investigate the possibilities that with her comfortable income, very modest fixed expenses, a no-upkeep home, and rather sizable bank accounts, she might start or invest in a small business somewhere abroad. "An excuse to go away for part of the year," she told her friends before leaving for Nassau. Her business preferences center around real estate, about which she has learned a good deal since her husband passed away, or perhaps a cosmetics boutique, a field she had worked in some years ago when her husband's real estate business suffered a slowdown. She had stayed with it longer than required because of what surprised her as a grand success. Despite much sorrow at the loss of her husband, she is determined that the best years of her life lie ahead, and with no small measure of confidence is embarking on what she feels is a fine adventure.

Mario is a good deal younger than our other two haven investigators, and of far different circumstances. At 38 he has lived a bachelor's life since his divorce 12 years ago. He has one son. He still lives in his native San Francisco close to his large Italian family, keeping one eye on his father's popular financial district bar and restaurant, the other on the books of a smallish peninsula computer firm of which he is financial vice president. Mario earns $35,000 a year, has a modest stock option program in his growing firm (they'll do nearly $4 million in volume this year, up from $2 million three years ago), and owns a fourplex on Russian Hill, one unit of which he lives in. His 40-minute commute to work is always against traffic.

Mario's interest in tax havens has been prompted from two sources. His 80-year-old grandparents still live in the old country on the outskirts of Rome, the locus of a biennial family gathering. The latest one had provided the revelation that Mario's family in Italy had accumulated a rather sizable estate, and shouldn't he, the "financial genius" from the Stanford Business School, help them provide for all the children and grandchildren outside of Italy? Somewhat reluctantly (the conflict between personal gain and his duty to assist the family was bothersome), Mario agreed to think about the matter.

A second prompting came from his computer firm which had recently opened what it believed to be a sizable foreign market for its products in Europe and South America. This trip was planned as a circuit of four havens to determine whether a haven company might further the financial cause for the parent firm in a sales, royalty, or manufacturing form. Conceivably it could even further the financial cause of Mario himself. Two of the firm's European salesmen had obliquely suggested that the size of the market might leave considerable room for competition should Mario wish to bring certain expertise into the establishment of a new organization. He hadn't liked the idea with its implication of leaving his present firm and San Francisco, but decided to keep an open mind while investigating all possibilities.

Each of our travelers has gained some familiarity with the U.S. tax situation they must confront in making haven use plans. We need only add that Doctor Fred and, to a lesser extent, Mario carried with them a belief in the fundamental truth of a statement made by a prominent tax attorney, "No one is smart enough to make a tax law that will not permit someone else to find a loophole in that law." The attorney had concluded: "Therefore all that the loophole-closing changes in tax laws do is create greater complexity and costs. What is the net benefit to society?"

The IRS rarely recognizes this concept. It can be very poor sport toward loophole finders. The Bahamas are one playing field in the great tax game where the IRS might have stretched the rules. Let us consider the case of Michael Wolstencroft.

THE ABUSER AND THE ABUSED

Was Michael Wolstencroft, B. Comm, FCIS, set up? Did he really have with him a list of his bank's clients and their account numbers at the time of the widely publicized "brief-case incident" involving himself and the IRS in Miami?[1] Or did an IRS agent already have that list on January 15, 1973, as Wolstencroft claims he has reason to believe, and simply planted it on him?

Quite possibly we will never know. Wolstencroft stands indicted by federal grand juries in Texas and Cleveland for alleged involvement with tax evasion schemes at Castle Bank & Trust Co. of Nassau, where he was deputy managing director. If he travels to the United States, he likely will be jailed and tried—a sufficient reason for remaining outside the country, but leaving the case unsettled.

Whatever the truth, however unlikely or possible Wolstencroft's claim in light of the known facts of the incident, it is largely academic now. The incident itself is not. It remains a silent reminder of the sociopolitical atmosphere in which Americans lived before Watergate. One can only wonder under what conditions or at what time such flagrant deception as practiced on Wolstencroft will again become government practice in probing for tax evasion evidence. Even if we accept the contention that U.S. tax evasion was going on under Wolstencroft's nose, one wonders who was the abuser and who was the abused.

It was a typically warm January afternoon when Wolstencroft caught an Eastern Airlines plane to Miami. He was making a rendezvous with an attractive woman at the Miami airport under circumstances which he had every reason to believe were quite innocent. It was, in a way, a matter of bank business. At least that's how Wolstencroft recalls his introduction to Sybil Kennedy by another new acquaintance,

---

1 "Probing the Tax Havens" *Newsweek,* June 28, 1976, pp. 52–56.

Norman Casper, during December 1972. It was to be two years and nine months before Wolstencroft discovered that both were paid IRS secret agents sent to dig up information on his bank and its customers.

Casper had, according to Wolstencroft, been introduced to him with proper references and a request for assistance, "in any way possible," during late fall of 1972. With Casper's 25 years of undercover experience, it wasn't long before he and Wolstencroft became apparently good friends. Thus Casper's suggestion that Wolstencroft meet a friend of his named Sybil, who might have business connections for the bank, seemed without malice, as Wolstencroft explains it. Even the subsequent date with her on January 15 seemed routine enough, he recalls. He believed he was on the track of sound business, although, married as he was, overnight business plans with a woman in another city might have suggested to some that he was skating on thin ice.

Kennedy met Wolstencroft at the Miami airport as arranged, whereupon they adjourned to her apartment for a time before going out to dinner around 7 P.M. at the Sandbar restaurant in Key Biscayne. They were gone for about three hours, leaving Wolstencroft's briefcase, allegedly containing names and account numbers of Castle Bank customers, in Kennedy's apartment.

According to the 1975 congressional testimony of Casper, it was during the dinner sojourn that he picked up the briefcase, visited a waiting locksmith, and then took it to a private home where its contents were photographed by IRS agents. Then Casper returned the briefcase to Kennedy's apartment. This is how the IRS says it came into possession of 300 names and account numbers of Castle Bank's customers.

Apparently that was not sufficient, however. About a month later, Kennedy made a trip to the bank's office in Nassau for additional details. She testified that while there she located a rolodex file containing the names, addresses, and phone numbers of the bank's customers. It was with this revelation that *Newsweek* broke details of IRS investigations into tax haven misuses.

The following is from the author's interview with Wolstencroft in Nassau:

Wolstencroft: "I couldn't understand this when I found out about it. I don't remember carrying any list of bank clients to Miami at that time. I knew them. I had them in my head."

"All 300?"

"Well, the most important of them. I didn't need a list for meetings with attorneys or anyone else. Besides, I have reason to believe the IRS already had a list."

"How?"

"I'm not able to tell you that."

"But why would the IRS (actually, Casper) say you had the list with you and they copied it?"

"I honestly don't know. Maybe they had to explain how they got it."

"So they planted it on a foreign citizen and took some highly questionable steps to 'obtain' it, which would be illegal if done to a U.S. citizen, all to cover up the true manner they got it?"

"If I didn't have a list with me, that would appear to be the case."

And there the facts and one opinion on the Wolstencroft briefcase incident rest. However, the ramifications have been sizeable. First, the U.S. Justice Department and at least five grand juries have been investigating the situation and persons allegedly involved with Castle Bank, off and on since 1973. The results have been meager to say the least. We have already noted that by August 1977, the Miami grand jury had come up with only one indictment after 18 months' work.

A Cleveland grand jury did indict a Jack Payner for a

violation of the Bank Secrecy Act in stating on his 1972 federal tax return that he did not have a foreign bank account, after the government contended it discovered Payner's account at Castle Bank, Nassau, contained some $100,000. The government claimed this evidence was obtained by means other than the Wolstencroft briefcase seizure. The case was decided on April 28, 1977 when the judge ordered the suppression of all government evidence relating to the means of discovering the existence of Payner's account in that it did apparently stem from an illegal search and seizure of Wolstencroft's briefcase. Those readers interested in the matter of individual due process rights in the United States will be heartened to note the comments of District Judge John Manos in his order on the case.

"The Court concludes that the United States was an active participant in the admittedly criminal conduct in which Casper engaged to procure the Castle Bank's documents in January of 1973." And later in the same order, "the activities of the Government agents Jaffe [IRS Special Agent in the Jacksonville, Florida field office] and Casper were outrageous. They plotted, schemed and ultimately acted in contravention of the United States Constitution and laws of Florida, knowing that their conduct was illegal. It is imperative to signal all likeminded individuals that purposeful criminal acts on behalf of the Government will not be tolerated in this country and that such acts shall never be allowed to bear fruit." The Justice Department has filed an appeal.

A second case involving one of Castle Bank's attorneys, Burton Kanter, whom we quoted earlier, arose out of a Nevada grand jury indictment against the lawyer on an alleged conspiracy to avoid taxes on $700,000 in proceeds of a hotel sale which utilized the Bahamas. He was acquitted by a federal court jury in Chicago in September 1977.

A third case, this not connected to Castle Bank, found Saratoga, California, attorney Harry Margolis, two others, and a Netherlands Antilles bank indicted on 24 counts of conspiring to cheat the U.S. government out of taxes due on $1.4 million in fictitious tax deductions, including phony loans, fraudulent interest payments on the loans, back-dating documents to make it appear the transactions actually had occurred, and the preparation of 22 fraudulent tax returns.[2] The chief of the Justice Department's Tax Division criminal section was quoted at the time of the indictment as terming it, "perhaps the biggest breakthrough we've ever had in the whole area of fraud in the widespread use of offshore tax shelters." He added it was "only the beginning." What it was the beginning of is not clear. In August 1977 a San Francisco judge threw out 18 of the 24 counts against Margolis et al., with a finding that the government had failed to present a *prima facie* case. The other counts went to trial. Margolis was acquitted within two months.

Where these initial government legal misfirings will lead is anyone's guess, except that they'll be in the courts for some time. Too many reputations and principles are at stake for the U.S. government to take the first defeats and give up. What is more, another government is involved.

Tim Donaldson, Governor of the Central Bank of the Bahamas, wasn't far from where the action at Castle Bank had been taking place. Physically, his modern two-story bank building is located on Frederick St. in Nassau, having been opened in February 1975 by Queen Elizabeth. Next to it is Trinity Methodist Church. Across the small street of Trinity Place stands a three-story Victorian colonial building called Norfolk House. Its ground floor houses the no-tellers, no-vaults Castle Bank & Trust Company.

Donaldson has clear opinions about the Wolstencroft affair, as might be expected of someone in his position. They are against both sides. First, he believes that Wolstencroft did have his bank client list with him on the sojourn to Miami, and he told me that he felt Wolstencroft had violated fundamental rules of banking in carrying that information, al-

2 *The Wall Street Journal,* October 6, 1975, p. 15.

though Donaldson was not aware of the problem until the story broke in the Miami newspapers two and a half years after the incident. "I was interested in policy matters in that case," he observed coolly. "We transmitted our comments to the bank (Castle) and advised them that we felt certain steps had been taken wrongly. It was not a matter of bank operations, rather someone's judgment."

About the IRS handling of the investigation into Castle Bank, he told me (before the Payner case decision), "either we believe in law or we don't. There is such a thing as due process. If they say the process of law is just too slow and frustrating, should we abandon justice?" Donaldson believed the proper action would have been for the IRS to swear an affidavit before the Bahamian Supreme Court to open the bank secrecy of that nation to an investigation of Castle Bank. That would, of course, have left the decision up to the Bahamian court.

Unfortunately, that might not have been as simple as Donaldson suggested. A prominent Nassau attorney told me the court's decision could well have come down against the IRS. He cited a March 1977 Bahamian Supreme Court ruling denying a U.S. Department of Justice request, along with that of an estate executor, that a Bahamian bank liquidator be required to testify in a U.S. Court in an exception to Bahamian bank secrecy. Of course, that ruling postdated the "briefcase incident."

A final observation may be taken from this whole affair. It should be clear, although time may slowly blur the image, that the Bahamas is an important point of focus for IRS, Justice Department and grand jury antiavoidance tax efforts, successful or not. For this reason, and the attendant cautiousness on the part of trust companies and banks in the Bahamas, this haven may be less attractive for purely tax considerations than some of the others we will visit, or a few that we won't observe firsthand. Good business reasons are always the most sensible foundations for haven use. The antiavoidance climate in Washington is sufficient reason for stressing business decisions over tax considerations in any haven. In the aura of the Bahamas' notoriety, the stress should be redoubled.

DOWN TO BUSINESS

There is no doubt that the Bahamaas has been the United State's most popular tax haven, and not an insignificant one for foreigners feeding funds here. With about 15,000 companies chartered in the islands, one for every 13 residents, plus a bank for every 600 citizens (nearly 20 times the U.S. ratio), something is going on there besides tourist frolics.

What is going on begins with the fact that the Bahamas levies no income tax or capital gains tax, has no gift, inheritance, or estate taxes, nor, to its disadvantage for certain business, is it a party to any tax treaties at present.

Going further, companies may be established in the Bahamas that do no business there but which are still legally domiciled there for tax purposes. Bahamian companies may be either resident or nonresident, but there are no "exempt" companies as in Cayman or Bermuda, where government guarantees against future taxation are exchanged for certain limited operating conditions.

Resident companies are the standard form for doing business *in* the Bahamas. They can be formed within a few days by a Bahamian lawyer for a filing fee of about $300 set by the Registrar General, plus the attorney's fees and a stamp tax based on capital. The latter is a progressive fee beginning at $60 for $5,000 capital. No financial information, other than details of issued capital, are required to be published or filed either upon formation or annually. Five or more persons must be named as shareholders; however, these may be nominees, such as those provided by local banks and trust companies, with the names of the true shareholders (beneficial owners) not revealed to the Registrar. Nor will these names be required by Exchange Control, except on specific request of the Bahamas Central Bank. However, officers of the company must be registered. No bearer shares may be issued. A company must have a local registered office, but it is not required that the company have actual employees, nor is the principal officer required to be present in the Bahamas. This accounts for the lists of 20, 30, or 40 company names mounted, usually on metal plates, outside the major banks, trust companies, and attorneys' and accountants' offices.

The significance of "resident" and "nonresident" companies develops from the existence of foreign exchange controls in the Commonwealth of the Bahamas. These restrictions are principally felt by Bahamian citizens and resident companies. The latter are defined as firms carrying on business in the Bahamas, or owned in part or all by Bahamian residents or by people who own property there. Resident companies must deal in Bahamian dollars, convert all foreign currency earnings into that currency, and cannot borrow or maintain a foreign currency bank account without Exchange Control permission. Such companies, when owned 60 percent or more by Bahamians, are charged an annual operating tax of $250. Others, $1,000.

Nonresident companies are specified as those with no Bahamian shareholders and not doing business within the Bahamas. They cannot deal in Bahamian currency, except through permission of Exchange Control, and then only for local expenses with funds supplied externally. Foreign currency accounts may be maintained in and outside the islands. These firms suffer the expense of a $1,000 annual tax.

Other than the fact that the Bahamas companies law is more than 100 years old, and necessarily requires lengthy filing and annual documentation, the foregoing are the principal points of reference for local incorporation consideration. However, as our Aunt Audrey will shortly learn, actually getting down to doing business in the Bahamas as she would like presents a financial and permission problem of some note.

TRUSTING

Use of trusts in the Bahamas, which has a long-standing body of trust law handed down from English law (and is therefore theoretically quite workable), is summed up by Vice President John Kitchen of World Banking Corp., Bahamas (WOBACO). "Our attitude is that we will only accept U.S. trust business where we are absolutely assured it's snow white." He explained, "We won't accept it unless it is sent by recognized U.S. tax attorneys or accountants or our shareholders" (the banks which own WOBACO). That is largely the attitude of the major trust companies in the Bahamas. Since TRA 1976 they believe that Americans can do little legally in the trust area, and therefore want to be assured that the business received is not speckled with illegalities. As the legitimate American uses of foreign trusts become better known, as is occurring now, trust company cautiousness will ease. "Where a trust company becomes the legal owner of funds," adds Bahamas International Trust Company vice president R. S. Owers, "we must go even further [in checking validity] than a couple of bank references." By that he means a check on personal references and on those of your legal/accounting advisors too, plus having the tax aspects of the potential trust analyzed by their lawyers. In all, a somewhat time-consuming process.

And don't forget the nontax aspects. "The name of the game," says Owers, "is not necessarily taxes. Exchange control is another." That's a reference to the social trend considerations we've noted earlier, as well as the other nontax advantages of foreign trusts.

The Swiss banks in the Bahamas are generally even more reticent about U.S. trust business now than they were before.

Swiss Bank Corporation (Overseas), Ltd., has three guidelines (subject to change): they will not accept trusts with *any* U.S. beneficiaries, in order to avoid U.S. tax problems; they require a minimum corpus of $250,000; and they won't accept "work-intensive" trusts, those which require extensive work by their people, except on a case-by-case basis.

Credit Suisse (Swiss Credit Bank) has both a bank branch and an overseas subsidiary in Nassau. They are even more adamant, and will accept neither trust nor corporate business "for at least two years" (until 1979), for the same reasons given by Swiss Bank Corporation. "Banking is a very personal matter," one of the bank's officers told me. "It has to suit that person, *and* his citizenship."

If this all sounds as though trust business in the Bahamas is difficult to arrange, remember that this is the public stance that the trust people believe necessary in wake of their much publicized reputation as a tax-dodge haven. Those who bring sound, well-planned, and reference-laden trust business to them will receive a friendlier welcome than suggested in public pronouncements. Also, smaller trust organizations and private attorneys and accountants may well open doors more readily. However, the most important aspect of any foreign trust is how it will stand up against IRS tests. A reputable foreign organization behind it will be helpful.

Above all, take the advice of Bahamas attorney Ralph Seligman on dealing in any tax haven. "Whatever you want to do, get it cleared with your tax people at home. If you're not connected, I'd be prepared to recommend someone. I won't undertake that aspect of work, nor will most members of the local bar."

INVESTIGATIONS

A first discovery for any tourist or business visitor, including our three traveling companions, is the high cost of living or staying in Nassau. This is where the no-tax facet of the

Bahamas comes home to roost. The most popular tourist area is Cable Beach, a $4 cab ride from the airport, and another $3 from downtown Nassau. The finest hotels are here, each of which has more than one excellent restaurant, and everything about them is pricey. Double rooms range from $65 to $85 per day at the Nassau Beach Hotel in season (November–March), dinners start at $9.50 a la carte, drinks run $2.50–$3.00, and a half bottle of a modest French wine (few American wines are available) costs $7.00.

Hotels downtown are less expensive, and older. Probably the best is the Sheraton British Colonial, where a new-wing double can be had for $55 to $70 per day (avoid the old wing), and a decent beach is available, although not comparable to Cable Beach. The hotel is within walking distance of almost all banking and trust firms, and therefore does a substantial amount of business trade.

Finishing coffee after a splendid meal at the Italian Renaissance restaurant on Bay Street, our friend Dr. Fred, his wife, and an official of a prominent trust company found their conversation turned to the political situation in the Bahamas.

"The legislative trend of the government, which was reelected in July 1977, appears favorable," the trust officer advised. "But foreign investors here are never quite certain which way the government may go. It's a function of the ambivalent position the government finds itself in. With a black majority electorate being pushed by the high cost of living and substantial unemployment (about 20,000 out of a population of 170,000), the Pindling government has a difficult time making the kinds of statements needed to reassure and induce foreign business. The result is something like dollops of nationalism interspersed with assurances to foreigners."

"Is the situation really safe for trust set-up?" queried Dr. Fred.

"We certainly hope so, and actually believe it is. Now that

Pindling is reelected, the government may take a more positive stance for foreign business. But the Bahamas needs money. So there is periodic talk about changing the tax situation, but the odds don't appear high for change in our opinion."

"You didn't really answer my question," injected Dr. Fred. "How do you establish a long-term trust plan under even modest uncertainty?"

"Well, we include provision for transfer of the trust to another haven jurisdiction within the trust documents. And we never leave the trust assets here. Their location depends upon the kinds of assets we administer. But there is no difficulty in having trust assets administered from here but kept in another nation. Not the United States, of course. Actually, this is quite common."

"Why go to that extra bother? If the assets are not kept here, why don't I set up a trust someplace where they can be directly watched over by the trustees?"

"Very simply because there aren't truly good investment opportunities in any haven jurisdiction, for one reason or another. The better investment opportunities are outside the havens, whether it's in securities or property. There are exceptions, of course, but not many. Take Cayman, for example. What do you buy down there? A turtle farm? The domestic market is just too small to justify investment in many local corporations, and sometimes these present tax problems besides. No, you'll find that good accessibility to the trustees, either by phone or telex, or even mail, is more important. So is the body of English trust law, and local banking, legal, and accounting expertise. All of this we have in the Bahamas, and this isn't likely to change. What's more, as trustees of your property we are fully responsible for it. We aren't going to place it somewhere so that we'll be exposed to undue risk, or on the other hand, low returns. That's what you engage us for."

"I'll bet y'all charge for extra work administering assets overseas, don't you?" queried Fred with a broad smile.

"It depends on the amount of work required. And that depends on the type of assets. If they were securities, there would be little or no extra fees. Real property would be a different matter."

"While we're talking about fees," injected Fred, "what sort of charges do you folks levy?"

Fred was handed a schedule of fees and was told they were competitive among the various trust companies in the Bahamas. They ranged from an initial fee of 0.75 percent of the first $200,000 assets; an annual administration fee of 0.4 percent of the assets; and ¼–½ percent of the amount involved in any sales, purchases, or conversions of securities or property; to a withdrawal fee for distributions of 1 percent of the amount distributed.

"In addition," the trust man pointed out, "we can act as executor or administrator of your estate."

As the numbers appeared in line with those incurred in the United States, Fred pounced on his favorite problem of hard currencies. "Do I have any advantage in dealing through here in placing trust assets in Swiss francs or Deutschemarks?"

"As you aren't a Bahamas resident, nor, do I suppose you intend to become one, yours would be a nonresident trust," replied the trust officer. "As such, its assets may be invested in any foreign currency. In fact, this is presumed. So that if you wish to invest trust assets in the Bahamas, say in income property, we would have to obtain Exchange Control approval from the Central Bank to buy Bahamian dollars and again to convert income from the property to the foreign currency. This," he added, "is usually freely given."

The prospect appealed to Dr. Fred. U.S. bank trust departments would rarely hold assets in a foreign currency like Swiss francs or Deutschemarks, let alone buy property abroad. Here he could accomplish both—if they could find some good income property, he thought.

The conversation meandered through other propensities of the Bahamas and Bahamians to a pleasant conclusion of the evening. Reaching for the dinner check, Fred wrapped up the conversation with an observation about his further travel plans and found himself staring at the bill. Including one drink apiece, a bottle of decent French wine, and gratuity, the tab was $71.00.

The next day our Aunt Audrey, having listened to the goombay native music show on the beach at her hotel and acquired a sunburn after only half an hour in the penetrating rays of the Bahamas, began the rounds of government agencies associated with immigration and business development.

At the Immigration Department she discovered that a permit would be required for any non-Bahamian citizen wishing to take up residence for more than eight months, or wanting to be employed, or wanting to engage in business, including even traveling salesmen. The requirement of a financial reference for persons wishing to become residents was no problem, nor was the need for an additional financial reference and two character references for anyone wishing to establish a business. The first problem was the fee. Permit fees ranged from a low of $250 per year for domestic servants to $1,000 for secretaries to a top of $5,000 annually for senior professional persons such as managing directors, attorneys, or accountants.[3] In establishing her own business, Aunt Audrey would fall into the top category.

This was not the only problem, unfortunately. In order to open a business, one is required to submit detailed particulars of business plans to the Director of Immigration. This proposal is then reviewed on the basis of (1) financial standing (no problem for Aunt Audrey), (2) number of Baha-

---

[3] *Bahamas Handbook and Businessman's Annual* (Nassau: Etienne Dupuch, Jr. Publications, 1976), p. 275.

mians to be employed (a potential difficulty, since there initially would be few in a real estate brokerage), and (3) the necessity to bring in foreign persons (yes, herself). Each application is decided on its own merits. There is no assurance it will receive approval. And, even when starting a business, one must still apply for a work permit.

What is more, Aunt Audrey was advised that since her proposed real estate office would be in competition with numerous Bahamian offices, and not initially employ more than one or two Bahamians, the possibility of her business application being turned down was real. The final, if relatively minor, difficulty was that Aunt Audrey would also be required to post a bond of $1,000 for each work permit or permanent residence permit issued. (Fortunately, since Audrey would not reside in the Bahamas for longer than eight months per year, she could avoid the $5,000 fee for the permanent residence permit, backed up by a property purchase requirement totalling about $50,000 and evidence of adequate financial support of $25,000 per year.)

The Bahamas intend to remain Bahamian, decided Aunt Audrey, as she unhappily walked down to the straw market on Bay Street.

Actually, had our Audrey wanted to go into the manufacturing of products which could receive government designation as "approved products," she would have found that she could enjoy several incentives including duty-free importation of raw materials and machinery, and tax exemptions. In a high-duty country, these could have been significant advantages. The Minister of Development's criteria for declaring something an "approved product" are that "such declaration is in the public interest and the manufacture of such a product will benefit the Bahamas, both economic and social considerations being taken into account." Products receiving such designations in recent years have ranged from oil refining to cement and aragonite mining.

On her way back up Bay Street toward the British

Colonial Hotel, Audrey passed by a cosmetics boutique, reminding her that while establishing such a shop would run afoul of the same problems she had encountered with a real estate office, perhaps investing in one would not. Her general inquiry of a pleasant British lady operating the boutique put a further damper on her spirits. Unless she was willing to enter into a partnership, any company limited by shares could not sell more than 39 percent interest to her or it would quadruple its annual operating tax to $1,000. Besides, if she intended to work at the business, Audrey would be subject to the usual work permit rules and would find the permit difficult to obtain because of the large number of Bahamians available as qualified salespersons. The business, she learned, would be required to advertise the job and interview locally to find a qualified Bahamian, and even if none were found, would still have to wait for the Labour Exchange to issue a certificate that no qualified person existed.

Well, at least she had one option: to find a company that might sell a minority interest strictly as an investment. She could come over for part of a year and visit her money. Or find some subterfuge to dodge the problem. Finding that in a foreign country didn't appeal to her. She decided on a piña colada at the British Colonial Neptune bar instead.

Our friend Mario was having somewhat better luck in his diggings into the usefulness of an additional haven country office for his computer products firm. He was already aware that a non-U.S. company has advantages over an individual in doing business outside the United States. Companies are granted tax advantages and concessions that U.S. individuals are not. Mario was also aware that if a foreign company is 50 percent or more controlled by non-U.S. persons, U.S. tax laws don't apply to its foreign income except in unusual cases. That type of company might be useful if he wanted to work out an arrangement with the two European salesmen, but he'd have to take the minority position, something he would prefer to avoid. In any case, he found that the percentage foreign ownership of a Bahamian company mattered only in regard to its annual operating tax. If the company was wholly owned by any given mixture of foreign shareholders, that was of no interest to Bahamian authorities.

For his company, a "Controlled Foreign Corporation" would be the likely designation under U.S. tax laws since it would probably be more than 50 percent owned by the U.S. firm. This is still satisfactory, as U.S. taxes apply only to certain kinds of foreign income in the Controlled Foreign Corporation: dividends, interest, or capital gains; insurance or reinsurance of U.S. risks; sales income where it is generated through purchase/sale of goods or services either from or to a "related person," and any increases in investments in U.S. property. Then, these types of income would be taxable to U.S. shareholders of the CFC if they owned 10 percent or more of the firm.[4] That "related person" category could be a problem in a straight foreign sales deal, Mario thought.

Mario was specifically interested in the possibility of producing computer components in the Bahamas, in establishing a sales office there, or possibly establishing a firm to deal in patent and copyright royalties on the products. He held conversations with a U.S. bank branch officer, a Bahamian attorney, and an officer of one of the "Big Eight" U.S. accounting firms which have offices in Nassau. The answers to his queries were quite straight-forward.

First, any income from sales of products or goods manufactured in the Bahamas is not subject to current U.S. taxation, even though the purchases of some items would involve the parent U.S. corporation. When profits are returned to the U.S. company in the form of dividends, they are taxable. And if he could gain a "designated product" declaration from the Minister of Development, probably based on the number of

[4] Ibid., p. 321.

local employees the firm would have, but still somewhat doubtful for computer products, he would gain the equipment importation duty advantages noted previously. In any case, there would be no local income tax on the firm. Mario noted the potential here and decided a feasibility study should be undertaken of the costs, available labor skills, plant location, etc.

As regards the viability of a sales office for U.S.-manufactured products, the situation was a bit stickier. Here the key determination was a U.S. tax problem. If the parent California firm was not involved in the purchase or sale of the products, there would be no U.S. income tax on the sales. But if the Bahamian firm was selling the U.S. company's products, clearly the U.S. company was "involved." This, Mario discovered, might mean that a separate firm, probably best established in a third jurisdiction, would have to acquire the products from the U.S. and re-sell them to the Bahamian firm. Even this presented possible problems. The activity might come under the anti-"re-invoicing" provisions of the U.S. tax code, and would certainly have to be done as an arms-length transaction at fair market value, or would cause an incidence of U.S. taxation.

With regard to the patent/copyright sales operation, Mario found the problem was again a U.S. tax incidence matter. The Bahamians would be pleased to have such a sales effort conducted there, and although the Bahamian market for such sales would be small, sales of patents to European and South American sources could be conducted from there, and income would be nontaxable in the Bahamas. The difficulty would arise in acquisition of the patents by the Bahamian company, and whether the sales would be derived from conduct of an active business in the Bahamas. In both cases, Mario was assured there could be a U.S. tax incidence if the patent was purchased by the Bahamian firm or was sold principally outside the Bahamas. He was advised to investigate a Netherlands Antilles company for these purposes as a more workable method of dealing in patents, even for sales within the United States.

The manufacturing operation appeared the best of Mario's three choices for the Bahamas. The other two would require additional investigation by the firm's U.S. tax attorneys, although the Netherlands Antilles idea appeared promising.

Mario's quest for trust information for the family estate largely paralleled that which Dr. Fred had pursued. One of the principal problems confronting the family in Italy was to find a means of transferring the assets outside that country, a task which fell to the family's *advocat.* Mario had been assured that a means could be found, possibly a *fiduciaria,* so that he need only be concerned with managing the funds for the children's and grandchildren's use.[5] His first belief was that they should be placed in a hard currency such as the Swiss franc or the Deutschemark for investment prior to distribution to either U.S. or Italian beneficiaries. In visiting one of the Swiss banks in the Bahamas, Bank Leu, he found that accounts could be opened readily, and that there existed an advantage in dealing through the Bahamas (or Cayman) branches. There would be no Swiss withholding tax on term account interest to bother with, nor would deposits be subject to so-called negative interest for accounts above 20,000 Swiss francs as would be true if held in Switzerland. The bank indicated it would accept a minimum of $25,000 or the equivalent for any term account, including investment in the Eurocurrency market. What was more, the bank would be capable of establishing a proper trust for all the beneficiaries, including those in the United States. The latter would be subject to the 6 percent interest charge upon distribution, but, Mario was advised, the long-term prognosis for the strength of the Swiss franc and the D-Mark against the dollar continued to appear favorable; and coupled with a tax-free accumulation in the trust and the fact that the interest charge

---

[5] Robert Kinsman, *Your Swiss Bank Book* (Homewood, Ill.: Dow Jones-Irwin, 1975), pp. 90–92.

was, in effect, a surcharge against the tax normally payable on a foreign trust's distributions, it was likely that the impact would not be too great if the distributions could be made before the beneficiaries had entered high tax brackets.

Mario said he'd take the whole matter under consideration and, as advised by the banker, have the family's Italian and U.S. attorneys prepare a list of requirements for submission to the bank's legal staff in Nassau.

Not a bad day, mused Mario as he rode in an elderly Cadillac taxi back to the Nassau Beach Hotel. Two available solutions to his queries, and he still had several days in Nassau, as well as three more havens to visit. Next stop: the Holiday Inn, Grand Cayman Island.

chapter 5

THE CAYMAN ISLANDS

WHILE NONE of our three travelers could meet him, they would do well to know about the most recently famous Cayman resident, a Canadian named Jean Doucet. Doucet resided for nearly six years on this small group of islands nearly 500 miles south of Miami, and in the spring of 1973 held assets of $52 million in two banks there.[1] His bank investments weren't deposits. As founder of a holding company which had established the banks, he owned them.

By September 1974, both Doucet and his banks were gone, he to Monte Carlo—his banks to liquidators. International Bank and Sterling Bank & Trust Company, both controlled by Doucet's Interbank House, now listed assets of only $4.2 million as against more than $40 million in liabilities. The demise has a lesson for all potential tax haven users, but especially users of private banks therein.

The *Wall Street Journal* viewed the collapse as "underscoring the risks of a tax haven."[2] More accurately, the situation emphasized the risks of not thoroughly investigating any use that one might have for a haven, even a bank deposit.

---

[1] *The Wall Street Journal,* January 30, 1975, p. 1.

[2] Ibid., p. 1.

The Doucet affair had warning signs blazing for anyone who took time to look critically: interest rates higher than those of competitors on term accounts, flashy equity investments in the bank's portfolio, and a flamboyant lifestyle among bank officers. Clear action is due when these warning signs occur in a tax haven. Regrettably, the signals do not always flash in time to save deposits or investments. According to authoritative reports, however, they were readily visible in the Interbank group.

One of the more reliable *long-term* warning signs about bank stability is interest rates on savings or term accounts higher than those offered by *local competitors.* (This applies to bank-versus-bank competition, not to competition between commercial banks and savings banks. Where legal differences in rates are permitted between different types of financial institutions, as in the United States, this interest differential is not a cause for direct concern.) Where one bank is outdoing the competition, or forcing other banks to raise rates to remain competitive, the chickens must home to roost eventually. Sooner or later the bank will have to reduce its interest rate expense or else it will run into difficulties. True, these may be offset by gains elsewhere within the bank. But a frequent result of this compensation effort is the taking of greater investment risks, as in the case of the Franklin National Bank of New York.

This was the first warning at Doucet's banks. He did pay higher interest rates than the other 160-odd banks in Cayman at the time of Interbank's demise. As late in the bank's life as September 1973, the Interbank Group was advertising 8 percent per annum interest on savings accounts in Cayman, Canadian, and U.S. dollars, compared to most other banks' rates of 3.5 percent to 5 percent in the same currencies. Whether this was a critical factor in Interbank's collapse is not known. It may well be that Doucet's banks had not been paying higher rates for a sufficient period of time for this expense, in itself, to generate liquidity-squeeze losses. But it was a clear warning sign. Another overshadowed it.

Most banks find it necessary to confine their lending activities to straight debt instruments such as construction loans, consumer loans, and general business loans. More commonly overseas than in the U.S., equity "kickers" are added, perhaps a profit participation in a real estate development project, for example. Where straight equity investments are made in the overseas bank's portfolio, they are usually small in relation to the debt portion. And these are not permitted at all in U.S. bank portfolios.

Not so with the Doucet group. A June 1973 brochure printed by the group announced several investments that came right out of the "gunslinger" U.S. equity markets of six years earlier. Some $75,000 went into 70 percent ownership of a Canadian subsidiary of New York-based Patents International Affiliates, which held rights to a device to determine the sex of an unborn child by testing the saliva of the expectant mother.[3] The brochure stated that Johnson & Johnson Company intended to market the device. A company spokesman later stated that plans had been dropped in late 1972. (Doucet did get his capital back on that one.)

Further adventures in the pharmaceutical field were indicated in the booklet. They included underwriting of a new stock issue in Dento Enzyme Pharmaceutical Corporation "along with 16 international banking and financing companies." The company was to manufacture an anti-tooth decay vaccine. Nothing came of the product.

A clear loss to the Doucet group was a $2 million investment in a planned $10 million townhouse and condominium project on Grand Cayman called Mitchell Creek Gardens. The $2 million went in prior to beginning construction. Nothing but a shell of a home for Mr. Doucet and family came out within a year of his banking group's demise. (The

[3] Ibid., p. 19.

project was restarted under the name Lime Tree Bay in 1975.)

These and other speculations in a turtle farm, a nightclub, two freighters, and a cattle ranch in Quebec became a substantial part of the bank group's investment portfolio. The liquidators charged in a 1974 report to creditors that the owners had tied up too much capital in speculative ventures, leaving too little in reserve for cash withdrawals. In some of these projects, according to the liquidators, the bank didn't receive any collateral, let alone such stodgy items as signed notes, trust deeds, or securities endorsements.

Thus, warning signal two to add to our original caution.

The final fillip came in the lavish spending habits of Doucet himself, allegedly on a $40,000-per-year salary as head of Interbank House. "Lavish and extravagant overheads," was the liquidator's phrase. It included a 1,000-guest party to celebrate the opening of a new bank office at Seven Mile Beach in Grand Cayman (about four miles from the main office on an island just 22 miles across at its widest point).[4] Beluga caviar and champagne were the staples of the night, which was less than a year before Doucet's departure. "He was spending money as if it were going out of style," was the comment of one Caymanian banker.

The pattern seems all too familiar: "He was a super salesman," observed another banker. "He advertised like hell and his public relations efforts were tremendous." An explanation comes from a colleague: "Doucet was depending on a continuing inflow of new money to fund all these schemes of his. He didn't make any normal allowance for reserves to protect against even modest withdrawals."

Before the real party was over, Doucet had opened banking offices in Miami, Montreal, London, and Geneva, imported a circular bed and $200 bar stools for his new home,

[4] Ibid., p. 1.

and managed to make friends with most of the island's businessmen and numerous local residents. He left 120 employees without jobs, 150 construction workmen on his condominium project without either jobs or a project, and a Cayman court occupied with his prosecution for nearly a year.

It will be a long time before the 15,000 residents of that three-island Caribbean oasis forget Jean Doucet. He was arrested in Monaco during May 1975 and returned to stand trial. Found guilty that November of "fraudulent conversion" (misapplication of funds), involving more than U.S. $1 million, he was sentenced to nine months in prison, the judge noting that his crime was apparently not for personal gain.

It should also be a long time before we forget there are danger signals to observe in small banks, especially private ones, and especially in tax havens. They may not be foolproof warnings, but as potential customers we don't need to *prove* that a bank is dangerous before we select another one.

Thus, it is important that you obtain detailed information from *privately* controlled banks. By detailed information we are not referring to a quarterly balance sheet and income statement. More is required. This point is expanded upon in Chapter 8 regarding Swiss banks, but deserves comment here because of its inherent applicability to the Doucet matter.

Of course, it is not simple to obtain data from any bank. In the case of a major bank with a multibranch international network and public ownership, you have reason to assume that the bank will *exist* over a period of time. But with a private bank you had better check out every detail concerning the bank and its owners. If you aren't fully satisfied, avoid the bank. Admittedly, this is hard on smaller private banks. But no depositor wants to become a personal charity. The problem should be the bank's, not yours.

We also must note that even major public banks are not immune to difficulties. Witness Swiss Credit Bank's Chiasso affair (see page 223). But they most often weather them. Few small, private banks can, and especially when management practices are open to question.

We by no means wish to suggest that all smaller private banks are risky. After all, most major banks started that way. What we do suggest is that a lack of published data for a private bank covering financial records, personal backgrounds (including the owners' investment holdings), and bank portfolio investments should make a depositor wary.

This also creates a difficulty in tax havens per se, since little detailed information is required by the banking authorities of any bank, and little of that is available or even meaningful. And no haven country has bank deposit insurance. As a result, we have established a series of specific criteria in haven bank selection for the use of our clients. In most tax havens, it comes down to avoiding any bank that is not part of an international banking group with a publicly held parent in either the United States, Canada, the United Kingdom, or Switzerland, that does not provide data in English, and does not use authorized accounting standards.

Despite the name of one of Doucet's banks, International Bank, his group would have failed our initial criteria.

SAND, STABILITY, AND SANCTUARY

Despite the ravages of the Doucet affair, and they were devastating in a small community that relies heavily on financial reputation, the Cayman Islands remain one of the most attractive tax havens for both Americans and non-Americans. For tourists, it may be the incredibly lovely long white sand beaches. For tax protection seekers, stability must be one of the major initial pluses. Cayman is one of the few remaining British crown colonies in the world, having decided to retain that status in 1962 when Jamaica, to which Cayman was formerly tied, gained independence. Cayman has a governor, appointed by Queen Elizabeth II, an executive council, a legislative assembly, and a new constitution dating from 1972. The population is without racial problems, with roughly 20 percent white, 25 percent black, and the balance of mixed blood. All are integrated socially and politically. There are no political parties, not by decree but from lack of interest or need.

Even crime is a negligible problem in Cayman. A diary of events for 1975 noted that the September opening of the Grand Court Session was, for the second year, without a criminal case on the docket.[5]

English is the official language of Cayman, and English common law is the basis for local jurisprudence. Thus English trust law provides a substantial body of practice for use with this financial planning device. Cayman has a modern companies law, has good professional facilities, despite its size, and has about 220 banks and trust companies operating within its perimeters. This latter fact gives Cayman one financial institution for every 70 residents, probably the highest ratio in the world.

This also reminds us of the biggest disadvantage of Cayman. It is very, very small. Out of the water, there is preciously little to do there, including no television and but one new (1976) radio station. The business climate is fine, as is the weather, but since only about 12,000 persons live on the main island of Grand Cayman, the product market is miniscule. Even the 50,000 visitors per year provide small business incentive.

A flavor of the island's happenings comes from the same 1975 diary noted above, which observes the important events in the country. A sampling for January:

> By far the most newsworthy event of January was the three-day creditors' meeting in the matter of the liquidation of the Interbank House Group.
>
> The Cayman Friends Hospital Fund went over the $1,000

[5] *The Cayman Islands Handbook and Businessman's Guide, 1976* (Grand Cayman: The Northwester Company), pp. 17–25.

mark at a fund-raising dance at the Royal Palms. Over 250 people, including the Governor, attended.

For February:

The Cayman Rugby Football Club registered the most remarkable achievement of its brief, three-year history when it won the Andrews Cup. . . . This was secured by individual victories over each of the six competing Jamaican clubs.

The Agriculture Show was held at the High School. This is a regular event of each Ash Wednesday. Future shows will be staged at the Department of Agriculture grounds on Smith Road, currently under development.

And from July:

At a well-attended evening event at the Holiday Inn, Miss Lovenia Miller of North Side, Grand Cayman, was chosen as Miss Cayman Islands, 1975. Along with the fanfare and recognition, Lovenia won a week-long trip to Indiana and U.S. $250.

So much for excitement.

On the other hand, this lack of crowded schedules and business pressures is precisely the advantage of relaxing in Cayman. And certainly one need spend little time there to take advantage of the tax planning attributes, as our three travelers from the Bahamas soon discovered. As with their former visit, two or three days is about all that is required to become familiar with the lay of the land.

Travelers arrive

Perusing their Cayman tourist literature aboard a Southern Airways DC-9 daily flight from Miami (on a midweek excursion fare of $106 roundtrip), the three discovered that, like the Bahamas, Cayman is expensive. When one looks at hotel prices, meals, entertainment, quoted from Cayman, one must remember that the Cayman dollar (C$) is worth

U.S. $1.20. While Cayman prices appear high when quoted in *their* dollars, they're 20 percent higher in U.S. dollars.

The in-season Holiday Inn rates (the only hotel in Cayman with more than 100 rooms) range from U.S. $58 to $73 double per day, depending on location, the latter on the beach front. This was slightly less than Nassau's Cable Beach hotels. Taxi fares to the Holiday Inn from the airport, the trio discovered after their 80-minute flight plus customs clearance, ran over $7.50 with tip, and would top $4.00 from the Inn to George Town's business district. Other common travel expenditures were comparable to those of the Bahamas, and were high for the same reason the Bahamas were high: stiff import duties on virtually all goods as the principal government revenue source. Plus the fact that Cayman has longer transportation routes.

Dr. Fred thinks of property

Looking over his notes from the Bahamas enroute to a meeting with an officer of one of the large trust companies in George Town, Dr. Fred noted that a Bahamian trust officer had suggested that there was less business expertise in Cayman, less experienced people and younger people. He had said that many bank and trust companies report to head offices in Nassau. And that there were many similarities between the two havens. "Interesting," thought the Doctor. "Is that why Cayman is growing faster, or is it because Cayman is so new?"

He was shortly to discover that numerous legal similarities between the two havens did indeed exist (the no-tax structure is virtually identical), but that it was also common practice among competitors in neighboring tax havens to put down each other's nation. The Caymanian trust officer later politely inquired about the stability of the black government in Nassau with that country's unemployment problems. (There are almost no jobless in Cayman.) From there on, Dr.

Fred found he was discussing an almost mirror set of circumstances for trust development as between the Bahamas and Cayman. There was one exception.

Cayman permits the establishment of *exempted* trusts (and companies), which carry a government guarantee that no taxes will be imposed on them for a period of 50 years from the date of establishment, provided no beneficiary becomes a Cayman resident. Moreover, such a trust may have a fixed duration of 100 years, an exception to the common-law rule against perpetuities. Cayman, Dr. Fred was advised, is the only tax haven to offer such advantages. However, when inquiring about fees, Dr. Fred uncovered the disadvantage of an exempted trust. A registration fee of U.S. $240 is required, as is an annual fee of $120, neither of which apply to ordinary trusts. Not much, but a factor. Investigating further, he found that since every properly drawn foreign trust should contain what is known as a "Cuba clause," permitting withdrawal of the trust to another jurisdiction under specified adverse circumstances, including the future imposition of taxes on it, the Cayman exempted trust may not be worth the extra cost compared to an ordinary one. Our friend Mario will find the opposite to be true about exempted companies.

Finding the body of Cayman trust law so similar to that of the Bahamas as to not require differentiation to him, and the number of highly regarded trust companies in the two havens offering him a wide choice, and the communications costs only slightly more expensive to Cayman, Dr. Fred was inclined to prefer the political and racial stability of Cayman over that of the Bahamas. He found he was weighing small, predictive presumptions in doing so.

One other matter occurred to him. In the Bahamas he had been inclined to consider purchase of any property. He wasn't certain that the sun-baked flatness of Cayman appealed to him, but perhaps there could be some advantage in purchasing if he selected Cayman for trust administration. He still preferred the idea of having trustees in sight of the trust property, however unnecessary they said it was. He delved into this subject and found that nonresidents could own Caymanian property through a trust or company, subject to certain stamp taxes. While property was expensive, it was less so than Florida's better areas, and according to one of the realtors on Grand Cayman, offered growth potential to match that of Cayman international business.

Dr. Fred also recalled that one possible use of the new U.S. grantor trust rules was to place a depreciable property in the trust, netting income against the depreciation, and taking any excess depreciable losses against his own taxes. Of course, upon retirement his income tax bracket wouldn't be anywhere near what it had been, but if the real estate income could build up tax-free in the trust, he could still receive the depreciable losses, however valuable, and with projected property appreciation, the concept might make sense.

However, a problem popped to mind. What about the currency? The Cayman dollar was pegged to the U.S. dollar. While that might change in the future, he felt he could lose much of the advantage he believed possible in holding hard currencies like the D-Mark or Swiss franc. A Swiss banker in George Town could offer no real help. If he established a trust there it could be nonresident for exchange control purposes, but once the trustees wished to purchase Cayman property, specific approval from the Controller of Exchange would be required. That meant an application for approval that set forth not only the terms of the proposed acquisition but also the benefits to the Island's balance of payments, and further a request to take the income, profits and, eventually, the initial capital out in a foreign currency. The banker offered no odds on approval. It was unusual enough that "we'd have to see." The banker had suggested an investment in some other haven, one that could be acquired with a hard currency and then be supervised by his bank as trustee in Cayman. This might even be done in Switzerland, he was told, under certain circumstances.

This appealed to hard money advocate Dr. Fred much more. But he was still going to have to separate the trust assets from the trustees. In this case, at least the same Swiss bank would be involved.

Aunt Audrey takes heart

At the time that Dr. Fred was completing his discussion with the local Swiss banker, Aunt Audrey had ascertained that, like the Bahamas, Cayman was highly protective of its local business community and workers. She found that any company wishing to carry on local business must be licensed by the Caymanian Protection Board as called for in the Local Companies (Control) Law. She was told that the Board's approval could be granted, but that it wasn't easy to obtain unless the firm had "substantial" Caymanian participation. Sixty percent or more local ownership would classify the company as Caymanian and permit a license to be issued "as a matter of course." The fees for obtaining this license vary by type of business, but will be about $200 on establishment and the same amount per annum, she was advised. This would be in addition to the normal fees for incorporating a company. (See the following section.) Thus, Aunt Audrey was faced with the same problem as in the Bahamas: the need to obtain extensive Caymanian participation in any company or face refusal on application for a business license. But, there was another difficulty. With less than 60 percent Caymanian participation, license approval, she was told, depended quite a bit on the type of business. Manufacturing and light industry would be fine, but a real estate brokerage, for example, would probably meet with difficulty unless she was willing to inject a substantial amount of capital.

Her discussions at the offices of the board now turned to the matter of the work permit (termed "gainful occupation license"). Aunt Audrey was told that, as she wished to be self-employed, she should give the Board a detailed letter setting forth the important aspects of the business, the number of local staff to be employed, and her financial status confirmed by her bank. She was also advised that as a foreign resident starting a new business in the islands she would not likely have any difficulty in acquiring the permit for herself, but that if she wished to bring in additional foreign workers they would not be granted work permits until the Board could be satisfied that no one now residing in the Colony was "suitable, available, qualified, and willing to undertake such employment."[6] Then came the pleasant surprise. The fee for each work permit was only $10. Immigration to Cayman was only a matter of application formalities, once the work permit conditions were met. After one year's residence, Americans could apply for permanent resident status.

Certainly the Cayman government welcome was less expensive than the Bahamas for foreigners wanting to do business, thought Aunt Audrey. But, the fundamental terms weren't much different. The government would still withhold approval if, in their minds, the business didn't do enough for the country. What she now needed to find was a Caymanian resident investor who would be interested in joining her in forming a real estate company on Grand Cayman. It was a thought she had skipped over lightly in Nassau because of the stiff work permit fee there. She decided that a visit to several of the major international bank or trust company branches in George Town was the first order of business in that process, coupled with a little background research on the local real estate market. The real question was whether, with 18 real estate firms already operating on Grand Cayman, there would be room for one more.

---

[6] Ibid., p. 194.

Mario has a good day

Mario had just received assurances from an officer of Barclays Bank International, Ltd., in George Town, that there would be no difference in the U.S. tax considerations between a company established in the Bahamas and one in Cayman. As before, the manufacturing concept appeared most viable, but he was introduced to two new thoughts (they could be accomplished in any haven). One was the establishment of a CFC that would inventory the computer products from California and make required adjustments and assemblies before reselling them to the European and South American markets. The other suggestion he received was on the importance of finding *several* foreign partners who would be interested in owning more than 51 percent of the company, so that it could qualify as a non–U.S.-controlled foreign corporation. The bank officer said that several firms were operating in Cayman in both of these ways. In one instance, where a U.S. firm owned the largest single block of shares, it had effective control over the diverse interests and locations of the other owners. To be sure, the others could agree to block the U.S. firm's interests, but that would only occur if serious problems arose. In another instance, a firm processing U.S.-manufactured products outside the United States and in a haven jurisdiction, the price the Cayman company paid the U.S. firm for the basic product was taxable to the U.S. firm, but the profits made between this price and the modified units' price when sold to the foreign markets were probably not taxable in the United States, and certainly not in Cayman, even if the firm were more than 50 percent U.S. controlled. Mario remembered a conversation with his firm's attorney that had brought out the importance of handling such connected firms' intercompany sales. First, the transaction must be made at fair market value under paragraph 482 of the Internal Revenue Code. And second, where foreign manufacturing was involved, it must be real manufacturing, not just adjusting a previously manufactured item.

Thus, he thought, if the California product were sold to the Cayman firm at slightly above the actual cost of manufacture, and a key item required for foreign use was purchased from another firm, it was likely that true manufacturing could be accomplished in Cayman with little taxable profit to the California firm. Moreover, the net profit between the total cost to the Cayman firm and the international sales price could be significant. The Cayman firm could then build up these profits tax-free.

Both ideas appealed to Mario. The products did require modification to meet certain European and South American specifications, but it was not a difficult process and could likely be learned by a local Cayman work force, with the additional advantage that the process would not require many persons, probably no more than eight or ten, the same as in the United States. Mario was told that wage rates would be about U.S. $3 to $4 per hour, the rates paid for heavy equipment operators in Cayman. That was certainly less than the plant was paying in California.

The idea of locating foreign investors for the company might solve an additional problem for Mario. He might offer his two European salesmen a stock incentive to stay with the U.S. firm, allowing them to pay for their stock out of commissions, and by having a bank or investment firm locate two or three other outside investors, a package could be put together giving that foreign group controlling interest, although effective control could be had by the California firm with its largest single block of shares. Either or both of these approaches would work equally well in the Bahamas, of course. It was at this point, however, that the Barclays officer brought up the subject of exempted companies in Cayman.

He told Mario that the exempted company device was for use by foreigners who wished to have the Cayman tax advantages but who did their main business outside the islands. Doing work in the islands in furtherance of business overseas would not be a disqualifying factor. Mario was also advised that an exempted company could obtain a government guarantee against any future taxation for a period of up to 30 years, the common period being 20 years.

In a booklet prepared by Cayman International Trust Company, which is owned by Barclays, Hambros Bank, N. M. Rothschild and Sons, the Bank of New York, and four other financial institutions, Mario found the other advantages of the Cayman exempted company:

1. No annual return of shareholders need be filed, nor need a register of shareholders be maintained or made available for inspection by the public.
2. No par value shares may be issued.
3. Bearer shares (fully paid) may, subject to Exchange Control approval, be issued but must be marked as not available to be held by Scheduled Territories residents.
4. While there is no requirement that a meeting of shareholders be held in each year, the Board of Directors must hold at least one meeting in each calendar year in the Islands. (Note: Such a meeting may be held by "Alternate Directors" present in the Islands.)
5. The name need not include the work "Limited" or "Ltd", and the name may be in a foreign language in addition to English, if desired.
6. An exempted company may not trade in the Cayman Islands except in furtherance of its business carried on outside the Islands.

None of these appeared particularly important to Mario in terms of his computer products firm, except the lack of need for a shareholders meeting, which could be helpful in maintaining control of the firm. But the lack of identification of shareholders might be important to the foreign investors, including his salesmen, as might be the possible issuance of bearer shares.

The costs of incorporating a Cayman company were certainly not expensive: less than in the Bahamas, more than in the U.S. The bank officer handed Mario the current fee schedule.

Government fees on incorporation	
Nonresident ordinary company	0.2 percent of authorized capital, minimum U.S. $366, maximum U.S. $1,220.
Exempted company	0.1 percent of authorized capital, minimum U.S. $732, maximum U.S. $1,952.
Government fees annually	
Nonresident ordinary company	Minimum U.S. $184 Maximum U.S. $610
Exempted company	Minimum U.S. $366 Maximum U.S. $1,220

Mario noted that an exempted company could have authorized capital up to U.S. $720,000 for the minimum fees, and was told that an ordinary company could be incorporated by the bank or Cayman International Trust Co. for about U.S. $850 in staff fees, and an exempt company for about U.S. $1,500, unless the company was very large or details quite complex.

One admonition was offered Mario by the Barclays officer: For any nonresident company, either ordinary or exempted, it would be important that whatever activity the firm undertook in Cayman be totally in pursuit of its foreign business. "If yours is a sales company," he said, "which does some inventorying and product adjustment in the islands, but does no other business here, even though it employs Caymanians, it should be granted the nonresident status. This will permit the firm to hold foreign currency accounts (in fact, it must do so, except for payroll and local expenses), and if it is sold or liquidated the proceeds can be remitted in foreign currencies. If it does not receive the nonresident status it will be considered a resident company, subject to Cayman exchange control, and required to hold all assets and accounts in Cayman dollars." He added that one exception may be granted under what is known as an "approved status," permitting transfer of funds into foreign currencies, but that this was not very common.

Upon leaving, Mario picked up the usual handful of literature describing the bank and its services, and those of its sister trust company. Glancing through the material on the cab ride to his hotel, he noted a couple of additional points of potential interest. First, that shares in a Cayman company may be issued for cash, property, or services. The latter means should permit a portion of the shares to be issued for organizational or promotional services: a means of reducing the capital contribution of his parent firm, as long as the other stockholders would buy the idea.

Secondly, he saw that a Cayman company may issue several classes of shares with different rights for each class. This could include voting versus nonvoting stock, or dividend versus non-dividend shares, as well as preferred stock. What's more, the latter could be a redeemable issue, unlike the common stock. These offered additional possibilities. Perhaps the foreign stockholders would prefer dividend-paying shares and his California company would not, at least for the time being. That might be accomplished by a redeemable preferred issue for the foreign investors plus a common share of 51 percent. They could receive dividends for a given period until the company wished to retire the issue and begin paying common stock dividends. By requiring that the preferred be fully paid in, the cash received could be kept in an interest-bearing time deposit, accumulating interest tax-free, if there were no other need for it is company operating capital. Provided the dividend payment was less than the interest, this would not only cover the annual dividend but add a bonus besides.

Mario also noted that Cayman had passed a new Confidential Relationships (Preservation) Law in 1976. It was their equivalent of the Swiss bank secrecy law, and from all indications very far-reaching in scope. It made the trading in or misuse of confidential information by anyone a criminal offense, and covered actions outside Cayman when related to Cayman subject matter, as well as acts within the islands themselves. He found the Act was brief, only two pages, and that a copy could be obtained from any bank or trust company or attorney, as well as from the government.

All in all a most satisfactory day, Mario felt. It wasn't that Cayman offered more different corporate vehicles or possibilities than the Bahamas. It was just that certain of them permitted small pluses, which taken together added up to more than minor advantages from his company's standpoint. And he could save some fee expense. Add in the government stability and attitude factor, and the scale was beginning to tip toward Cayman.

He still had the Netherlands Antilles royalty point to unearth, plus the Channel Islands and Liechtenstein to delve into.

He was looking forward to the flight to London as a jumping off point for the Channel. Too bad there wasn't a golf course on Grand Cayman to absorb some time until the return flight to Miami.

chapter 6

TWO EUROPEANS: THE CHANNEL ISLANDS AND LIECHTENSTEIN

"THE QUEEN'S OWN ISLANDS," "Pieces of France Fallen into the Sea," and "The Sunny Islands" are appellations attached to the covey of land bits lying in the English Channel, 14 miles off the hook of France's Cherbourg peninsula. We know them simply as the Channel Islands. The two largest, Jersey and Guernsey, account for almost the entire population, and certainly all of the financial matters of concern.

Another island, Sark, is of interest for its charm, lack of any motorized vehicles, and hereditary ruling Seigneur. It also acquired some fame in the early 70s as a pivot point in the United States's largest insurance fraud: The wholly notional Bank of Sark, with an "audited" balance sheet of $72 million, was identified as administrator and guarantor of multimillions of equally fictional insurance company assets.[1]

Alderney, Herm, and a half dozen other land chunks are usually named as part of the Islands, depending principally on how large a rock one calls an island.

Historically, the Channel Islands were battled over by England and France for half a dozen centuries until 1781, with

[1] *The Wall Street Journal,* September 20, 1973, p. 10.

England prevailing at the last decision. Great Britain is now responsible for their defense and foreign affairs, and they are part of the few scheduled territories of Great Britain for exchange control purposes. Other governmental matters are handled by local legislative bodies called "States," one each for the Bailiwicks of Jersey and Guernsey.

The Channel Islands are probably the most accessible tax havens in the world, if measured by the frequency of arriving/departing transport during the summer season (although access is still good from October through March). From either France or England, by water or air, travelers have no trouble reaching these quaint combinations of British and French heritage. British Airways sends five flights daily into Jersey from London (three on weekend days), and three into Guernsey every day. Aircraft will vary from BAC 111 jets to Trident jet-props, with fares about £20 ($35) one-way for the 50-minute flight. Coming from Paris is only a bit less handy, and all flights are on privately owned airlines. Hydrofoils and ferries make runs too numerous to mention from the French coastal towns, and a few from England.

The Channel Islands may be the Queen's Own, but their residents are highly jealous of their prerogatives. One of these is taxation. As the Islands are not part of the United Kingdom, they retain full powers to establish their own levels and means of taxation. This they have opted to do at the point of 20 percent of net income for both corporations and individuals. Thus the Islands' designation as a low-tax rather than no-tax haven. However, an important caveat to this taxation law makes certain companies subject to only an annual £300 (about $525) tax, in effect similar to the annual fees paid in the Bahamas or Cayman under no-tax conditions. Mario will shortly discover that the key consideration in this exemption is where these companies are resident and where they are managed (controlled).

While the Channel Islands do control their own taxation, Britain has recently (December 1974) enacted a tax bill levying a capital transfer tax on the worldwide assets of anyone either domiciled or deemed to be domiciled in the United Kingdom. Its effect on the Channel Islands will not be of concern to any of our three haven investigators (except to cause banks or trust companies there to be more interested in U.S. business), but is of much concern to Channel Island residents. The law prevents any resident of the United Kingdom prior to November 12, 1974, from transferring assets to the Islands without payment of a stiff tax penalty. Its effect has been to substantially slow the flow of business into the Islands from their primary source, and raise serious questions about the United Kingdom's future ability to negatively affect Island residents through tax legislation.

Our travelers will discover that Jersey and Guernsey are substantially different islands, with different laws and governments, different business facilities, and even different methods of levying the same basic tax. Jersey has the more developed tax haven business facilities and is consequently used more frequently, except where there is occasion to use both jurisdictions—an occasion which arises more often than one might expect because of a legal distinction involving the location of corporate management. However, they share one important advantage for our travelers (and any others). The Channel Islands are without question the least expensive of any of the tax havens we are dealing with. And notably so.

Arriving in the off season in March, as our trio did, even the sinking-pound-reduced prices of London seemed substantial in comparison, while those of the Bahamas and Cayman were astronomical. Any of the three top hotels in St. Helier, Jersey, provided single rooms with full board of three meals for £11.50 ($20.63)! Add £3 to £4 for double occupancy. And, of the £11.50, only £2 represented meals, a substantial encouragement to attend one of the hotels' regular "seatings" for lunch or dinner. Still, dinner in one of the good restaurants, some with fine French cuisine, and nearly all with good French wines, will rarely run more than £4 per person (about $7). An inclination toward Bass, Charington, Courage, Whitbread, or Watney's ales will cost not more than 40p or about $0.70 a pint, usually less. Pubs are open all day.

The reason for the low cost of staying: the Channel Islands compete with Spain, Brighton, and France's Normandy coast for tourist dollars, not with Rome or Paris.

Dr. Fred takes courage

Dr. Fred, during lunch with a local trust company officer, had heeded the pub sign "Take Courage" and polished off a half pint of its adequately chilled brew. He pondered the belief that there was going to be little more he could discover about trusts in tax havens. The trust officer had initially advised him that with trusts there was really no advantage between one tax haven and another. Fred had to admit that thus far he had found only technicalities; however, he had been told that trusts could be a problem for U.S. tax purposes in the Channel Islands. The problem arose, he was advised, because these islands have no specific trust law per se. Rather, they assume the existence of common-law trusts, and courts there have upheld them. Whether the IRS, which has not specifically stated whether it will treat Channel Island trusts as falling under French civil law or English common law, will challenge them in the future, is problematical, Dr. Fred had been told.

The trust officer couldn't enlighten him as to U.S. IRS policies, of course. However, he did point out that Jersey was considering a new trust law, and that with the past establishment of so many trusts there it would be difficult to imagine that the IRS would treat them as nontrusts for tax purposes.

"But, nevertheless, a possibility," Dr. Fred mused, to which the trust officer observed, "With revenue agents, anything is possible. In any case, we ensure that trusts are drawn most carefully here."

In addition to this concern, Dr. Fred found out that in order for a trust to be declared nonresident of the Islands, the tax authorities there must be convinced that the trust's settlor (grantor) and beneficiaries are nonresidents. Then the trust will be taxed only where it is created (resident) on income arising there. It was common for a trust to be established in Jersey and to do its banking in Guernsey. There was no tax in Jersey because it earned no income there, and no tax in Guernsey because it wasn't resident there.[2] However, both islands now permit exempt trusts established by nonresidents to pay no income tax on interest earned by bank deposits within their jurisdictions, eliminating the need for that modest bit of location fiction.[3] In addition, nonresident trusts are exempt from Exchange Control regulations of the Bank of England when trustees are, in effect, an authorized depository of the Bank and guarantee that its actions are proper.

No estate taxes or death duties existed in the Channel Islands, Fred discovered, but that was also true of the other havens, and unfortunately had no bearing on U.S. estate taxes.

Dr. Fred had returned briefly to his old theme of having trustees direct and control the trust assets close at hand, inquiring whether it wouldn't be possible for a Jersey or Guernsey nonresident trust to acquire income property in the Islands. Yes, it could, he was told, but there were conditions. First, it would have to be done with pounds Sterling, probably through a leasehold or freehold, and after Bank of England exchange control permission, which was obtainable, and permission from the local Housing Committee. However, the income from the property was subject to the 20 percent Jersey income tax, and any initial cash balance to be used to acquire the property would first have to be invested in Guernsey to avoid a Jersey tax. Finally, the income after

2 Marshall Langer, *How to Use Foreign Tax Havens,* p. 209.

3 Practicing Law Institute, *Foreign Tax Planning, 1977,* p. 187.

tax could be accumulated in the trust and reinvested in a foreign currency with Bank of England concurrence.

The trust officer thought one other point was worth mentioning to Dr. Fred.

"We can execute a document known as a Declaration of Trust, whereby we accept trust funds to hold and manage under terms set forth in the Declaration. Your name, as settlor, need never appear in the trust documents."

"If I've got nothing to hide," asked Fred, "why handle it that way?"

"We never know what the future might bring, do we?" queried the trust man. He had a point.

But the point that Fred got was the tax liability on income arising from within the island where the trust was created, even though it was nonresident type. This was a worse problem than in Cayman or the Bahamas.

Fred had little more to pursue, except the matter of costs for trust establishment and oversight. Here he found some apparent differences. Barclaytrust quoted an acceptance fee of £250 plus about £250 for legal work, where Wobaco Trust (Jersey) stated their fees in a printed schedule as $450 legal, $250 acceptance. Both subject to change, of course. But the difference, Fred learned, was largely one of current exchange rates compared to those on the date the schedule was printed. The annual maintenance fees were 0.75 percent of trust capital at both institutions, and 1.25 percent on capital distributed to beneficiaries. They each got something going in and going out.

Going out was Dr. Fred's plan for the afternoon, and after lunch, the Freds set out by taxi for St. Brelade's Bay, one of the 20 beaches on Jersey basking in sunny 60°, if somewhat windy, weather that March day. London had been 39° and raining the day before. The difference had something to do with the Gulf Stream in the Channel, Fred recalled.

Our Aunt Audrey had been shut off just as she was beginning her inquiries of the day. She had been told by a local bank officer that he was terribly sorry to have to advise her that the right of occupancy of a piece of property was difficult to obtain and that immigration into the islands had all but been closed off to foreigners. No, he had said, there was no work permit required in the islands similar to the Bahamas or Cayman, and business licenses could be obtained, so long as the use of the property didn't change. A new small business could replace an old one in a building devoted to small business use, but the building could not be converted to, say, residential use. Audrey was a bit confused. "I don't need to buy or lease a property," she explained, "just to begin a small business. It can be in a shop which has gone out of business." In that case, she was advised, her real problem would be one of finding such a location. If that could be accomplished, and she didn't require much labor, a business license probably would be approved. She was relieved, but the feeling was short-lived.

Unfortunately, there was still the problem of how to live in Jersey (or Guernsey) while operating the business. The island was accepting about 15 families as immigrants per year, each agreeing to pay a minimum tax based on the 20 percent income tax rate. That fact hadn't seemed too bad to Audrey, compared with her U.S. and state income tax rates in California, until the banker said that the *minimum tax* would be £10,000 per year (about $17,500) ! In addition to that, there were virtually no apartments available, modest townhouses didn't exist, and the occasional executive estate leaseholds could reach £150,000, *if* the owners wished to move and not remain as renters. One didn't automatically receive occupancy rights with purchase. The alternative would probably be staying at a guest house or hotel and traveling to France every three months to reestablish her tourist status. Plus, of course, her business income would be subject to the 20 percent tax rate.

The charm of the narrow hilly streets of Jersey were apparently meant for long established residents and tourists, with no category in between, thought Aunt Audrey, as she politely thanked the banker for his time. Maybe she was giving up too easily, she thought, but she could do better in Cayman. Why couldn't it be as charming as Jersey?

Mario investigates the Companies Law

Mario had developed a fondness for the town of St. Helier, as had our other haven seekers, but more for the quiet little shops laid out by the dozens on several streets in the central part of town. As with most tax havens, many items were offered under special duty exemptions; watches, some jewelry, and perfumes were the common lures. Scattered among the vendors were the island's 25 banks and associated trust companies. Numerous law offices and chartered accountants displayed their tax haven accoutrements: rows of managed company names on plates outside office doors. Mario stepped in one such office to visit an attorney in his quest for haven company information that morning. The well-known French lawyer stated the islands' case for U.S. business first-off.

"The advantages of the tax haven," he offered bluntly, "are greatest when farthest away from the eyes of the relevant regulatory authorities, I think." He cited the 1974 British law applying the capital transfer tax to the Channel Islands and the Isle of Man on a permanent basis. Those moving elsewhere from the United Kingdom were only penalized if assets were moved within three years. "That," the attorney opined, "is–how you say–discrimination, no?"

Mario then delved into the sometimes confusing Channel Islands nonresident company, known as the corporation tax company. Once established as nonresident, it need pay only an annual tax of £300 unless it earns income, other than bank interest, in the Islands, in which case it is taxed at the rate of 20 percent on that income. In order to be nonresident, either the place of formation or the place of control of the corporation, the latter evidenced by where directors' meetings are held, must be outside of Jersey/Guernsey. As a result, companies owned by nonresidents of Jersey/Guernsey, but formed in those islands, have long engaged in a piece of legal fiction. The directors, often provided by a local bank, trust company, or associated attorneys, travel once a year to Sark (which has no corporate law) or France or elsewhere to hold board meetings for a list of firms. This satisfies the requirement.

The French attorney noted that the other side of the coin could be advantageous too. Companies nonresident for exchange control (the Channel Islands, as part of the scheduled territories, fall under the strict exchange control of the Bank of England), or those owned by nonresidents, must have approval of the Bank upon establishment. This is usually done by certification of a local bank which is an "authorized depository" for exchange funds. While the Bank of England has agreed to give names of shareholders full anonymity, they must still be provided to the Bank by the Island bank. To avoid this, and still keep nonresident status, a company could be incorporated elsewhere, say Bermuda or Bahamas or Cayman, and be managed in Jersey, with the directors still taking their customary annual journey outside the two islands for establishment of offshore control.

That could only make sense, thought Mario, if the company had something to hide. Otherwise, why pay an annual fee to the governments of two havens? Just to blur the traces?

The attorney indicated that before a company was established in Jersey/Guernsey, he would want to check out the company's "scheme" or plan for doing business. He said he wanted to insure its viability so that it wouldn't fizzle after six months and not pay its fees. "The banks and authorities want to know what you're doing and why you're doing it," he explained.

"Neat combination of tell them something, but not everything," observed Mario. The attorney smiled. "We must be aboveboard here," he replied. The implication was to do the tricky things elsewhere, hardly an unexpected stance for a lawyer in a small town, thought Mario.

The other provisions of local Companies Law were quite straightforward. A company is required to keep a list of its shareholders at its registered office, to file an annual return with specifics of capital and shareholders every January, to hold an annual General Meeting of shareholders and of directors, keep minutes, etc. Several points caught Mario's attention in the list of particulars provided by the attorney: The purpose or object of the company's being in business cannot be changed under the Companies Law, although the name and capital may now be altered by Special Resolution. Secondly, bearer shares are not permitted, and while shareholders must be identified, this can be accomplished through use of three nominee shareholders, permitting the beneficial owner (s) to not be identified anywhere in the Islands. Finally, the capital and books of a nonresident company must be expressed in currencies other than British Sterling or Swiss francs. Can't hold Swiss francs? wondered Mario. The attorney explained the books must be kept in a foreign currency other than these two, but that the firm can hold cash in *any* currency.

Mario now filled in his last piece of required information as he discovered the attorney's belief that an inventory/adjustment activity for a computer products sales firm in Jersey/Guernsey, as long as it met the outside control/management test, could be a perfectly viable nonresident company. It had the advantage of being close to the European market, if not the South American, which might sit better with Mario's European salesmen. Whatever the case, Mario recalled that redeemable preferred shares were permissible under the local Companies Law, giving his firm the same option available in Cayman.

"And what about formation costs?" queried Mario.

"They will vary a little from attorney to attorney and some with the trust companies," was the reply. "With the new stamp tax, we should charge about $750, plus an additional $200 for undertakings to the Bank of England by an authorized depository in the instance of nonresident companies for exchange control purposes."

"Corporate establishment fees don't vary much from haven to haven, at least the ones I've been to," remarked Mario.

"We stay competitive," commented the attorney, "but here we are a little less than the Bahamas or Cayman, if you compare the exempted company in Cayman."

It was to be at his next inquiry locale that Mario would discover major differences: the tiny principality of Liechtenstein. It would be the most interesting, but unrewarding stop of the four havens.

A LOOK AT LIECHTENSTEIN

Getting to Liechtenstein is not the easiest undertaking. One either drives or takes the train, usually from the nearest jet age connection in Zurich, Switzerland. The country, smaller than the District of Columbia with a population under 22,000, has no airport, although the government occasionally issues airmail stamps. In fact, the train from Zurich doesn't stop in Liechtenstein at all (there is no railroad station either), but rather halts just across the Rhine river from the capital of Vaduz in Buchs, Switzerland. A bus takes travelers into Vaduz. The Transalpin Express leaves Zurich daily at 11:20 A.M. for the one-hour, 20-minute trip to Buchs enroute to Salzburg and Vienna. Round-trip fare including bus was SFr. 35.40 (about $14.25) at the time of our visitors' sojourn.[4] The auto trip is 110 kilometers via a good highway for about half the distance and an average mountain road for

---

[4] Author's note: By December 1977 the dollar value had increased by 25 percent.

the balance on one route; on the other, longer route there is an expressway nearly the whole distance. Scenery is lovely by either road or train, but not of the spectacular alpine variety on this generally southeastern passage from Zurich.

The nation itself, best known to art lovers, stamp collectors, and European industrialists, is frequently described as amazing.[5] Its magnificent scenery ranges from the low valleys of the Rhine to the 8,500 foot grandeur of the Grauspitze. Its population is one-third foreign, the limit prescribed by law, and yet it is almost impossible for a foreigner to become a citizen. A foreigner seeking citizenship must obtain approval from the town of prospective residence, from the national government, from the 15-member Diet, and finally from the Ruling Prince himself. Few people remember when the last foreigner was granted citizenship in this way. The alternative is to be born of a Liechtenstein family or for a foreign woman to marry a Liechtenstein man.

It is a Catholic, German speaking country where divorce is unknown. Women still do not have suffrage (it was voted down in 1973), largely because they don't want it. The ruling family governed from Vienna for several generations, taking up permanent residence in Castle Vaduz during the Nazi occupation of Austria in 1938. The current Prince, Franz Joseph, is the 12th in a line traceable back more than 800 years. He is considered to own the greatest private art collection in the world.

Liechtenstein is a constitutional monarchy, does not have its own currency (it uses the Swiss franc) and is largely dependent on revenue from stamp issuance and from its tax haven business. Ninety percent of the principality's operating revenue comes from the 25 percent tax on business and individuals. Actually, Liechtenstein is a highly industrialized country, with companies like Hilti, Hoval, Balzers, and IDAG Plastics Processing headquartered there. They employ

---

[5] For example: Joseph Wechsberg, "Liechtenstein," *Gourmet*, December 1976, p. 26.

thousands of locals and some 1,500 foreign workers. The Prince is the largest stockholder in several of the companies. There is no unemployment.

Aunt Audrey thinks of California

Our Aunt Audrey was about to receive the shortest shrift of her four country trek. It was put in the politest of terms by a Doctor of laws at a trust company, a contact provided her by Swiss Bank Corporation during a day's stopover in Zurich.

Yes, she was told, she could form either a company limited by shares or an establishment in Liechtenstein to do business there, but was she a Liechtenstein resident? No? That was unfortunate. A permit to work or do business could not be granted unless she was a resident. But what about all the foreigners she had heard about working in the principality? Oh, they were special cases. They were brought in under special conditions because of a shortage of local workers at certain companies some time ago. The conditions no longer applied, and would not have done so anyway for a foreign citizen wishing to operate a small business in the country.

Well, what about residency? Of course, one may become a resident when one gains citizenship; otherwise a stay of a few months is all that is permitted. And citizenship? The Doctor of Laws spelled out the circumstances. He said the probability was about 99.5 to 1 against obtaining it.

The whole process is a Catch 22. One can't operate a new business without having a working permit; a permit can't be obtained unless residency is; residency can't be gained without citizenship; citizenship can't be had at all; therefore, a foreigner can't operate a new business in Liechtenstein. (The situation is the same in Switzerland; it is a common problem in small popular countries.)

Aunt Audrey wished the flight back to California was much shorter. She'd have gotten the late afternoon train to Zurich and gone immediately. Not that there was anything unpleasant about Liechtenstein. Foreigners were just no longer welcome to operate in the business world of that small country. Reluctantly, she'd stay overnight as planned at the Hotel Real, try some of the local fine wines (a Süssdruck perhaps), and maybe even visit the village of Planken the next day to see some of the countryside. The weather was fine for March; and to look on the cheerier side, at least she had missed the tourist crush of summer when as many as three thousand autos come through Vaduz *per hour,* usually stopping only long enough to buy a few stamps and maybe a bit of wine. Might as well make the best of it, she thought.

A new discovery: The Stiftung

Both Dr. Fred and Mario had, in separate meetings, come across a fascinating new concept, the Stiftung (foundation), along with the rather unusual fact that Liechtenstein has a trusts law despite being a civil-law country. In making their discovery they both quickly learned that a Stiftung and an Anstalt (establishment) were highly creative devices. They were legal hybrids: a foundation/corporation and trust/ corporation respectively. And therein lay the problem. How would the IRS treat them for tax purposes? As the officer of General Trust Corporation with whom Dr. Fred was talking said, "Our business is Liechtenstein tax and company law. We can't advise about American or German law. It's much too dangerous. We leave it to you to know whether a Liechtenstein entity can accomplish your purposes from the U.S. tax standpoint." Both Mario and Dr. Fred had been warned about the possibility that if either a Stiftung or an Anstalt became involved with the IRS, it might be challenged and assigned whatever status—corporation, foundation or trust—would yield the most taxes. The U.S. concept of an association taxable as a corporation could well be the catch-all into which these entities might fit.

Mario, with his Italian family, might be able to make the

best use of the Stiftung, certainly for the non-U.S. beneficiaries. Dr. Fred felt it would probably be a waste of time for him, but the concept was intriguing.

A Stiftung, the two discovered, was most similar to a U.S. charitable foundation, with one significant difference: the beneficiaries would be private, noncharity individuals. The person founding the entity does not acquire the traditional founder's rights of control or ownership of funds. In this way the Stiftung is similar to a U.S. discretionary trust. The Stiftung is endowed with a given amount of funds which may be added to by anyone in the future. The responsibility for administration of the funds is vested in a board, and, although the members do not have title to the funds, the founder may be a member of the board. The funds can be used for any purpose set forth in the enabling articles, most often for the maintenance of a family. The board is usually given broad powers to amend the articles, issue by-laws, add or delete beneficiaries, and even dissolve the foundation. The only limitation of note is that this entity cannot be used to engage in business, and is therefore fundamentally a passive being. It must be initially capitalized with a minimum of SFr. 30,000 (about U.S. $12,000), fully paid-in. Formation costs would include a 2 percent constitution fee based on paid-in capital, although the tax authorities may reduce this to 0.2 percent if satisfied that it is a family foundation not doing any business or commercial transactions. Deposit fees for documents can range from SFr. 250 up to SFr. 2,500 ($100–$1,000), and an annual tax of 0.1 percent is payable on foundation capital and reserves, with a minimum of SFr. 1,000 ($400) payable in advance.[6] Adding legal fees, the formation of a Stiftung could run to about $1,500.

Clearly, at least two problems arise where U.S. persons are involved. First, if the founder is a U.S. person, what will he be designated under U.S. tax laws? A grantor of a foreign

---

[6] "The Family Foundation under Liechtenstein Law," The General Trust Corporation, Ltd., Vaduz, January 1976, p. 28.

trust? A donor to a charitable foundation? The founder of a corporation? And where do the assets come from? Will there be a taxable transaction at the time of transfer of the assets? Secondly, how will U.S. beneficiaries be treated? As foreign trust beneficiaries under TRA 1976? As shareholders of a foreign association taxable as a corporation? As owners of a foreign personal holding company? The proper answer is likely to be any of the above.

Conceivably Mario might make use of such an entity, assuming capital transfer problems from Italy could be solved, to benefit the non-U.S. family members, as long as he was not the founder. He certainly could be a board member. Also possible would be the establishment of a foreign trust in conjunction with the Stiftung to benefit the U.S. family members. If the foundation was the grantor, there would be no U.S. tax incidence likely to that entity, and the U.S. beneficiaries could receive income under the 6 percent penalty rule, with both the Stiftung and the trust able to accumulate funds almost tax-free until the distribution. Clearly, privacy would be maximized. On the other hand, the foundation might be able to make direct payments to U.S. beneficiaries, as long as they paid normal taxes upon receipt. They would not be able to have control over the assets either.

Dr. Fred still had the matter of the civil-law trusts to pursue in Liechtenstein, but quickly came to the conclusion that these could be rather dicey entities. Again, the question was what they might be designated as for U.S. tax purposes. The problem was that Liechtenstein trusts are really quasi-independent enterprises of their own, carrying their own assets and liabilities, independent of the trustee. The trust enterprise is usually established by a contract between the grantor and the trustee, which need not be registered in the Public Register.[7] But since the trust can acquire liabilities independent of the trustee, which is not possible in common-law trusts or U.S. trust law, Fred rightly felt the potential risk of

[7] Marshall Langer, *How to Use Foreign Tax Havens,* pp. 239–40.

being designated an association taxable as a corporation or a foreign personal holding company was not worth accepting. Not when there were other jurisdictions in which he could deal on surer ground.

The more well-known Liechtenstein entity called an Anstalt or establishment brings certain characteristics of a trust into conjunction with the personal corporation. It is a corporation without issued shares, controlled by the founder for his/her benefit or for others. The founder (or the current holder of the founder's certificate, which is a bearer instrument evidencing all the ownership rights of the entity), has the power to amend the articles of incorporation, appoint or remove directors, and also give the Anstalt beneficiaries. The founder may be one person or a group. However, the Anstalt's board of directors is the operating mechanism responsible for the conduct of the Anstalt's affairs: the relationship between persons acting for the company and third parties. The Anstalt or establishment must have one director or can have more, at the discretion of the founder, with at least one director domiciled in Liechtenstein. The directors serve at the founder's pleasure, usually for a period of three years, and it is the founder alone who may liquidate the entity.

An establishment need not be profit-making, nor does the object of it have to be an operating business: it can hold financial interest in foreign firms or exercise control over them, for example, in the sense of a holding company or an investment company. As a result, depending upon how its articles and objects are drawn and practiced, it could readily be designated as having any of the forms of income falling into U.S. Internal Revenue Code Subpart F: the "pentapus" noted in Chapter 3. The founder's peculiar role could also cause it to be treated as a form of trust or an association taxable as a corporation. As such, the Anstalt appeared to be a risky means of accomplishing any of Dr. Fred's or Mario's purposes. It also required paid-in capital of SFr. 30,000, would cost around U.S. $1,600 to set up, but would have the local Liechtenstein tax advantage of paying only 0.1 percent annual tax on capital with a minimum of SFr. 1,000 due, insofar as it did no operating business in the principality. It would have no income tax under those circumstances except a 4 percent withholding tax on dividends if it had dividend capital.

It was after discovering this much about Liechtenstein entities that Dr. Fred decided he had sufficient time to catch the afternoon train back to Zurich and spend his leisure more usefully. He drew a thick black line through Liechtenstein in the notebook where he listed interesting potential uses of tax havens for his upcoming retirement. Next to it he wrote, "Not for U.S. citizens like me!"

Mario still had an avenue open to explore, the European corporation known in German as the Actiengesellschaft (AG). It is a company limited by shares and, in Liechtenstein must have paid-in capital of SFr. 50,000 (about $20,000) minimum. Capital must never fall below this minimum. If it carries on business in the principality, it is subject to both an income tax ranging between 7.5 percent and 15 percent and a capital/reserves tax of 0.2 percent with a minimum of SFr. 1,000, plus a 4 percent dividend/interest tax. (Aunt Audrey wouldn't have found it to her liking even if she were a citizen.)

Two forms of the AG in Liechtenstein are given preferential treatment, however. When it holds investments in other companies or intangible property rights such as copyrights, patents, and so on, it is designated a holding company. When the AG has its headquarters or domicile in Liechtenstein, but carries on no commercial activities there except operation of an office, it is termed a domiciliary company. Both of these corporate types pay no regular income tax, but only the 0.1 percent annual tax on capital and reserves (minimum SFr. 1,000) as with the Anstalt and Stiftung, plus a 4 percent tax on most dividends and interest. In order for these taxes to be properly paid and verified, the AG will usually be required to submit financial statements to the government. However, audits are not required if no share certificates are issued, or the initial capital does not exceed the minimum required, or if there are fewer than 20 shareholders.

Two other features of the AG caught Mario's attention. All share capital must be subscribed; if it is not fully paid-in at the time of incorporation, the shareholders are liable for the fully subscribed amount. With registered shares, at least 20 percent of full subscription must be paid-in (and it must total SFr. 50,000). However, bearer shares are permitted, comprising either the total capital or some part, and all bearer shares must be fully paid upon incorporation.

Costs of formation of an AG, as provided to Mario by General Trust Corporation, were noted as a chartering fee of SFr. 1,200 ($480), a registration fee of SFr. 500 ($200), a representation fee of SFr. 500, and about SFr. 1,500 ($600) for annual administration in addition to bookkeeping and accounting charges by the hour.

Weighing the potential of a Liechtenstein AG for his company, Mario felt that the paid-in capital was clearly a negative, insofar as the company would be principally a sales office for the European market. Holding patent rights was only useful where double taxation treaties existed, and Liechtenstein had none. Because of the work permit problem and shortage of labor, manufacturing in the principality wouldn't be feasible. This left the possibility of direct sale of the computer products manufactured in California at "fair market value" to the Liechtenstein AG as the principal alternative which could justify the paid-in capital requirement. And this represented a problem in obtaining a U.S. revenue ruling under Code paragraph 482 as to fair market value. If, in fact, the sales price in Europe for the units was much above the price the Liechtenstein company paid for them, the first sale might not be considered "at fair market value." The alternative would be to add value by certain adjustments in Europe, in which case he was back to the labor force problem. It began to look more and more as though the direct foreign manufacturing or the non-CFC route was going to be his answer, with a tax haven entity woven into the process. For the non–U.S.-controlled foreign corporation he had the alternative of the U.S. company giving up 51 percent or more to foreign investors, or to increase the number of U.S. shareholders to more than ten with no stockholder owning more than 10 percent. Either way, his parent company would lose control.

Mario would learn, as we will discover in the next chapter, that while a Netherlands Antilles company could hold his company's patent rights for sale to foreign nation companies, the advantage would depend upon which countries the Antilles held double taxation treaties with, thereby saving *foreign* taxes. His company could gain no advantage on U.S. taxes if it was in any way associated with the Antilles firm. And the issue would also depend upon obtaining an IRS prior ruling on the proper transfer of the patent rights to the Antilles company under IRC paragraph 367. The net effect would be to make the royalty concept only marginally workable, even in the case of a favorable IRS ruling.

The tax haven Grand Tour for our friends had come to a close. Certainly Aunt Audrey had fared the least well in terms of viable alternatives. Anti-foreigner prejudices carry widely these days, from "bloody wogs" in England to Switzerland's "guest workers" and Arab nations' mistrust of any connection with Israel. The mood is not uncommon in tax havens either, at least where possible residence or business with the locals is concerned.

It would be up to both Dr. Fred and Mario to make personal decisions among the revealed alternatives upon return to their home areas. The most important fact they had learned was that there is no precise and single answer for the use of havens under any circumstances. There are only relative alternatives, and the great bulk of the decisions to be made about them are based on U.S. tax considerations, not on those in the haven. The haven considerations largely involve technicalities with a smattering of personal preference thrown in.

They had also discovered something that most reputable tax attorneys in the U.S. will advise: for U.S. persons, either individual or corporate, who wish to benefit U.S. persons, there is no advantage in trying to dodge U.S. taxes through foreign gambits. Where there are legitimate business reasons or personal concerns, such as those expressed in Chapter 1, prompting the use of foreign entities, the approach should be as straightforward and legitimate as possible. Tax haven users are swimming upstream against a strong current. It may require double effort, but one should not risk being drowned in a morass of illegalities.

chapter 7

THE MISSING

As we can surmise from the previous three chapters, a detailed look at any haven is not only quite space-consuming but is also repetitive in certain respects. Havens resemble each other. But most of them also have unique advantages or disadvantages that are worth pointing out. Having explored two of the no-tax and two of the low-tax havens, we can use these as a basis from which to approach the next half dozen with an eye to their key differences.

BERMUDA

Bermuda is an important tax haven for Americans, but we omitted it from our magnifying glass view for several reasons. First, it is one of the more difficult havens in which to physically incorporate a company; one must undergo a tedious screening of bank and personal references to determine one's stability and standing in the community. The docket requires approval of the Minister for Finance's Advisory Committee, a process which can take over a month. Second, for exempted companies, the costs of formation are about double those of the other havens we visited. In addition, this British

Crown Colony has experienced a spate of violence in recent years. The Governor, an aide, and the chief of police were assassinated in 1972–73, and upon execution of the convicted assassins in late 1977, the island was rocked with riots. The racial and political motivation of these acts has generated a period of uncertainty and change—a hazard one can avoid in other close offshore havens.

Most important, however, there have been two inroads on the no-tax status of Bermuda in the past four years. While they are not substantial, they are important. In 1973 a 5 percent payroll tax was imposed on local companies, based on the amount of total salary paid employees—an obvious form of local income tax. It did not apply to exempted companies, for which there was a 30-year government guarantee against future taxes.[1] However, in 1976 a hospital tax was instituted covering Bermuda residents working in *both* local and exempted companies, at the rate of 1.5 percent of salary, to be paid equally by the employee and employer. To get around the law's provision that exempted companies are not required to open their books to government inspection, a notional salary of $18,000 per year was set for exempted company employees.[2] To paraphrase Shelley, "if a salary tax comes, can corporate be far behind?"

Bermuda still holds substantial benefits for persons wishing to incorporate a captive foreign insurance company, or a holding company for which tax treaty benefits are not important, and it is good for trust establishment.

HONG KONG

By far the most important tax haven in the Pacific is the British Crown Colony of Hong Kong, the gateway to the People's Republic of China. Its principal advantage lies in a

---

1 Marshall Langer, *How to Use Foreign Tax Havens,* p. 122.

2 Practicing Law Institute, *Foreign Tax Planning, 1977,* p. 180.

lack of taxes on any foreign-source income for companies incorporated there. The local-source tax rate is now 17 percent. The colony has also had political and economic stability throughout this century, which, despite the Japanese presence during World War II, has seen the Hong Kong government remain intact. Headed by a governor appointed by the Queen, with an executive and legislative council each appointed by the governor, the government has maintained a staunchly probusiness attitude since World War II.

The Chinese Communist power has made its principal contacts with the outside world through the auspices of Hong Kong, and trade increased tenfold over the past decade as a result. China's lease with the United Kingdom for Hong Kong has more than 20 of its original 99 years to run.

The Chinese attitude toward Hong Kong has made the Colony one of the three major business centers of the Far East. Nearly 30,000 businesses operate within its space of just 33 square miles. The investment climate of Hong Kong has been, and remains, highly conducive to foreign capital. Free exchange rates exist for nearly all currencies, including the nonconvertible Chinese Yuan, through more than 75 foreign banks and innumerable exchange dealers.

Of principal interest to potential users of Hong Kong as a tax haven is an aggregate income test that is used to determine whether or not income is earned within the colony or outside. According to Langer, this is a matter of substantive fact with a sizable body of case law on the subject.[3]

A second point: interest income is subject to a 15 percent tax, usually withheld at source, and applied to bank interest if the rate is more than 3.5 percent. For this reason, many bank deposits are placed outside Hong Kong through local banks acting as agents, with Singapore the principal beneficiary.

Hong Kong makes a distinction between "public" and "private" firms. Private companies may have up to 50 share-

---

[3] *How to Use Foreign Tax Havens,* p. 165.

holders, and must submit audited balance sheets to shareholders and the government annually. There is no restriction as to the location of shareholders' and directors' meetings, unlike the laws of the other key havens we visited. Bearer shares are not allowed. Public companies are defined as those with more than 50 shareholders; they are required to publish audited annual balance sheets for public inspection, but otherwise are similar to private firms. To incorporate a private company usually costs about U.S. $750. There is no requirement that there be local directors.

Hong Kong has a common-law basis for trusts as well as a specific trusts law, making it a good jurisdiction for creation of a foreign trust. However, trust assets must be invested outside Hong Kong or be subject to local taxes.

The Colony has excellent communications and professional facilities. The currency unit is the Hong Kong dollar.

LIBERIA

We have already noted the importance of this African tax haven in the shipping world. Because it encourages the use of its flag as a flag of convenience, it has the world's largest merchant shipping fleet. Liberia is the only tax haven in Africa and has a few other significant tax features of potential interest: it levies no tax on the foreign source income of nonresident corporations more than 50 percent foreign owned, but does tax their domestic income. The country's corporation law is patterned after that of Delaware. Assistance in establishing a company may be had through a Liberian trust company office in New York. Despite its distance from the United States (almost nine hours by jet from New York), it uses the U.S. dollar as its currency and English as its official language. The nation has no exchange controls and has been an independent republic since 1847.

Liberian corporations can be formed quickly, sometimes within 48 hours, by cable from the United States, and have several other handy features. Annual meetings can be held anywhere, as with Hong Kong companies, but there are no government reporting requirements and bearer shares may be issued. The articles of incorporation need not specify corporate purposes, and corporations may become directors as of 1977. There is no residence requirement for officers, directors, or stockholders, although each corporation must have a resident business agent in the country, a task usually performed by a local trust company.

MONACO

This principality is better known in recent years for its Prince Rainier, Princess Grace, and their daughter Caroline than as a tax haven. The opposite was true until 1963, when a tax treaty with France diminished Monaco's importance as a haven. Nevertheless, it is still of interest in two tax regards: companies doing more than three quarters of their turnover in Monaco pay no tax. (Hello, Aunt Audrey.) And a company with administrative offices in the country but doing no business there, for example, one running a firm incorporated in another haven, pays an effective tax of 2.8 percent of its local office *expenses* only.

NAURU

This is the tiniest and one of the newest of our tax havens, covering only eight square miles of phosphate-rich land virtually on the equator, but nearly 2,500 miles from the nearest major city of Melbourne, Australia. There are no cities, and only one road running around the island. The government enacted new corporation and trusts laws in 1972 to attract tax haven business. Because of this it deserves inclusion as a haven, but there is little else to commend it. The legislation was designed to promote an alternative source of business when the island's enormous phosphate deposits are used up. While Nauru has not taxes of any kind except import duties, it also appears to have an aversion to both immigrants and visitors (visitors' visas are difficult to obtain). It also has no trust company or professional service infrastructure, offers poor telephone and telex service, and is directly accessible by air from only Melbourne, Australia; Kagashima, Japan; and Majuro, Marshall Islands. Unless one is intrigued with "ground floor" developments, Nauru seems to demand to be ignored.

NETHERLANDS ANTILLES

The six islands of the Netherlands Antilles chain, less than 50 miles offshore from South America in the Caribbean, are a principal center of European, and lately Mid-Eastern, financial interests in the Americas. The major Dutch, Swiss, German, and French banks have offices here, principally in Curaçao, and significant business is done through them, including foreign investment in U.S. real estate and the floating of sizable Eurobond issues. Tax regulations here are complex, partly because of the involuted Dutch legal codes, but they offer most advantage to Americans through the U.S.-Netherlands Antilles Tax Treaty. There is also a "free zone" where the tax on companies operating in it is just 2 percent of net.

In considering use of a Netherlands Antilles company under treaty provisions, principally an investment company or a holding company, it is important to recall that if a permanent U.S. entity is involved in business with the Antilles firm, the latter firm is taxed in the United States. Also, in the case of transfer of patents or royalties to an NA holding company by a U.S. firm which controls the NA company, a prior ruling from the IRS on the terms of the transfer and its tax incidence should be obtained under Section 367 of the Tax Code. The effect of these caveats should be to prevent U.S. persons and corporations from anticipating a tax-free transfer of patents or copyrights to a CFC which could then earn income even from U.S. sources in the use of the patented item, also nontaxable in the United States. U.S. source income from such rights can be nontaxable in the United States if the foreign corporation is non–U.S.-controlled, if it is not connected in business with a permanent U.S. entity (such as a distributor), or if the product covered by the license rights is created outside the United States and held by a non-CFC.

Keeping these facts in mind, we can now look at the key provisions of the U.S.-N.A. treaty. We are indebted to Marshall Langer for a summary of these points, and recommend his detailed analysis of the treaty in his fine book.[4]

> Income of whatever nature derived from U.S. real property is taxable only in the U.S. (Article V). The same rule applies to interest from mortgages secured by real property.
>
> Article VII reduces to 15 percent the rate of U.S. tax on dividends derived from a U.S. corporation by a Netherlands Antilles corporation which is not engaged in U.S. business through a permanent establishment. A further reduction to 5 percent is provided for under some circumstances.
>
> *Interest* derived from U.S. sources by a Netherlands Antilles corporation not engaged in U.S. business through a permanent establishment is ordinarily exempt from U.S. tax (Article VIII). However, the exemption does not apply to interest paid by a U.S. corporation to a parent Netherlands Antilles corporation which controls more than 50 percent of the voting power in the paying U.S. corporation. Nor does it apply to mortgage interest.
>
> *Royalties* derived from U.S. sources by a Netherlands Antilles corporation not engaged in U.S. business through a permanent establishment are exempt from U.S. tax (Article IX). The exemption covers royalties for the use of copyrights, patents, trademarks and other industrial property as well as motion picture film rentals.
>
> A Netherlands Antilles corporation deriving rentals from U.S. real property may elect for any taxable year to be subject to U.S. tax on such rental income on a net income basis (Article X).

[4] Ibid., pp. 195–96 and 315–43.

> Dividends and interest paid by a Netherlands Antilles corporation are exempt from U.S. tax unless the recipient is a U.S. citizen, U.S. resident, or U.S. corporation (Article XII).

The effect of these provisions is to give a Netherlands Antilles investment or holding company a tax election between the United States and the Antilles. A corporation of this type in the latter country will usually elect to pay the Antilles profit tax on *net* income. This will vary considerably, depending upon the type of income received, but will usually range between 15 percent and 27 percent of *net* income versus the 30 percent U.S. rate on *gross* payment made at the source.

A final word of caution. Because of the apparently favorable conditions of the treaty, U.S. investors may be tempted to ignore the exempted conditions of the "permanent U.S. entity" which includes U.S. individuals, and use the treaty to evade U.S. taxes on property or rights holdings through a Netherlands Antilles company. Consider this no longer possible and don't try it. Do consider the use of a Netherlands Antilles company to reduce taxes in a foreign country with which the Netherlands Antilles has tax treaties, namely Denmark, Norway, the United Kingdom, and the Netherlands itself. Our inquiring visitor Mario would have found this aspect of the Antilles most useful.

NEW HEBRIDES

It may be fairly said that despite a handful of monumental obstacles, the government of this 5,000-square-mile South Pacific enclave east of Australia is probably as determined to promote tax haven business, or more so, than any other we will come across. That is, if we can call its dual administration a single government. The country has literally two sets of laws and two administrations, one for British subjects, the other for the French. Everyone else elects to be governed by one of the two, except the natives who are governed by their own tribal system and are therefore technically stateless since the British and French form the state.

Nearly all of the true tax haven business developed in the New Hebrides has been accomplished under British legal auspices, although both the British and French laws allow for no taxation.

In developing their own body of laws, the British administrators appear to have overcome the dual legal system as major obstacle number one. Remaining are (1) the islands' remoteness–approximately 14 hours' flying time from Los Angeles via either New Caledonia or Fiji, not counting layovers; (2) poor telephone and telex links with the rest of the world, despite some recent improvements; (3) a very recent turn toward tax haven business, with most haven-type legislation dating from the early 1970s; and (4) anti-tax haven attitudes on the part of Australia, from which most of its companies business has so far developed. Also bothersome for foreigners considering development of haven business in the New Hebrides is a visa requirement for travel into the islands (although visas are readily attainable), and Bermuda-type prescreening of prospective corporation founders.

As evidence of its interest in expanding haven business, the British government made effective regulations in 1977 permitting the transfer of domicile of companies in other countries to this jurisdiction, unless prohibited by the original country, a relatively rare move among haven-promoting nations.

The islands also permit exempted companies similar to the Bahamas' offshore companies: no tax guarantees, but instead a privacy assurance for companies doing business offshore. These exempted companies are relatively expensive to form in the New Hebrides, approaching U.S. $2,000.

All companies must submit audited financial and directors' reports to the government, which in turn guarantees their confidentiality with criminal penalties for violations.

The New Hebrides banking and professional facilities are now quite adequate, though still small in number: they include a half dozen or so each of accountants, lawyers, and trust companies, plus about a dozen banks.

Trusts may be established under the British common law, but there is no trusts law per se. The Austrialian dollar is the unit of currency.

PANAMA

Despite the important question of political stability in this significant Latin American crossroads nation, and the potential for U.S.-Panamanian problems over the canal in the future, Panama has several favorable attributes as a tax haven. What is more, Panama has been *the* favorite western hemisphere haven in the past. Langer estimates that over 35,000 companies have been established there, probably more than in all other American tax havens combined. However, many of these may have been established by U.S. firms before the 1962 addition of Subpart F to the U.S. Internal Revenue Code, which made reinvoicing operations taxable in the United States. Certainly Panama's shipping laws have contributed by making its flag a flag of convenience.

The key attributes of Panama as a haven include not taxing foreign source income of either companies or individuals, the low cost of company organization compared to other havens, and use of the U.S. dollar currency with no exchange controls. It also permits: change of corporate domicile both into and out of the country, bearer shares, and shareholder or director meetings in any location. Panama is also a banking secrecy country where numbered accounts are allowed, and has become a major banking and financial center with nearly 100 banks. No tax is collected on bank interest.

Panama has a trusts law but it is of the civil law variety, making other jurisdictions more useful in this regard.

TURKS AND CAICOS

These islands are geographically an extension of the Bahamas chain, but were a dependency of Jamaica until the inhabitants elected to remain under the British crown at the time of Jamaican independence in 1963. They were then attached to the Bahamas government until Bahamian independence in 1973, when they were given separate colony status.

If ever there was a need for a group of islands to develop a revenue source, the Turks and Caicos appear to have it. Possessing a population of only about 6,500, with less than one third of that number on any one island, and no industry of any note, including tourism, the group survives on the largesse of the British government plus customs duties and expatriate remittances. Consequently the government has been moving as rapidly as it can to develop tax haven business, somewhat stymied by the opposition of the present British government.

A new constitution introduced in 1976 provided greater self-determination. By keeping the costs of company formation low (the government fee for companies with minimum capital is under $100) and matching the annual fee with it, the government has enticed the tax haven user community to "discover" Turks and Caicos. One discovery is that companies formed in these islands can be operated from the Bahamas, where good companies service exists, and avoid the $1,250 annual fee imposed by Nassau. Since the Turks use the U.S. dollar as their currency, there are no exchange controls.

Accessibility remains a problem, with only infrequent air service from Miami and modest service to Nassau.

Trusts are not advisable, since no trusts law exists and the trust company infrastructure is not satisfactory.

ON TO SWITZERLAND

We have traversed the sometimes rugged, often treacherous, and rarely smooth terrain of the most important tax havens worldwide, with the exception of one of the world's most famous rugged nations, Switzerland. As we have suggested earlier, our coverage was not intended to be exhaustive. Purposes, needs, and circumstances vary too widely, and space is too short, to embrace the myriad of personal aspects which would bring out the minutiae. We have accomplished, I believe, what might be termed "a broad survey with depth in the most often appropriate points."

We have omitted, for example, a discussion about Costa Rica, which is not normally considered a tax haven but which has many haven characteristics including an exemption from taxation on a corporation's foreign source income, permissibility for bearer shares, and a minimal cost for establishment. But the most significant aspect of Costa Rica is outside our purview: It is an excellent place to retire, with legal conditions permitting not only the easy establishment of residence but also the rapid obtaining of a passport and eventual citizenship. We probably should have devoted a chapter to Costa Rica just for Aunt Audrey. However, the company incorporation procedure is elaborate; trusts are not appropriate; and numerous other countries share its non-taxability of foreign income. We had to draw the line somewhere.

We are now prepared to devote considerable time to a country which properly qualifies as a low-tax haven, but which has two most significant characteristics: It is one of the most important financial centers outside the United States, and it provides access unparalleled in privacy and expertise to virtually any other important tax haven one might consider. The road to Switzerland is open, if occasionally misty.

chapter 8

THE UNUSUAL CASE OF SWITZERLAND

ALMOST ANYONE traveling the road to money privacy will early-on come upon its most famous waystation, Switzerland. This small country, about the size of Maine but with a population nearly seven times as great at 6.4 million, has come to epitomize money security and privacy in almost every conceivable way. Widely circulated rumors of Mafia infestations and stealthy foreign exchange manipulations notwithstanding, the Swiss' closed-mouth security and worldwide investment expertise have given their nation a more positive image in the world of finance than any other country except the United States. Because of that reputation, Switzerland has no need to offer tax advantages and even promotes a few disadvantages, but can still be technically considered a low-tax haven, as the aggregate of federal, cantonal, and municipal taxes, while rising in recent years, is still low by most comparisons. However, its inclusion in this book is primarily for other reasons than as a pure tax haven. Its privacy, security, and stability, its unsurpassed range of financial services, and its availability as a quiet entre to other havens are the principal benefits of concern to us.

In their storied land of primal grandeur, precision watches, and maximum privacy, the so-called gnomes pursue their policies of hard money, secure caches, and other principles of financial conservatism with sealed lips, certainly to foreigners. (It's said they gossip much amongst themselves, usually by the same people who say they drink too much. I don't know.)

It certainly isn't difficult to get your Swiss banker to talk about money. He'll have a general opinion on any financial matter you might mention, no matter how remote. He'll discuss the details of your monetary needs with great care. Politely frowning, he will decline comment on the specifics of other persons' dealings. His silence is more than a tradition, although that is an important ingredient in a country with a century and a half of banking privacy.

As is now widely known, Switzerland has formulated its banking privacy into the most stringent law on the subject in the world. (It has been copied by a few nations in recent years, notably the Cayman Islands.) The law was ratified by the Swiss National Council in 1934 and updated in 1971. It was prompted by the Nazi pursuit of fleeing German money in the early Hitler years, and has served the Swiss well, in their opinion, in the ensuing decades. The law simply makes the revelation of information about any bank customer's dealings punishable by prison and fines, at any time in the violator's life, even if the act is one of negligence.[1] The mere existence of the law is sufficient to deter most potential violators. It rarely has to be invoked to the point of punishment.

One of the most interesting cases involving the banking

---

[1] Article 49 of the law reads as follows:

1. Whoever divulges a secret entrusted to him in his capacity as officer, employee, authorized agent, liquidator or commissioner of a bank, as a representative of the Banking Commission, officer or employee of a recognized auditing company, or who has become aware of such a secret in this capacity, and whoever tries to induce others to violate professional secrecy, shall be punished by a prison term not to exceed six months or by a fine not exceeding 50,000 Swiss francs.

2. If the act has been committed by negligence, the penalty shall be a fine not exceeding 30,000 Swiss francs.

3. The violation of professional secrecy remains punishable even after termination of the official or employment relationship or the exercise of the profession.

secrecy law is the now famous Clifford Irving caper. It offers prime evidence of the lengths to which the Swiss will go with their banking privacy, even allowing protection of criminals until proper court action has its way.[2]

The Irvings, Edith and Clifford, while involved in a proposed Howard Hughes biography for the McGraw-Hill Book Company of New York, committed a special crime against Swiss banks.

The Irvings didn't violate bank secrecy. They used it to fine advantage, for a time. But they did something worse. They defrauded a bank, and that itself was sufficient to force an opening in the fabled curtain of Swiss bank secrecy.

The scenario unfolded quietly enough. As was later revealed, on May 13, 1971, a blonde, long-haired woman about five-foot-three opened an ordinary bank account, numbered 320 496, at the Swiss Credit Bank's Paradeplatz main office in Zurich. She identified herself with a Swiss passport in the name of Helga R. Hughes and signed her opening deposit slip for SFr. 1,000 (paid in cash), "H. R. Hughes," matching the name and initials of billionaire Howard Hughes. In addition, she presented a check for $50,000 for collection.

On May 27, a woman of similar description opened an account at the Winterthur branch of Swiss Bank Corporation, using a West German I.D. card issued to one Hanna Rosenkranz. The family name was later revealed to be that of Edith Irving's former husband. So far, so good for the Irvings. During the balance of 1971, Mrs. "Hughes" made several deposits and withdrawals of substance at Swiss Credit Bank. To bank officials it was obviously a relatively sizable account.

Next, at Clifford Irving's insistence, three checks totalling $650,000 were made out by McGraw-Hill in payment for all rights to Howard Hughes' biography and presented for col-

---

[2] Robert Kinsman, *Your Swiss Bank Book,* pp. 10–13. Note: The chapters on Switzerland herein contain numerous quotations from *Your Swiss Bank Book* which will not be footnoted to avoid repetition.

lection in favor of H. R. Hughes to Swiss Credit Bank's Zurich main office. The account number into which they were deposited was 320 496, in the name of H. R. Hughes.

In December 1971, Helga Hughes appeared at the same Swiss Credit Bank office and asked to withdraw the balance in her account. After withdrawing all but a small amount she took the proceeds, in more than 1,200 one-thousand franc notes, from the bank in an airline flight bag. Later that same day, Hanna Rosenkranz deposited $450,000 in her Winterthur Swiss Bank Corporation account to be managed in an investment portfolio by the bank.

Meanwhile, the legitimacy of the Irving biography of Hughes was in the midst of swirling controversy. In the course of it, Howard Hughes' attorneys asked for an affidavit from Swiss Credit Bank in Zurich that he *did not* have an account there. This caused some consternation at the bank. Swiss banking secrecy requires that the bank reveal no information whatsoever about any account. But was a request to reveal that there was *no account* considered the same as revealing information about a real account? The bank satisfied itself that the Hughes attorneys' request was legitimate. Then, after extensive consultation within the bank, it was agreed that the request was not a violation of banking secrecy in this case, and so advised Hughes' attorneys: Howard Hughes had no such account.

Now McGraw-Hill was in a fix. Its money had disappeared into an account made out in the name of H. R. Hughes at Swiss Credit Bank and they couldn't touch it, nor find out anything about who really held it. It belonged to an H. R. Hughes. But they had been told that Howard Hughes had no account there. Swiss banking secrecy was now operating in favor of what McGraw-Hill knew was a fraud against them.

On January 19, 1972, a group of officials and attorneys from McGraw-Hill met with chief counsel Hegetschweiler of Swiss Credit Bank. Hegetschweiler confirmed the fact that Howard Hughes did not have an account at his bank. But then who opened the "H. R. Hughes" account which held their funds? Hegetschweiler demurred. "Private bank information," he said; to reveal it would be a violation of bank secrecy laws.

Fortunately for McGraw-Hill, little in this world is absolute, even in Switzerland. The company had one option and they took it: ask a Swiss court to compel the bank to reveal the true H. R. Hughes account holder. In a rare parting of the bank secrecy veil, the court agreed that there existed substantial evidence of fraudulent use of the bank account through falsification of the account papers. This, it was decided, was a crime committed primarily in Zurich which, according to that canton's laws, made it obligatory to reveal information about the account. The bank was directed to comply with McGraw-Hill's request. One Helga R. Hughes was named as holder of the account. Local journalists identified her as Edith Irving, and later Swiss Bank Corporation added the Hanna Rosenkranz twist to the story. The Irvings were immediately charged with fraud, as well as falsification of bank documents, and subsequently jailed.

In the short-run analysis, Swiss bank secrecy acted to protect criminals, an argument critics often use in lambasting Swiss banking practice. But it later functioned to convict them, an ultimate justification for their system, argue the Swiss. In Switzerland, no one is in a great hurry for *final* justice. The morally right end justifies the means. And the means—in this case, bank secrecy—protects the account holder, a noble enough objective. Swiss bankers believe their handling of the Irving case was most sound.

However, a less sanguine view of the secrecy situation is offered by a U.S. SEC official familiar with Swiss banking practice. "Swiss bank secrecy can be pretty much what they want it to be," he told me. "If they want to divulge information they will find a way to do it."

I wonder if that isn't fundamentally possible with any national law. And there the argument rests.

FLAVOR

Financial privacy in Switzerland is best pursued by going there, although one can open a Swiss bank account by mail just as in the United States. A far better feel for the country, its ethics, mores, and practices can obviously be had through a personal visit. And since there is much to learn from this little nation, a visit is strongly recommended.

Some 8 million foreigners travel through Switzerland every year, and nobody need know they've been there. Swiss customs officers do not stamp passports, a fact which quietly reminds us that not everyone going to that lovely land wants it to be known. And what sort of people are they, these visitors to this land of money hiding? The bulk of them, as might be expected, are neighbors—French, Italians, Austrians, and Germans. The Swiss banks are usually not the prime point of their visit, except for the Italians. Most Americans head for Zurich or Geneva first. The Arabs prefer Geneva. Both groups are often on banking sojourns. But the diverse flavor of the country is revealed best in its smaller cities: the German-speaking St. Gallen and Lucerne; French-speaking Lausanne and Neuchatel; and Italian-speaking Lugano.

The second-floor reception area in the Union Bank of Switzerland's Lugano branch is typical of rooms into which potential money hiders are ushered. It is a rather brightly lighted modern room, about 30 feet long with large, curtained windows and a purple (not magenta nor violet, but purple) carpet. Seven stuffed leather chairs and a semicircular sofa of similar material are grouped casually and face low, glass-topped tables. The large reception desk sits opposite one of two elevator doors at the end of the room near a long office corridor. It is presided over by an efficient-sounding guard in dark blue coat and tie with UBS emblems. His white shirt is starched: proficiency personified in Lugano. At the opposite end of the room is a door leading to a large conference room next to a second elevator door.

Similar reception rooms receive important and minor seekers of privacy at major Swiss banks. Most visitors to them have made one decision in common—to make use of a Swiss bank. In this reception room they will meet their first bank officer, usually prior to being taken to a second, smaller visitor's room, separate from his private office, where banking business will be discussed. *Sitzimmers,* the latter are called in Zurich.

Out of the UBS, Lugano, conference room poured, at the moment of my arrival, two bank officers, a secretary, and a wealthy-looking, well-dressed businessman of obviously Italian lineage. The latter's briefcase seemed ordinary enough. His clothes, though expensive, revealed little. He conversed with easy smiles in Italian. The bankers' persiflage was given with similar smiles. The businessman didn't look like a money runner or drug dealer or racketeer. But what do those people look like? Few higher echelon money runners, drug dealers, or racketeers *look* the part. Common hoods aren't common hoods, given sufficient money. I decided he looked more like a Milan industrialist or attorney. It was that private room with the bankers that had added a degree of the sinister. That, plus the popular American image that private meetings in secret Swiss banks *must* be dealing with something illegal.

I looked at the other inhabitants of the reception room. They'd each made a decision about this bank, or someone had made it for them, otherwise why would they be here? Bankers don't meet purely social luncheon dates in this sort of room.

One was a lower-income Italian in undershirt with a rumpled jacket hanging over it, sporting new leather sandals, with his wife and two children. There were also three European businessmen in suits, all in their 60s, and all quietly reading either newspapers or bank literature taken from a large rack in a corner. A fortyish Frenchman with coat and no tie was staring at the ceiling. Another man—an Italian in his 50s or so (how do you tell the age of middle-aged Italians?) —was wearing crushed velvet pants and jacket with a shirt open to his chest, the vogue. His younger female companion was chatting brightly. He paid little attention. There were no other signs of circumstance evident among any of those waiting.

A diverse lot. They apparently all had needs for this bank. They may have all lived in Lugano or its environs. Or perhaps not. Their banking decisions may have arisen out of the bank's pure convenience, or come from pure fear for their money, or out of motives of asset diversification, or simply to hide funds. Whatever. There was no way of knowing. And yet, I somehow felt I should know. This was a *Swiss bank* in one of the liveliest money movement areas in the world.

There were no Americans waiting for a Swiss banker at UBS, Lugano, during my brief dalliance in its reception area. That was not surprising. Lugano is "out of the way." Still, the presence of several nationalities among the customers of the bank and the absence of Americans during that particular hour prompted some questions.

Could Swiss bank services be so uniquely European or established for use of non-Americans that they are too "foreign" or unusual for U.S. citizens' banking habits? Are their services better than, competitive, or noncompetitive with those offered by U.S. banks? Or, on the other hand, are there special factors which make Swiss banks especially attractive for Americans? The reception room offered no clue.

Research later revealed that while banking services worldwide do differ, it is mainly in terms, not form. Most major banks offer savings and checking accounts, trust services, and some degree of investment capability. Americans will be inclined to use Swiss banks most logically through their wide range of services offered. They truly make up a full laundry list and one which few American banks can match. The Swiss bank service list, however, would rarely be of interest to Americans without their having some concern about the antiprivacy, anticapital trends we noted in Chapter 1. For all of the fine Swiss services, the effort of using a Swiss bank will offset its service advantages unless there is an interaction with those privacy and capital concerns, and possibly with some special services such as tax haven support. Exceptions will occur for those who travel frequently to Europe and persons doing business there. Otherwise the above generalization will prevail. However, it is my belief that the negative U.S. social trends are more than sufficient to outweigh Swiss bank use problems over the long term. This is despite the reduced financial attractiveness of the country. It is a subjective matter, not one which can be discussed in absolute terms. Still, there are some generalizations that can be made.

NORMALCY

Everything we do with our money must have its advantages and disadvantages. Swiss banks are no exception.

But there is a problem. The reasons listed in favor of Swiss bank accounts by most potential depositors aren't "normal." That is, they don't fit the usual pattern for choosing one's bank. Normally we consider quite simple reasons for selecting one bank over another, and the banks promote them in vying for our cash. Inevitably they are: convenience, costs, personal relationship, or services. However, Swiss banks are inconvenient for everyone but the Swiss, and most offer little in a personal relationship potential as a result. They are also more expensive to use than U.S. banks. That leaves only services in the usual list, and, as we will see, these they have in abundance. You just have to overlook the inconvenience, impersonality, and costs to obtain them, and, in so doing, ignore three out of four advantages which most banks think are important. The question is, do you want to do that?

Most major banks are so determined that a branch on every corner is the formula for success that they are virtually falling over one another seeking space. Among the more vehement in the branching vocation has been Barclay's Bank of Great Britain. Through its International Division (renamed from DCO: Dominion, Commonwealth and Overseas) Barclay's has acquired more than 5,000 branches in nearly 50 different countries. More than 45 percent of these are outside the United Kingdom. Other British banks are nearly as aggressive. National Westminster has about two thirds the foreign branches of Barclay's, and Lloyd's Bank in 1974 acquired the near 50-branch system of California's First Western Bank in a major competitive move against Barclay's in the Golden State. The two most expansive U.S. banks, Bank of America and First National Citibank of New York, have 104 and 252 foreign branches, respectively. While this represents a considerable falling off from Barclay's pace, it also reflects a sharp difference in the size of domestic markets and the fact that a bank doesn't go afield to obtain what it can get at home.

And the Swiss? Domestically, they are the greatest of branch bankers. Their convenience is spread through 473 banks with over 4,500 branches in their small country. However, the Swiss branch banks combined have only ten true branches outside Switzerland. In the United States, they have opened only seven branches. Swiss Bank Corporation has three branches in New York, and one each in Chicago and San Francisco. Swiss Credit Bank will accept deposits through New York and Los Angeles. But Union Bank of Switzerland, with nineteen "representative" offices worldwide, has only three in the United States, and none accept deposits. They are in New York, Chicago, and San Francisco. What is more, the banks in Switzerland jointly agreed to limit their domestic expansion until 1977. Hardly aggressive banking at all.

This suggests the Swiss know something about their drawing power. Given their deposit growth in the past few years, they clearly haven't needed to open convenient branches to get foreign deposits. Convenience simply has not been nearly as important to Swiss banks' foreign operations as to major American or British banks.

Swiss banks certainly cannot have the personal relationship factor working for them with Americans. It is rather difficult to hold a "personal" relationship across an ocean, even though a correspondence can be developed. They emphatically do not advertise themselves as "friendly," either, and in offering depositors a four-language statement only once or twice a year can hardly be considered warm communicators. Swiss banks also do not have a list of free services or giveaway items as are often touted by banks in the United States to tempt your money into their vaults. Indeed, the personal touches offered by Swiss bankers are few, and usually, when given, follow the arrival of your deposit rather than precede it.

Certainly cost savings aren't a forte as far as customers of Swiss banks are concerned. Not only is the cost of communication with them significant, but their "unbundled" charges (separate fees for each service) will rapidly add up to more than those of U.S. banks for all but inactive accounts.

Having pointed out why selection of a Swiss bank will fall outside "normal" banking consideration let's now consider the Swiss bank pluses, the real reasons why they could well be attractive to you.

PRIVACY

The Great Theme upon which the strongest Swiss pluses are built is privacy. It plays counterpoint, background, and main melody at varying times. Probably the most demonstrable evidence of its main melody role came with Swiss determination to maintain monetary privacy in the early 1930s, when Switzerland reacted to Hitler's fanatical despotism in Germany. The Nazi regime in 1933 had become infuriated over the flight of capital from Germany, a flight which frequently stopped just over the border in Switzerland. Literally thousands of Germans had sent funds out of their country in anticipation of Hitler's suppression of civil liberties. Accordingly, a law was promulgated in Germany ordering all citizens to declare their foreign holdings. Failure to comply carried the death penalty. Most Germans who had exported capital felt they had no choice but to put their trust in the Swiss not to reveal information on their personal finances, and a great many Germans did not report their accounts across the border. And a great many Gestapo agents were sent into Switzerland as a result. The latter's methods and techniques included not only bribes, but efforts to deposit funds under suspected account names at various Swiss banks. If the funds were accepted by a bank, this was considered proof that the person named held an account at the bank. If that fact hadn't been reported, the death penalty was invoked. One famous inducement case involved a young lady employee of a Swiss bank who had made a few offhand comments about depositors to her boyfriend, undoubtedly, as it turned out, with some prompting. He, of course, was later exposed as a Gestapo agent.

As these methods of ferreting information became known to the Swiss government, it reacted with the 1934 Bank Secrecy Act. This law and the new practice of numbering accounts protected a great number of Germans, despite the Gestapo efforts which continued for many years. It remains the key for any individual's belief that his money matters will remain private while they are being dealt with in Switzerland. It is a virtually unique concept in the world, and with the backing of history, has made Switzerland both famous and wealthy, and made several million persons more confident about their financial resources. Quite clearly, this privacy has attracted many persons of doubtful intentions who have made the system work for illegal gains. This has led to some highly celebrated court cases, all of which served to focus the world's attention on Swiss banking secrecy. Some of this attention has been highly critical. However, as an editorial in *Barron's* (January 20, 1969) put the matter: "Just because almost all other countries have given up what for centuries had been a globally upheld financial freedom, the Swiss are not believed to have the slightest inclination to follow suit. . . . Why should the Swiss banking system give up the very discretion for which it is world-renowned and respected?"

It would seem that this is the context in which potential depositors should view Swiss bank privacy. Governments have great abilities to deny privacy. It is up to individuals to take personal steps to protect it.

Complete privacy?

As was pointed out in our discussion of the Irving case, Swiss bank secrecy is hardly absolute. When one wanders into the quasi-legal world of tax avoidance or potential fraud, privacy can disappear as quickly as the spring alpine snow.

As the Big Three Swiss banks stated the matter in their booklet, *The Truth about Swiss Banking:* "Contrary to popular belief, there are limitations on banking secrecy in Switzerland. Banks are obliged to furnish pertinent information when the higher interest of the public or the state are involved, particularly in cases defined as crimes by Swiss law. The purpose of banking secrecy is to protect the innocent, not to shield the guilty, and history has demonstrated its usefulness."

If that sounds a bit smug, you should ask the Irvings.

One important aspect of Swiss bank privacy, the difference between numbered and regular accounts, will be discussed later. Suffice to say here that there is no legal difference and only small practical differences between the two. The availability of numbered accounts cannot be considered a plus for Swiss banks in any legal sense.

What is more, Swiss bank secrecy has been under attack around the world, as well as in Switzerland. It has seen the effects of what in 1974 Hans Bär, then partner and now managing director of the large private bank, Julius Bär & Co., told me would be "salami tactics": a steady cutting away of bank secrecy. It has taken many forms, some far more damaging than others. The U.S.-Swiss Mutual Assistance Treaty, which went into effect in January 1977, is one of the smaller cuts, although until there are sufficient cases testing its efficacy, it is open to wide interpretation. Quite erroneously, I think, it is frequently cited as being a major inroad to bank secrecy.

The treaty is the culmination of several years of negotiations between the Swiss and American authorities over the issue of illegally gotten money flows from the United States to Switzerland—principally underworld money. The treaty was prompted by pressure from criminal law enforcement officials, securities law regulators at the SEC, monetary authorities at the U.S. Treasury, and the Internal Revenue Service. They all wanted the cooperation of the Swiss in tracing alleged criminals through name- or event-associated data. The Swiss staunchly refused to cooperate in investigation of alleged crimes on the basis of tax avoidance because they don't see it as a crime.

The matter of tax fraud versus tax evasion requires some clarification as there is a fine line between the two. Basically, fraud is involved where a statement is made or documentation given about alleged nonexistence of certain income. Tax evasion is the omission of reporting the income without any supporting statement or data. This technicality is one upon which Swiss and American authorities agree, but act upon in different ways. The distinction is not usually important in the United States except in fixing the degree of penalty; both evasion and fraud are crimes. With the administered tax system in Switzerland, only fraud is a crime. (Legitimate tax *avoidance* is legal in both nations.)

This distinction is recognized in the Mutual Assistance

Treaty and was a fundamental point of argument during the Swiss National Assembly's ratification process. The treaty precisely defines certain criminal acts in Switzerland which might come under provisions of their existing statutes and require some lifting of secrecy when requested. Tax evasion, which is not a crime per se in Switzerland, can now come under provisions of the treaty if crimes of gambling, narcotics, poisons, firearms, or an association with organized crime are also involved, if the accused cannot be convicted under any other evidence, *and* if the U.S. government requires Swiss government assistance to convict. Then, under specified terms, bank secrecy can be lifted. Prior to the treaty no U.S. tax evasion case could receive Swiss assistance. Now, under the conditions above, it can. The treaty also spells out antitrust and fiscal crimes (nontax) where organized crime is involved, plus detailed procedures for protection of accused persons, and evidentiary procedure for both requesting and requested (in terms of initiators of action) states.

Two other points deserve mentioning as they both deal with time factors: Now that the treaty is in effect, its provisions apply to acts committed *either* before or after it went into effect. And the treaty may be cancelled by either government after January 1982 with six months' notice.

A copy of the treaty may be obtained from the U.S. State Department for further details.

A final point is worth noting about the treaty and its ultimate bearing on banking secrecy. The Swiss, who have stood pat on the secrecy issue for over 40 years, have now shown a willingness to bend a bit in unusual matters. The question that only time can answer is whether this treaty is the camel's nose under the tent.

There are other movements on the Swiss bank secrecy front, many of them within the country itself. One finds Swiss bankers a bit more willing to admit possible changes in the area. Dr. Hans Mast of the Swiss Credit Bank: "Discussion here is not yet at the serious stage, but there is pressure, both internal and external, for this discussion. Political opinion of the Swiss people is against any change, but we will have one: certain aspects of tax evasion will be defined as fraud, and will be punishable as a crime, a special category."

Nicholas Bär, chairman of Julius Bär & Co., takes a broad view but arrives at a similar conclusion: "I believe Swiss banking success has been very much helped by banking secrecy. But if the banking secret existed in a lousy country with largely lousy banks and bankers, it wouldn't mean much. If there is true erosion in banking secrecy, it will be a major shock internally, and such shocks must be avoided. Besides, any change in banking secrecy will hurt the little fellow more than the big one. I am also quite sure that legally the system will not be changed *for many years,* if ever. But there will be more agreements of the type we have made with the United States." (Italics mine.)

Another banker at a small Zurich bank was more specific: "Bank secrecy will not change from today to tomorrow. If change should occur it would not be in the next 20 years."

Whenever an elimination of Swiss banking secrecy may occur, if there should ever be a finite date, it is not as important as the new readiness on the part of Swiss bankers to admit that change is in the air. These quotations were taken in March 1977. On none of my previous half dozen visits to Switzerland from 1973 to 1975 was any suggestion of change in banking secrecy admitted, other than in Hans Bär's "salami tactics." It appears that the modified attitude about it on the part of at least some important bankers may, in itself, hasten further changes.

In terms of actual developments, the most important cuts into banking secrecy recently have been made outside of Switzerland. That receiving the widest notoriety was the SEC case against American Institute Counselors of Great Barrington, Massachusetts, and its resulting pressure via court order against Swiss Credit Bank as custodian of certain securities partially backed by gold. In November 1975 the SEC charged AIC, Swiss Credit Bank, a Liechtenstein corporation, and nearly a dozen other companies and individuals with fraudulently selling unregistered securities worth some $280 million "in violation of virtually the entire panoply of federal securities laws." The securities in question were "metric accounting units gold storage agreements" and "gold coin securities." The SEC obtained a U.S. federal district court order freezing the assets behind the securities at Swiss Credit Bank in Zurich, and a demand that the bank deliver some $150–$200 million to its New York branch office while an accounting of the actual assets could take place.

The bank demurred, citing Swiss bank secrecy, and asked the court to rescind the order. The court refused. After about a month's delay, and with an obvious eye on its U.S. subsidiary, a New York Stock Exchange membership, and branches in New York and Los Angeles, not to mention untold millions of dollars worth of U.S. securities held for customers, the bank deposited a $122 million letter of credit with its U.S. attorneys in satisfaction of the court order.

Thus, the effect on bank secrecy was to raise a serious question: Can money or other assets falling under jurisdiction of a U.S. court act as a hostage to compel a break in Swiss bank secrecy, where existing laws would otherwise be insufficient?

Perhaps the "hostage" need not be cash, as one Anthony Field of Grand Cayman would confirm. Field, a Canadian citizen and managing director of Castle Bank, Cayman Islands, an entity made famous by IRS efforts in Project Haven, had the misfortune to be subpoenaed by a Miami grand jury on his way through the Miami airport during the grand jury's investigation. He refused to testify about accounts or activities at his bank, claiming both U.S. Fifth Amendment protection and his likely indictment in Cayman for violation of their bank secrecy law. Found guilty of contempt of a federal district court for his refusal, an appeal went all the way to the U.S. Supreme Court, which denied *certiorari* and let stand a Fifth Circuit Court decision that both his defenses were invalid: the former on the grounds that he was not testifying about matters occurring in the United States and therefore could not incriminate himself under U.S. law in so doing; the second on the grounds that since the court had *in personam* jurisdiction over him, it could compel testimony which need only be balanced by the equities in the case—the importance to the grand jury of his evidence, versus his possible penalty in Cayman for testifying. Interestingly, however, he never testified; the mandate of the grand jury had expired before the Supreme Court refusal to hear his petition.

A larger slice of the salami went with that case, as the ramifications are wide. For example, a Swiss attorney argued before a Practicing Law Institute seminar in February 1977 that, under the U.S.-Swiss Mutual Assistance Treaty, a Swiss banker could not be forced to testify under circumstances similar to the Field case. His argument was that the treaty "contains important restrictions about the personal appearance of a witness in the requesting state [the state requesting assistance]. A person other than a national of the requesting state who has been served for appearance in the requesting state, shall not be subjected to any civil or criminal penalty because of his failure to comply. On the basis of the abovementioned disposal of the treaty, a Swiss banker cannot be compelled to appear as a witness before a grand jury in the United States." He added, "It is important to notice that the treaty avoids conflicts of laws between Switzerland and the United States. In this way, a Swiss banker may avoid disclosing in the United States facts which he is required, according to Swiss law, to keep secret. Only a Swiss authority has the right to compel a Swiss citizen to give testimony."

On the assumption that the Swiss attorney knew whereof he spoke with regard to the treaty, a respected New York tax attorney and law professor apologized for disagreeing with him, but then asked, "What if a grand jury or court asked for testimony *outside* the purview of the treaty?" His reasoning was that the treaty deals with permissible government authorities' actions in a list of specified matters, while a court or grand jury is not a government entity but rather a separate legal authority. "The existence of a treaty," he concluded, "is no defense in a U.S. court of law."

If this attorney was correct, and there appeared to be general agreement among the 100 or so attorneys attending the seminar that he could well be, even Swiss banking secrecy had taken a drubbing in the Field case.

In another area, the SEC has attempted to open the securities ownership aspect of foreign bank secrecy through a proposal filed in February 1977. The proposed regulation would require all U.S. stockbrokers to obtain an agreement from their customers to supply to the SEC, on request, the identities of the beneficial owners of their accounts. The SEC already has subpoena power to obtain this information from domestic brokerage firm customers, so the new proposal is aimed at foreign accounts where brokerage business is often done in the name of banks, not in the name of individual customers.

The New York Stock Exchange, in opposing the proposal on the grounds of potential loss of business to foreign markets (that is, no Swiss bank could possibly conform to the proposal under current bank secrecy laws), estimated that 6.6 percent of the NYSE's 1976 volume, or about 1.4 million shares per day, came from foreign sources.

A final area of consideration in the secrecy matter is a very practical one: that prompted by a pending or threatened dissolution of marriage. Lawyers say that such actions may be one of the major instigations of Swiss account openings. Here, Swiss authorities have little interest in providing exceptions to their fabled privacy. A husband may stash away funds in a Swiss account and even swear to its nonexistence in an American court (running risk of perjury, of course), and face little chance of being discovered. Even if the American court requested assistance of a Swiss court in determining bank balances, experts say it is doubtful if the Swiss court would find sufficient exception to banking secrecy to check all Swiss banks for the existence of family assets. Sequestering funds from relatives, including a wife, is not a crime in Switzerland.

Interestingly enough, however, a wife may not be given the same protection in legal matrimonial proceedings under Swiss courts. Husbands can sometimes obtain permission to inspect a wife's account under Swiss law, an extension of the highly male-dominated society of the Swiss which only recently gave women full suffrage. Women's liberation is hardly considered an "in" concept in Switzerland.

Perhaps the most that can be said about this range of recent developments in banking secrecy is that the "salami" is indeed getting shorter. As one law professor later observed, "It is clear that there is much that is not clear in this area. The law is changing very quickly."

For those readers interested in legal details out of professional or other curiosity, the following case citations regarding bank secrecy may be useful:

United States v. *First National City Bank* 396 F 2d 897 (2d Cir. 1968).

United States v. *Field,* 532 F. 2d 404 (5th Cir. 1976).

Arthur Anderson & Co. v. *Finesilver,* 546 F 2d 338 (10th Cir., December 1, 1976).

In sum, Switzerland does indeed provide privacy that is almost unique in the world, notwithstanding the "salami effect." Why you might wish to make use of that privacy, for positive or negative reasons, out of legal or illegal motives, is a personal consideration which must color that uniqueness for you.

STABILITY

A final major factor weighing on the plus side of Swiss accounts is stability. Stability of the government, stability of the economy, stability of the currency. Change or uncertainty is probably the most important irritation giving people sleepless nights about their money. Whether it is money in the stock market, money in a strike-torn, economically wracked nation, or money caught in the throes of a political coup or other upheaval, the fact of pending or threatened change in dramatic form is one of the most significant stimuli to our collective money-protective natures. The relative absence of these changes in Switzerland for the past 125 years has led invariably to its positive image as a safe haven for money. Here history weighs so heavily that there can be little argument that political and economic stability of the country is a major plus for anyone considering a Swiss bank account. A brief return to that history can be helpful here.

The neutrality of Switzerland has been guaranteed by the major European powers since 1815, a factor which has not been changed by the colossal political and economic upheavals surrounding the tiny country since then. The Swiss, of course, would be the last to wish a change in neutrality status, and the European powers have largely found Switzerland to be a useful island in their stormy history. The Swiss federal government has flowered since 1848, not seriously threatened in its decentralized democratic form to this day. No other important country in the world has been excluded as a combatant in a war or untouched by revolution for as long. The Swiss are determined to keep it so.

As a result, when Americans on rare occasions are beset by concerns about a political change or a social upheaval in their country, as many have been over the past decade, they turn naturally to the political stability of Switzerland. It matches that of the United States, and, without a civil war in 125 years, even tops it.

Switzerland and America did undergo revolutionary changes within a decade of each other just before the turn of the 19th century. In Switzerland this was also the period of the establishment of the major private banks, giving them a lengthy record of stable growth after the upheaval. Of those formed at that time, the largest are now Lombard, Odier, Pictet, and Julius Bär (the newcomer of nearly a century later). They are estimated to account for approximately $7.5 billion in portfolio assets among them. The Big Three public banks date back nearly as far, with the oversubscribed sale of Swiss Credit Bank stock to the public in 1856 being the first, and the 1912 merger birth of Union Bank the last. These giants are now believed to control assets and portfolios worth well over $100 billion, making them distinct rivals of New York and London banks in the Goliath world of high finance. In age alone, however, Barclay's of Great Britain is the Methuselah: over 350 years have passed since its birth. Interestingly enough, despite the century-old beginnings of most important Swiss banks, it wasn't until 1907 that the nation formed a central bank. This was largely a function of the decentralized federal concept of government; there simply had been little need for one. Now the country is the home of the best known *central* bankers' central bank, the place where so many of the monetary crises of the late 1960s were thrashed out—the Bank for International Settlements in Basle.

While the Swiss banks were founded as an outgrowth of manufacturing or as a refuge for political escapees' funds, they emerged shortly as most deft and experienced dealers in money and its investment for their clients. Three and four generations of families have held their accounts at the same bank and have been rewarded not only with success in investments, but with numerous favors. The banking establishment and its clients have grown apace in service to country and local civic causes. Their ties are often inseparable.

By the time of World War I, Swiss banks had established

themselves as important purveyors of funds to the country's own cantons and several foreign nations as well. This followed a traditional Swiss interest in capital export. In the aftermath of the war, the banks became major lenders to war-ravaged countries and furthered their reputation as bankers who kept their pledges and were willing to take measurable risks in doing so. Through Zurich, Swiss bankers provided assistance to Germany in repayment of war reparations and floated loans to the French National Railways, the government of Italy (yes, under Mussolini), and several South American nations.

But it was not until the Depression, when the Swiss banks withstood the Nazi inroads on their privacy and also kept their doors open at the time everyone else was closing theirs, that they set their reputation in granite. In 1931, Germany froze foreign assets and declared a moratorium on foreign payments. By 1933, there was a General Transfer Moratorium throughout Europe which also involved foreign assets in the United States. The U.S. bank holiday occurred in March 1933. This was the infamous time when "the American experiment in self-government was facing what was, excepting the Civil War, its greatest test. . . . In 1933, the fate of the United States was involved with the fate of free men everywhere. And through the world the free way of life was already in retreat."[3]

The Swiss banks did not retreat. Throughout the Depression they remained open and paid all deposits demanded. The penalty was financially heavy. Swiss bank assets declined by more than 50 percent between 1930 and 1936. From 1935 to 1942 some 35 banks were closed, but only 7 through bankruptcy. Others were dealt with through various forms of grace periods with creditors, or taken over by Swiss Bank Corp. and Swiss Credit Bank. Union Bank of Switzerland was reorganized with a smaller capitalization. But all deposits were

[3] Arthur Schlesinger, *The Crisis of the Old Order* (Cambridge, Mass.: Houghton Mifflin Co., 1957).

paid. And the Swiss banks' stature in the financial world and in the public mind increased immeasurably.

Swiss economic stability is militarily backed up, not only with troops, but with a national mentality that accepts the military as an important fact of life, probably dating from mercenary days. Every man who is physically capable of doing so serves in the army reserves between the ages of 20 to 50. This includes annual drills of two to three weeks, plus an active duty period in the early years. Hardly a home in Switzerland is without a gun, and reservists carrying a weapon and pack during the summer are seen all over the country, including main city streets and rail stations, on the way to annual drills. The exercises of the 650,000-man militia and the willingness with which the men accept the concept have been the backbone of Swiss neutrality. They deeply believe that the best way to stay out of war is to prevent one. Their army and reserves are their ounce of prevention.

As might be expected, clothed in such trappings of political stability as we've noted, the Swiss currency has been just short of unique in its own record. It is the only major trading currency of the world not to suffer a devaluation since the Depression, and that devaluation, in 1936, was the only one of this century. Contrasted with the 14 suffered by the French franc, the 7 of the Italian lira, or even the 5 of the British pound and 3 of the U.S. dollar, not counting floating rate declines, the record is unusual. Since the fear of devaluation is one of the prime movers of funds out of any given country, Switzerland has become the natural refuge for monetary protection. This is despite the fact that the small country does not belong to the International Monetary Fund, should it need assistance, and it has been forced to take important steps to stop the inflow of funds in order to avoid hyperinflation from currency surges. Steps such as the negative interest rate imposition on foreign holdings of Swiss francs, first in 1972 and again in 1974–75, and the limitation on foreign purchase of Swiss securities in 1972 (rescinded in

1974), and even the initial float of the franc in February 1973, were considered necessary to protect the franc for the Swiss. (See page 185 regarding the negative interest concept.)

However, the Swiss economy, having withstood the Depression, the Nazis, and World War II in determined isolation, joined in the recovery of Europe after 1945, and in so doing fell prey to the greatest economic ravage of the 70s—inflation. From December 1971 to December 1973, the Swiss consumer price index jumped 19 percent. By 1975, the country was in two-digit inflation. But in 1976 a dramatic reversal occurred: the Swiss consumer price index gained only 0.9 percent for the full year. Even so, prices in Switzerland for foreigners who have suffered currency devaluations in addition to the Swiss inflation are now a real deterrent to visiting the country. Such is the price of success in lack of devaluations for the Swiss, who, while finding tourist and watch trade down, are not notably complaining about it (at least no more than their normal level of lament at lost business, which is hardly a stony silence).

Taken together, the total record of stability in Switzerland is an important advantage in holding a Swiss bank account. And yet, political stability there is meaningless unless you fear for it in your own country. A banking record which not only includes overcoming the vicissitudes of history, but a willingness to band together to solve the problems of the future as they arrive, is of little use to you unless you believe this might not continue to be the case at home. A currency more stable than the dollar is not a great advantage to the average bank account holder in the United States, unless he or she is looking for an opportunity to profit from dollar declines in the floating money market.

In sum, something must precede the "plus" mark for the value of Swiss stability; either fear, a profit motive, or some illegality. But when you want the warmth of stability the Swiss have it in historical abundance.

Having tasted the flavor of this unusual little nation, we

can now examine some of the changing considerations about Swiss banks. Later, we will look into their larder of financial services. Some are bound to tempt you, be forewarned of that.

chapter 9

SWITZERLAND: NEW CONSIDERATIONS

NEWSPAPER headlines in early April 1977 trumpeted, "Prime Minister's Secret Bank Account Admitted." The related stories explained news media pressure on the prime minister of a small Middle Eastern country that had resulted in his admitting he held a bank account with his wife in a foreign country. It had been held secretly, contrary to his nation's laws on capital transfers. His chagrined resignation followed "clarifications": there were two accounts, larger than earlier admitted, and both in his wife's name.

If the name of the country where the accounts were held wasn't emblazoned in the first line of the story, today's casual reader would have presumed their location to be Switzerland, the land of infamous bank secrecy.

But that's not quite the way things were in the monetary milieu of spring 1977.

Israeli Prime Minister Yitzhak Rabin's wife's accounts were in Washington, D.C. She did not admit holding anything in Switzerland. In fact, the United States was probably more attractive to her. Whatever the reality, first and foremost the "Affair Rabin" revealed the state of international monetary freedom and privacy that year.

Israel is one of the majority of countries which find it necessary to control their citizens' cash transfers. Of 109 nations listed in *Pick's Currency Year book 1975–76,* only 19 had no restrictions on currency movement out of their respective nations. The United States and Switzerland were, of course, among them. U.S. restrictions can now be termed mild—only the reporting of transfers—while Switzerland has none except a limit on the importation of banknotes dating from April 1976. Israel's controls are strict: no foreign bank accounts permitted unless in the foreign country of a citizen's temporary residence (ala Rabin), and then only until six months after return to Israel. Great Britain, Sweden, and a host of other countries have blunt restrictions on *any* capital outflows. This international potpourri of controls quickly prompts the old query, could the United States slap on absolute controls? The answer: certainly, probably by as simple a device as a Treasury Department regulation. What is new is that a further question of *would it?* now poses some problems.

The Rabin accounts imply that the decision to do so could be more complex than "discovering" a need to control U.S. citizens' outflows of cash. A major problem is the amount of foreign funds like the Rabins' on deposit with U.S. banks. Including demand and time deposits and negotiable CDs, foreign interests of all types had stashed $32.73 billion in U.S. banks as of June 30, 1976.[1] Another $74 billion was parked with U.S. bank branches and subsidiaries outside the United States. While the first figure was less than 5 percent of total deposits at all U.S. commercial banks on that date, it is a sizable number. And it had increased by one third in the previous two and a half years.

That raises some pertinent points: Could U.S. citizens' funds be restricted and not those of foreigners? As a practical matter, could foreign funds be restricted at all? Would the

1 *U.S. Federal Reserve Bulletin,* December 1976, pp. A62–63.

banking lobby, on the other hand, accede to any action that might scare away those funds? Finding answers to these questions suggests that the issue of controlling transfers of funds from the United States has some intriguing caveats to it. Moreover, Congress again in 1976 failed to institute a withholding requirement on foreign account interest. The United States remains one of the world's great legal tax havens.

Thus the Rabins mutely tell us that in the current state of international monetary affairs, U.S. banks with 5–7 percent interest plus insured principal offer a most attractive place for anyone's funds. The Rabins might have been naive about legalities and U.S. bank privacy, but they were following a popular trend in holding U.S. accounts.

Indeed, the matter of banking privacy for the Rabins was a far different game. A close observer of the methods used by newspeople to discover their accounts saw *deja vu.* Offering a deposit for a suspected account holder at the suspected bank worked as well in Washington in 1977 as it did when used by the Nazis in Switzerland during 1932–33. When the bank accepted the funds in a depositor's name, the existence of the account was confirmed. The Swiss eliminated this privacy abuse with their famous Bank Secrecy Act of 1934, and set the cornerstone of their financial privacy upon rock. The United States, to the Rabins' pain, has yet to do so. Our accounts remain as transparent as a Salome veil. Finding an account balance is a problem of only slightly greater translucence.

So the "Affair Rabin" set very neatly the dichotomy of a U.S. bank account at interest: It is safe, financially attractive, possibly tax free for foreigners, and has a relatively free transfer horizon. But, it is irretrievably public.

It is principally this latter aspect that has tempted many Americans to keep a portion of their funds in Switzerland or other banking secrecy nations (notwithstanding the "salami" problem) at the same time that large amounts of foreign cash were finding a haven in the United States. Not surprisingly in our shrinking world, great cross flows of capital take place. There is nothing unusual in this: What is financially attractive to an Israeli, Pakistani, or Frenchman may not be as interesting to an American.

THE CURRENCY ISSUE

An early consideration in the use of a Swiss or tax haven bank must involve the matter of foreign exchange and dealing in foreign currencies. It is highly doubtful that one would consider a Swiss bank account while expecting to deal only in one's domestic currency. As the matter of foreign exchange is complex for most persons, a few concept and flavor expositions are in order here.

The gains of several foreign currencies against the U.S. dollar have been well publicized in recent years, as have the collapses of the British pound and Italian lire. For the record, the Swiss franc showed a 72 percent gain versus the dollar in less than five years up to early 1975, while the Deutsche mark rose over 60 percent and the Dutch guilder over 50 percent in roughly the same period. The pound, meanwhile, fell nearly 40 percent against the dollar in three years prior to October 1976, while the lire sank 26 percent over a similar time. These price swings point up both the dangers and possible rewards in holding foreign units for investment purposes. Decisions to do so must now involve the complex interactions of national economic prospects, political developments, and market psychology on an ongoing basis, more so than was the case in the wake of the dollar devaluations of 1971–74. The market is simply more settled and responsive to longer range forces now, despite temporary aberrations.

Whatever your specific inclinations, your Swiss bank will hold foreign currencies in separate accounts at your direction, providing you have sufficient capital. This is a task far less familiar to your U.S. banker, if not outright impossible for him. For the Swiss it's an everyday mundanity. The excitement comes in trading the currencies, especially in futures contracts.

If we may view the price relationship between any two currencies as being a seesaw contest between the respective countries, the price of one country's currency in relation to another's may be moved up or down by an increase or reduction in pressure on either of the two currencies situated at opposite ends of the seesaw. The two most important, though by no means the only, pressures are the inflation/recession prospects in one country relative to the other, and the balance-of-payments prospects in one country relative to its business partner.

In simplified terms, if domestic inflationary pressures increase in one of two nations riding a currency price seesaw *relative* to its seesaw partner, the seesaw tends to drop on the inflationary pressured end, attendantly raising the price of the currency on the other end. In addition, the relative lowering of general interest rates, a recessing economy, or a worsening balance-of-payments expectation, will have a similar downward "seesaw" pressure for the country experiencing these difficulties, relative to another with better prospects.

The following seesaw example should be helpful in understanding the manner in which currency prices fluctuate, and references to them in the financial papers.

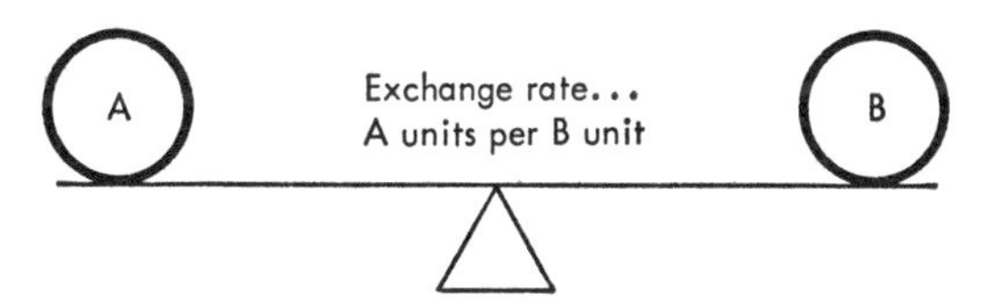

Countries A and B sit on opposite ends of a seesaw with the exchange rate of their currencies stated between them. If we designate A as the foreign currency, say, the Swiss franc, and B as the U.S. dollar, and utilize a 1977 rate of 2.5 francs per dollar, we have a real-life example:

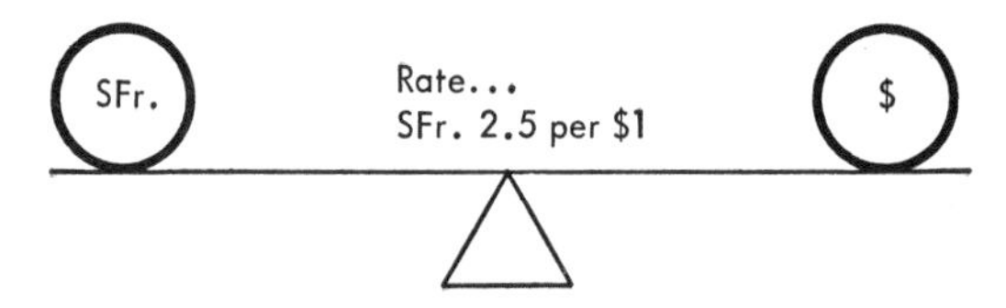

Now if we look for a stronger or higher *dollar,* which way will the seesaw move? Upward on the dollar side, of course, and attendantly lower for the Swiss franc. This can only be accomplished in terms of the exchange rate by adding more "weight" or larger numbers on the franc side. Thus if we have an increase to 4.3 Swiss francs per dollar, we get a lower franc-higher dollar relationship. In fact, it's the one which prevailed from World War II until late 1970.

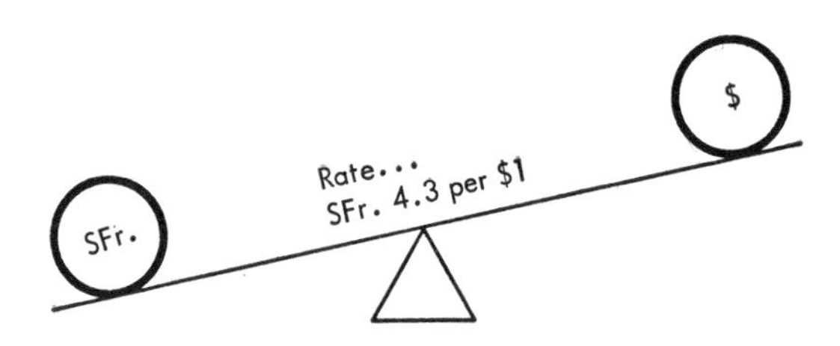

This is how the financial press quotes exchange rates in foreign units per dollar. When they indicate that the dollar rose against the franc from 2.54 to 2.58, they are saying that a buyer of francs is receiving more francs per dollar. Conversely, if the dollar fell to 2.50 from 2.54, a buyer would receive less francs per dollar. If you keep this seesaw relationship in mind it will help explain the workings of floating currencies.

With floating currency rates, the strength or weakness of a currency in relation to any other is a direct reflection of how the financial world perceives that country's *relative* economic prospects. This position is transmitted by official statistics and both published and private opinions offered by foreign exchange dealers, bankers, and corporate treasurers, who create a pervasive psychological mood which is akin to that surrounding that great confounder of public logic, the stock market. Over the longer term there is often a more predictable direction to single currency prices than to individual stock prices. But currency prices swing day to day by the tenuous thread of psychology. Daily or even weekly currency price undulations can be just short of maniacal.

The key to understanding currency price movements in the world of floating rates, is to identify which of the myriad forces acting upon a given currency seesaw are prevalent at a given time. As an example, the Swiss franc/U.S. dollar rate began a dollar uptrend in late October 1976. With an October closing rate of 2.43 francs per dollar, the dollar gained to 2.55 by early March 1977. In analyzing this rather sharp climb, the first question should be whether this was a positive dollar move or a negative franc move, or a combination of the two. All three possibilities could produce the same effect.

In early 1977, the potential for emergence of worldwide inflation was a key preoccupation of economic thinkers and doers. And on the surface at that time, inflationary factors appeared positive for the franc versus the dollar. Switzerland had just recorded a less than 1 percent inflation rate for 1976 versus a 6.5 percent rise in the United States. The gold price was surging higher, flirting with $150 per ounce, and in so doing was forecasting greater inflation ahead. And the new Carter administration was creating a nervous U.S. stock market by proposing significantly stimulative economic measures. What was more, interest rates were rising in the U.S. short-term money markets. All of these were signals which *should* have led to *downward* pressure on the dollar versus the franc, the opposite of what occurred. (Note in Figure 9–1 the drop in the dollar when worldwide inflation and interest rates were notably rising during 1974. It was accompanied by a rise in the price of gold to a record by December of that year.)

Obviously, the market was reading the dollar/franc seesaw in another way in early 1977. One reason was revealed in a *Wall Street Journal* article of February 23, 1977. A. G. Becker & Co. (whose parent is the European merchant bank of Warburg-Paribas), predicted that the franc was "in the early stages of a substantial devaluation," the ultimate goal of which could be a scary 3.33 francs per dollar or more. Their reason: a sharp growth in the Swiss money supply in 1975–76. The franc reacted against the dollar but returned to near 2.50 by late April. Nevertheless, the situation was unnerving. Not since the initial rise of the franc from its postwar peg in 1971 had a prediction of a franc devaluation received any real credence.

Some perspective is needed on that money supply growth, however. The 1975/76 average growth in the Swiss monetary base was 9.2 percent versus a 12.3 percent growth in their M1 money supply. This is relatively high by Swiss standards to be sure, but it occurred against that Swiss economic background of very low inflation in 1976, continued slack loan demand, underused industrial capacity, and predictions of only slow growth in GNP for 1977. Monetary purists were saying the money growth rates were too high and that sooner or later that meant an inflationary pressure in Switzerland. Whether it finally occurs was not as important as whether it was expected to occur. The expectation temporarily drove the franc lower.[2]

Another example of this quixotic foreign exchange market occurred with the Swiss National Bank's imposition of 40 percent negative interest rate in January 1975. It had both temporary and artificial effects on the franc/dollar rate. The initial movement went against monetary theory and the desire of the Swiss National Bank, a common perversity. The franc rose against the dollar and most other currencies for about a month. This was followed by a four-month period of

---

[2] Author's note: A. G. Becker's prediction was dead wrong. The weak dollar of fall 1977 sent the franc to a record high of SFr. 2.0 per dollar.

uncertainty, and finally five months of lower franc rates against the dollar, the hoped-for effect.

Both of these examples illustrate the importance of identifying the prevalent factor affecting the market for any given currency in relation to another at any specified point in time. Clearly, this is easier said than done. The risks and rewards, with normal three- or four-to-one leverage in futures contracts, are patently great. Regrettably, we must complicate the problem a bit more.

The foregoing discussion has treated the currency seesaw as being bilateral, that is, involving only the exchange rate between two currencies. Of course, the relationship is more complex. A general trend in a given currency's price affects its seesaw relationships with all other monies. The dollar was in a general downtrend vis-à-vis several currencies from 1971 to 1975. The downdraft was against those with relatively fewer national economic problems than those perceived for the United States. By 1975, when the recession was becoming worldwide, the dollar was still sliding against those currencies which represented countries with apparently less troublesome problems. This trend reversed in mid-1975 as predictions of a more rapid U.S. recovery compared to other major industrial nations became prevalent.

In this multilateral sense, the seesaw analogy becomes a group affair, with a given major currency weighing on one end of the board and group of relatively better-off currencies on the other end. At the same time, the original major currency is riding a seesaw with another group of nations doing relatively poorly compared with it. The analogy becomes a bit tenuous here, but is valid. Whether one discusses bilateral or multilateral exchange rates, *both* favorable and unfavorable relative pressures can weigh on *either* end of the seesaw, giving us four directional variables to affect the exchange rate itself. These variables are psychologically activated by a group of special financial opinion makers over the short term, while longer-term trends have shown a momentum which has been more universal.

FIGURE 9–1

Spot exchange rates (dollar and weighted-average prices)

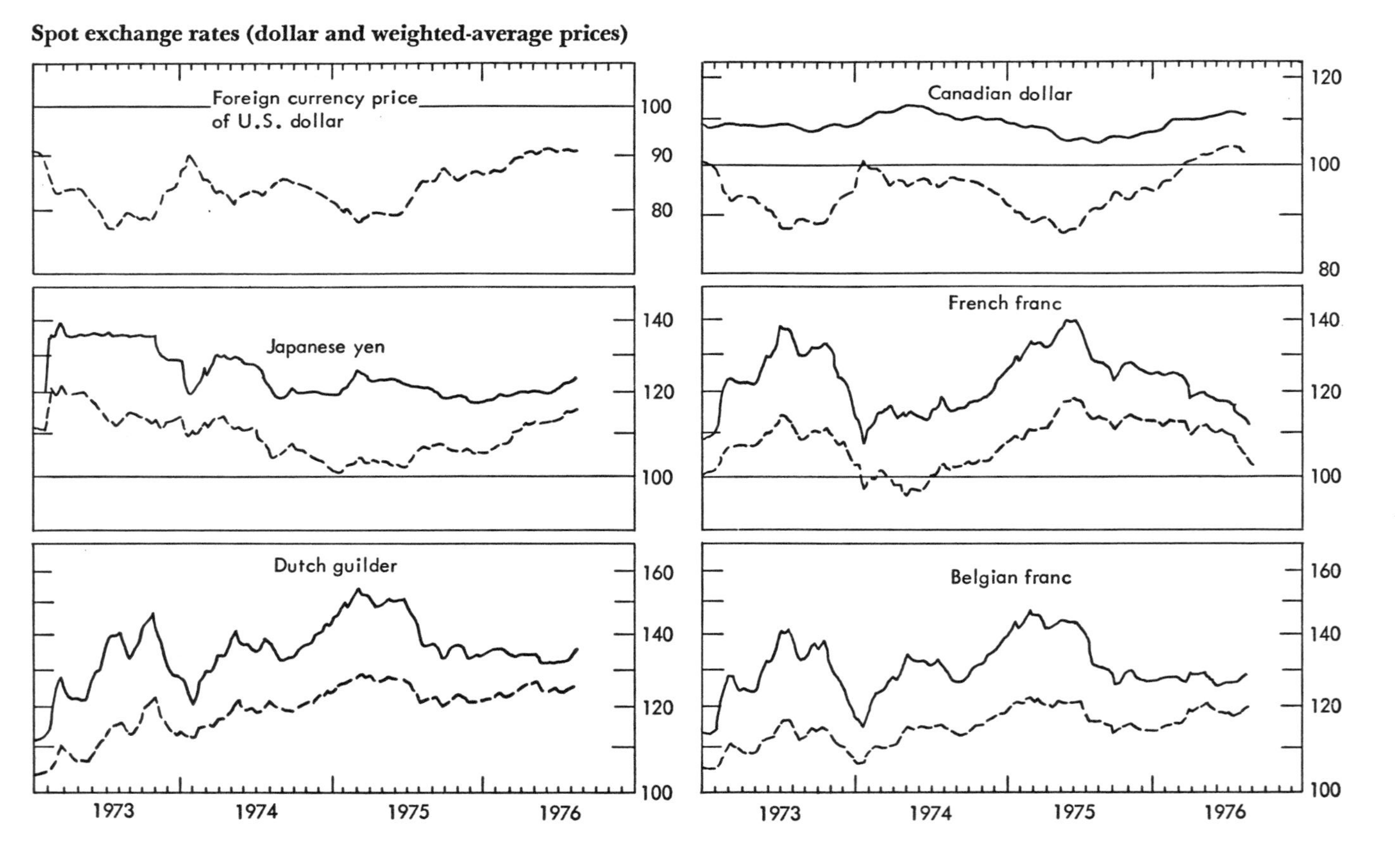

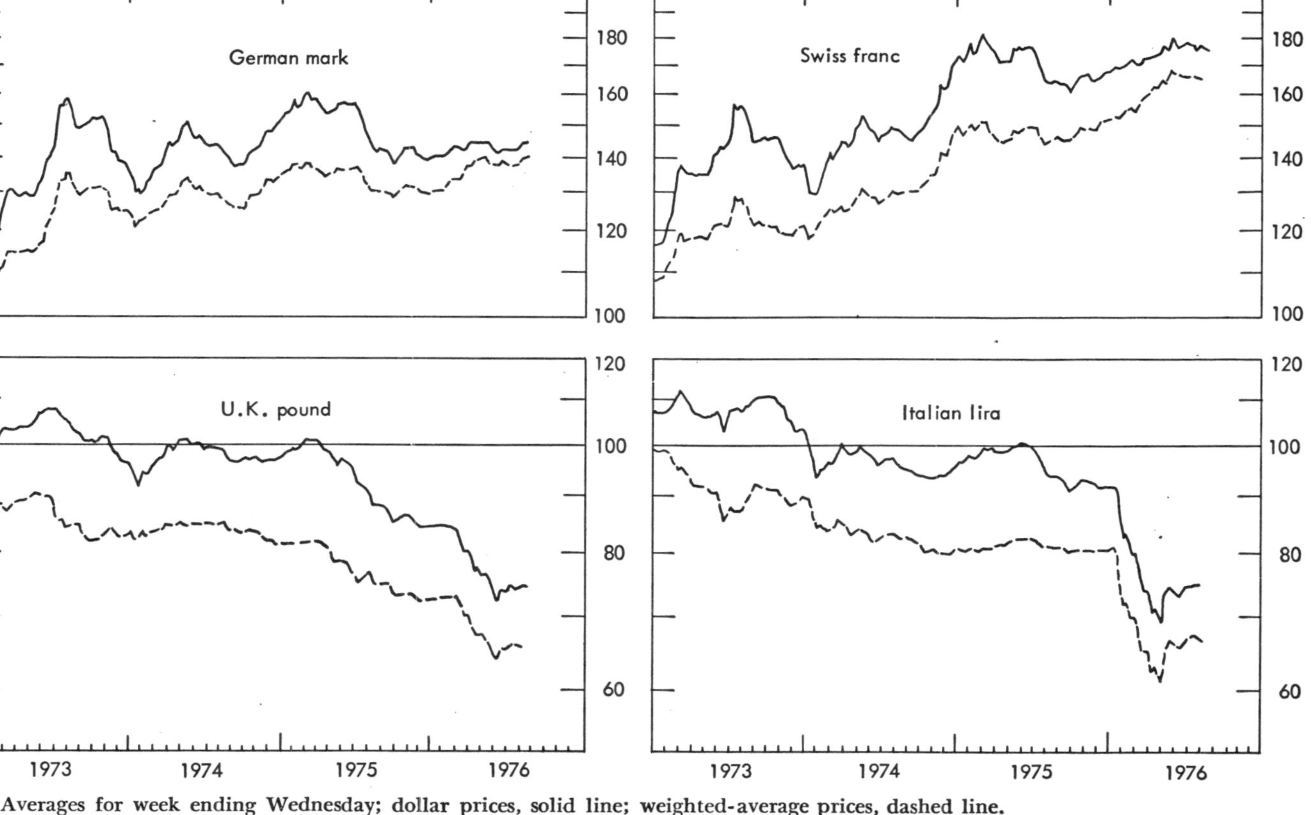

Averages for week ending Wednesday; dollar prices, solid line; weighted-average prices, dashed line.
Source: *Historical Chart Book,* Board of Governors, Federal Reserve System, 1976.

Unfortunately since the world has had only a brief modern experience with floating exchange rates (since 1971) we have a limited amount of data upon which to build long-term currency price patterns. However, the Figure 9–1 charts show price action against the dollar for nine trading currencies 1973–76, based on a parity with the dollar in 1970.

We have offered the foregoing examples and description to provide a taste of the factors involved when dealing in foreign currencies. Suffice it to say, *trading* in them for short-term profit is both a highly risky and a sophisticated game. But selecting times to buy and hold long-term some of the hard foreign currencies as a means of asset diversification has, and likely will, continue to make sense, if one watches the long-range picture regularly. This reasoning stems primarily from the danger of further capital accumulation problems and tax-driven social pressures in the United States, a theme which we have been expounding since the opening pages of this book. We are not alone in this analysis, of course. The once highly popular "New Jeremiahs" as *Newsweek* called them—Dr. Harry Schultz, Harry Browne, James Dines, and others—have been trumpeting this tune for years. Their siren song to early riches in a new Armageddon of financial collapse has been premature, to say the least. But they have not been proved entirely wrong. (And at least Schultz, whom I interviewed for U.S. television in February 1975, switched his theme out of gold into the U.S. stock market with fine timing.) The full story has not yet been written, and may not be for years. But the trends are there; asset diversification under such long-term pressures is thus only prudent. Swiss bankers naturally agree. They have expounded this cause for most of their lives, and, in offering probably the world's most efficient means for accomplishing it, have done well by it.

A 1972 quotation given in my book on Swiss banks remains valid today. In discussing capital flows, economist Albert Wojnilower of the investment firm, First Boston Corporation, observed, ". . . even those Americans with no

TABLE 9-1
Swiss franc record 1970–1976 (francs per U.S. dollar)

	1970	*1971*	*1972*	*1973*	*1974*	*1975*	*1976*
January	4.30	4.29½	3.86½	3.63	3.28	2.49	2.60
February ...	4.29½	4.29	3.85	3.13	3.12½	2.40	2.57
March	4.31	4.28½	3.84	3.23½	2.99	2.54	2.54
April	4.29½	4.29	3.86	3.24¼	2.93	2.56	2.51
May	4.31	4.08¼	3.86	3.09½	2.98½	2.50	2.46
June	4.30½	4.09	3.73½	2.93	3.00½	2.50	2.47
July	4.29	4.08	3.77	2.84	2.97	2.69	2.48
August	4.28½	3.99	3.77½	3.03	2.95	2.68	2.47
September ..	4.31	3.95	3.80	3.01½	2.93	2.74	2.44
October	4.32	3.98¼	3.79½	3.09	2.87	2.56	2.43
November ..	4.30½	3.94½	3.77¾	3.20	2.71½	2.67	2.44
December ..	4.30½	3.94	3.76½	3.23	2.55	2.62	2.44½

Sources: Franz Pick, *Pick's Currency Yearbook* (New York: Pick Publishing Co., 1970–74), Commercial and Financial Chronicle, 1975–76.

particular international business connections [will] learn, like everyone else in the world, not to keep all their eggs in one basket, and gradually and modestly diversify their assets among different currencies."

The Swiss franc, despite a narrow trading range from late 1974 into 1977 (2.70–2.40 per dollar), and the Becker predictions, had again proved by December 1977 to be an important currency to consider in any diversification steps.

THE SOLID GOLD FRANC?

Probably the most pervasive myth about Swiss banks and their currency has to do with the government's gold backing to the Swiss franc. A point made somewhere in seemingly every investment or market letter, advisory service, and treatise on international finance, is that the Swiss franc is 100 percent backed by gold, and that this fact provides an unusual safety and store of value in the franc. If we use the Swiss National Bank's official figures and agree on the same definitions of currency and gold reserves, the backing is notably less than 100 percent. What is more impotant, this backing or "cover" as it's officially termed, is of little practical value to the holder of Swiss francs. Psychologically speaking, however, we have a different matter.

Taking bank notes in circulation as the measure of currency, at year-end 1975 $7.4 billion was in float.[3] The gold reserves were stated at $4.6 billion on the same date, bringing the gold cover to 62.2 percent. This was down from 71.4 percent three years earlier. And, when final 1976 figures are available, it will probably place the cover under 60 percent due to the spurt in the Swiss money supply that year.

The value of the gold was calculated on the official reserve basis, that is, $42.22 per ounce, as done by all central banks. This admittedly opens the matter to some quibbling, as the free market price was then nearly 3.5 times higher. Making this adjustment obviously raises the cover of the franc to well over 100 percent; 217 percent to be precise. Wherever you wish to place the gold price, it will still not change the true practical value of this cover for the simple reason that the Swiss franc is not redeemable in gold. A Swiss franc holder cannot demand and receive gold for francs from the Swiss central bank any more than a holder of dollars can redeem them for gold at the Federal Reserve banks. Of course, one can buy gold with francs, dollars, and most other currencies in Switzerland, but this is not the same as redeeming them. There is no guarantee as to what the value of the franc will be in terms of gold at any future date, nor is there any promise that the Swiss National Bank will buy francs for any specified price or number of grams of gold. Those would be the conditions necessary for redeemability to exist. Since they don't, one might logically ask, of what value is this gold cover, then?

In fact, there is a value to the gold cover, but not the one that is popularly believed. It is the value of the gold as a potential support to the currency in international trade as a

---

[3] "Switzerland in Figures, 1976," Union Bank of Switzerland.

reserve behind the balance of payments of any given country. In this regard a far more important statement about the gold cover in a country is its backing to the balance of payments or trade account deficit/surplus. But that sounds complicated, so the "cover" to the currency is quoted instead.

Gold backing to a balance of payments deficit simply provides the country with one means of settling that deficit without printing new money or borrowing internationally. While settling such deficits by gold payment has been something most nations are loath to do, the availability of gold to do so provides one more psychological factor behind a nation's finances.

This balance of trade/payments consideration touches upon still another myth about Switzerland, which is that the nation's trade account is very solid. Historically, it has not been. Switzerland has run a chronic balance of trade deficit. In 1975, imports to Switzerland were $13.3 billion versus $12.9 billion in exports: a $400 million trade deficit. Against this figure, the $4.6 billion in gold reserves is meaningful. It means that the country could finance over ten years of similar trade deficits out of its gold stock alone. In this sense, the gold backs the currency because theoretically the franc would not have to be devalued to bring this account into balance. However, we are overlooking the fact that nearly all of that trade deficit is also covered by the so-called invisibles of the payments account: direct dividends from Swiss firms abroad, banking, tourism, and insurance. In fact, there was a balance-of-payments surplus in 1975.

With this additional bolstering to the franc, Switzerland's gold resides in unused splendor in the National Bank vaults, "backing" a currency which cannot be exchanged into it, and "covering" a nonexistent balance-of-payments deficit. It is plainly a powerful reserve, and one which is not likely to change negatively in the foreseeable future. Its existence and expected immutability provide significant psychological reasons for international interest in the Swiss franc.

One piece of evidence of the psychological factor at work where gold reserves are large, was provided by a *Wall Street Journal* report on currency strength versus gold reserves.[4] It quoted results of a study made in late 1974 by a Boston-based statistical services firm comparing the gold coverage of a nation's money supply with the price change of its currency against the dollar. While the relationship was not stated as causal, it is interesting. Valuing the gold portion of reserves at $168.50 per ounce over the period 1970–74, the Swiss franc had gold equal to 76 percent of its money supply, and the franc gained 51 percent against the dollar. The Netherlands' gold was 64 percent of money supply; the guilder gain was 36 percent. Austria: 60 percent gold, 41 percent currency gain. West Germany: 38 percent gold, 41 percent currency gain. The Boston firm's conclusion: "The strong currencies aren't necssarily that way just because of the gold, but because they [their respective governments] tend to think along broad monetary policy lines which assign weight to gold reserves, among other things."

In sum, the gold backing to a currency carries either psychological or disciplinary weight in the Great Money Game, but not redeemability. The Swiss franc is not "as good as gold," but is thought to be. That's what counts.

THE HAVEN ASPECTS

Switzerland is far less used for companies' business than most other tax havens due to a few relatively important disadvantages. The Swiss federal government requires a withholding of corporate interest and dividend payments in the amount of 35 percent of the sum paid, a factor not found in the no-tax havens. In addition, the disadvantage found in Liechtenstein of substantial minimum corporation capital of SFr. 50,000 is also found in Switzerland. In fact, the tiny

---

[4] Charles J. Elia, "Heard on The Street," *The Wall Street Journal*, April 7, 1975.

principality derived its requirement from the Swiss, as it did its requirement that all authorized capital must be paid in at least up to 20 percent of its value, with shareholders personally liable for the full value thereafter. When bearer shares are issued, all capital must be fully subscribed. Finally, a majority of directors of a Swiss corporation must be Swiss citizens residing in the country, and they must each own a qualifying share of the corporation's stock. The directors, as is the case with most other corporations elsewhere, determine the individuals who are empowered to obligate the corporation by signature, and these signatures are published as a matter of public record. Financial statements of a Swiss corporation must be audited annually.

Location of the corporation within Switzerland is important due to the notable variation in cantonal tax laws and rates. It is these rates which will have a primary bearing on the overall tax rate as federal taxes on most Swiss corporations have a maximum rate of under 10 percent per annum.

Also, Switzerland recognizes several different types of corporations, and these are taxed at differing rates by the various cantons. *Holding companies,* where the primary business is the administration of holdings in other firms, receive the most favorable tax treatment in all cantons, usually no cantonal or municipal income taxes, but rather a small tax based on paid-in capital, plus a low federal income and net asset tax.

Participation companies are mixtures of a holding company and an operating company, with the distinction that administration of holdings must not be the primary business. These are given favorable tax treatment in about one third of the cantons.

Service companies and *domiciliary companies* are those based in Switzerland but primarily serve foreign interests, servicing foreign firms in the first case, and not engaging in any business in Switzerland in the second (similar to nonresident companies in the Bahamas and Cayman). The domiciliary company is given the most favorable tax treatment of the two, similar to that of a holding company in about 80 percent of the cantons. Federal income and capital taxes are applicable to both types of firms.

In delving into the special considerations about Switzerland, we have discovered a new set of disquieting circumstances involving their banks and a few long-standing deterrents to initiating companies' businesses there. As we now look into the Swiss larder in some detail, we will come across more negative comparisons. In total, they have prompted my belief that the net weighted comparisons between U.S. and Swiss banks on one hand, and Switzerland and other tax havens on the other, make Switzerland relatively less attractive than at any other time in this decade. I stress the word relatively in the tax sense. Switzerland is still the most important *money* haven in the world.

chapter 10

THE SWISS LARDER

IF SOMEONE asked you whether you'd be willing to pay your bank to hold your savings, and what's more, to pay it at a rate of 10 percent per quarter, 40 percent a year to do so, you'd think the inquirer either mentally unbalanced or a joker with words, or worse. Unless you'd heard of the Swiss "negative" interest rate. Since January 1975 that's exactly what Swiss bankers have asked for. Needless to say, they haven't gotten it, but the requirement remains. And it's doubtful they've lost many deposits as a result.

There must be an angle to this, you say? Well, yes, if you consider a cut-off point for the charge to be an angle. The 40 percent so-called negative interest applies only to amounts per account of SFr. 100,000 or over ($40,000 at 2.5 francs per dollar). Single accounts with SFr. 20,000 to SFr. 100,000 balances are paid no interest, nor "charged" any. They ride free. Balances under SFr. 20,000 are paid the prevailing interest rate.

All of this promotes some inconvenience for would-be savers, which is precisely what the Swiss had in mind in levying the charge: reducing the attractiveness of Swiss franc holdings for foreigners. Their stable, sound, and recently valuable little franc had become just too popular. It was causing double-digit price spurts in the franc versus most other currencies from 1971 to 1975, thereby reducing the attractiveness of Swiss exports and inflating the Swiss money supply to keep some sort of pace with demand. So, at this writing, all foreigners with Swiss savings-type accounts keep less than SFr. 20,000 in them and draw their interest. True, this has caused many people to open several accounts at different banks, or at different branches of the same bank, or in different family members' names. One is not legally allowed more than one account in the same name. Thus the saga of the "negative" interest rate in Switzerland.

It has been noted earlier that the Swiss banks offer a wide and unusual range of services. That list must be weighed against the inconvenience of dealing several thousand miles from home, costs, and a number of other personal factors, to determine the real value of a Swiss account. In order to provide quick answers to two of the most common queries about Swiss bank services, the capital requirements, and where to find a given service, Table 10–1 is offered as a guide. Regrettably, I was required to generalize on the capital categories because of the wide range of circumstances with which the banks must deal. One general rule will prevail, however: the more of the services you utilize, the less the bank will require in the way of minimum capital on any one service. The suggested capital levels are stated for new customers and tend to be on the high side for those with established relationships.

SAVING MONEY

In my first book on Swiss banks I was able to discuss the interest return on Swiss savings accounts as a reason to at least consider them for a portion of your funds. In 1974–75 they were paying 3.5–5 percent, depending on type, and were then competitive with U.S. accounts, even with Swiss reductions due to withholding taxes. This was especially true if a holder's principal reason for use was to hold Swiss francs in anticipation of an improved exchange rate versus the dollar or other currency. They provided a modest interest bonus. While this is still true, the bonus has become notably more modest. Swiss banks have cut their rates twice in the 1975–77 period. They are now at the point of utter disenchantment with a 3.5 percent top rate in effect since April 1, 1977. These rates are significantly more sensitive to international money market rates than are their U.S. counterparts, and because of the drop in interest rates as a result of the worldwide recession of 1975–76, they have fallen apace. Europe has been much slower to recover from that slump than the United States, as well. A second related reason for the cuts in Swiss bank savings rates has been a slack loan demand and reduced lending rates. As savings accounts are a large source of loan funding in Switzerland, there existed a strong downward pressure from this source, too.

Key savings account rates at the major banks and withdrawal terms are given in Table 10–2 on page 190. Be advised they are subject to frequent change, and that many smaller banks have discontinued offering them entirely as a result of the SFr. 20,000 maximum forced by the negative interest rate regulation.

Note the terms of withdrawal, first. The three categories of interest-bearing accounts have progressively longer time periods under which withdrawals can be made. They form the equivalent of U.S. bank time savings certificates. In a deposit account, for example, you may withdraw *up to* SFr. 10,000 in any single month without notifying the bank of your intention to withdraw. But you'll have to give them three months notice for any larger withdrawal, or lose the interest paid on the amount exceeding the SFr. 10,000. While this may be unusual to Americans, it is common practice in Europe. It gives the banks a clearer control over their savings deposit liabilities.

TABLE 10–1

A guide to services available to depositors in Swiss banks

Service	Type of bank	*Capital required* Under $2,000	$2,000–5,000	$5,000–10,000	$25,000–50,000	$50,000–100,000	$100,000–250,000	Over $250,000
Certificates of deposit	All				X			
Checking	All	X						
Corporate underwriting	Public, private							X
Factoring*	Public							
Fiduciary deposits	All				X			
Foreign exchange	All	X						
Foreign exchange futures trading†	Most				X			
Foreign trade financing*	Public, some private			X				
Investment advisory	All (see discussion)				X		X	X
Investment funds	Public		X					
Letters of credit	Most		X					
Precious metals futures‡	All			X				

Savings accounts	Public, few private	X	
Safety deposit	Public	X	
Travel	Public, private	X	
Trusts	Public, special arrangements		
Wills	Public, private, closely held banks		X

* Based upon degree of banking relationship established, not dollar amount.

† Based on minimum margin requirement of 30 percent at major banks for new accounts; will vary from bank to bank.

‡ Based on minimum margin requirement of 30 percent at major banks; subject to frequent change.

Discussion: Note that this table is a recommended guide, not a precise series of cutoff points. As seen above, of the 17 services listed, 7 may be obtained for a deposit of less than $5,000 at the major banks. The real breakthrough comes at the level of $25,000–$50,000, where 13 of the services may be utilized. These levels are not precise, of course. For example, investment advisory services may be obtained at approximately the $25,000 point at the smaller branches of major banks, at some small banks, and at Bank Leu. The stated minimum at the major offices of the Big Three banks is over $100,000, although with a solid banking relationship in other areas they will accept less. The important private banks begin their advisory services at around the $250,000 level, but again are subject to variation depending on the total banking relationship.

Other services offered by the major banks are generally not related to any specified amount of capital. These include: serving as members of boards of directors (or trustees); incorporation, corporate operation; capital goods leasing; legal advice; tax information; and personal loans. These are generally available at the larger banks, both public and private.

TABLE 10–2
Interest rates*

Account	*Interest payable*	*Withdrawal terms*
Current (checking)	None Annual fee of SFr. 2., or 0.1 percent	No limit
Deposit account	2.5 percent	SFr. 10,000 per month without notice in advance; 3 months notice for larger amounts.
Savings account	3 percent	SFr. 5,000 per month; 6 months notice for larger amounts.
Investment savings account	3.5 percent	SFr. 10,000 per calendar years; 6 months notice for larger amounts.

The quoted rates and terms are those prevalent at the major banks. They may vary among other banks and are subject to frequent change.

Another point to note: Savings interest is paid only once per year, at year end, and is not compounded daily, monthly, or even quarterly. The stated rate in the table is the true annual percentage rate.

Another negative point with Swiss savings accounts is that the interest they pay is taxable in Switzerland and withheld by the banks and savings institutions for the government, a fact most Americans are unaccustomed to. This is a true tax disincentive, although it is not as serious a negative as it might appear, as long as you're planning to handle it legally.

The withholding rate is now 35 percent of the net interest paid, increased from 30 percent on January 1, 1976. This means that for every SFr. 150 interest paid into your account on December 31, the first SFr. 50 will be tax exempt; of the remaining SFr. 100, SFr. 35 will be withheld for Swiss taxes. While this is a healthy bite out of your already smallish savings yield, it won't be quite so deep if you declare it to the IRS. This is accomplished by obtaining Swiss certification of interest withheld on their Form R-82, sending it to the IRS for their approval, and returning it to Switzerland. Once cleared, all but SFr. 5 of the SFr. 35 withheld per SFr. 100 interest paid is returned to you. This paperwork exercise is the result of the United States-Switzerland Double Taxation Treaty, if that's any consolation.

Calculating your interest yield after Swiss taxes isn't difficult. For example, suppose your investment savings account has had a SFr. 10,000 average balance for the full year. On December 31, the bank credits the account with 3.5 percent interest, SFr. 350, and deducts the required withholding.

Interest earned	SFr. 350
Less exempt portion	– 50
	300
Less 35 percent withholding	–105
Interest paid	195
30 percent treaty recovery	90
Net interest received	
Exempt portion	SFr. 50
Interest paid	195
Treaty recovery	90
Total	SFr. 335
Yield as percent of SFr. 10,000 = 3.35 percent	

A FIDUCIARY ROLE

Given these problems of low initial return, withdrawal restrictions, and withholding tax, it's little wonder that the Swiss have come up with a way around the drawbacks. Unfortunately, it requires more capital, usually a minimum of $25,000, although if your banking relationship is solid it can be accomplished for less by pooling. This is the fiduciary deposit, made by your bank in the Eurocurrency market. It can be handled by a Swiss bank U.S. branch, an offshore branch or subsidiary in the Bahamas or Cayman Islands, or by any bank office in Switzerland.

The fiduciary deposit is not widely known outside Switzerland as it involves separating the risk (largely theoretical), from the name in which the funds are held. This occurs through your authorizing your Swiss bank to place the given deposit for a specified period of time with another bank outside Switzerland. The funds are placed in the name of the Swiss bank but at your risk, thus the fiduciary connection. The interest rates obtained are quoted daily in several major currencies from which you will select. These are the rates which helped push down Swiss savings returns over the past three years, but at the height of their popularity in 1974 they were running between 11 and 13 percent per annum. As seen from the table below, those were halcyon days.

An important advantage to these deposits is that they are neither subject to the 35 percent withholding rate nor the negative interest restrictions, as the interest earned is outside Switzerland.

There are two drawbacks: they cannot be used to purchase Swiss francs, a prohibited currency by Swiss bank regulation (a U.S. bank may purchase Swiss francs in the Eurocurrency market, but it will be done in your name, not the bank's). And the Swiss bank will charge a fee for this service, usually ranging between 0.25 and 1 percent. Again, this depends on your banking relationship and the size of the deposit.

Since any deposit made in a bank is a form of loan to that bank, there can be a private loan aspect to this fiduciary deposit concept. Your bank may act in its own name between a client wishing to loan (deposit) funds in Deutschemarks, for example, and another client wishing to borrow them in Germany. If you as lender are assured of the quality of the borrower, say a creditworthy brewery or small vehicle manufacturer, and the size of your deposit is sufficient, your bank may act as fiduciary between you and the borrower. This

TABLE 10–3
Euromarket rates

Running period	*US$*	*SFr.*	*DM*	*£ sterling*	*FF*
On call	5¾%	1½%	3⅛%	7 %	9¾%
One month	6⅛	2¼	3⅝	7⅜	12⅜
Three months	6⅛	2½	3¾	7⅞	11⅝
Six months	6¼	3	3⅞	8⅜	11⅜
One year	6½	3¼	4	8¾	12¼

Euromarket average interest rates (bid) as per August 5, 1977 in percent per annum.
Source: The Union Bank of Switzerland.

entails more risk on your part, but will attendantly increase your return. It will also be tax exempt in Switzerland.

Table 10–3 shows the wide range of interest rates available in the Eurocurrency market for five key currencies. In general, the lower the interest rate relative to other funds, the more in demand that currency is, with an attendant belief that it is safer, that is, less likely to float downward against the other quoted funds. Note that the Swiss franc was considered the premier currency on the date, with the French franc the least desirable in terms of potential risk.

These rates change daily, and over time, they change substantial amounts. On February 11, 1977, six months earlier, the three-month rates were:

U.S.$	*SFr.*	*DM*	*£ Sterling*	*FF*
5%	1¼%	4½%	13⅝%	10½%

SWISS TRUSTS

Swiss bankers are eminently practical fellows. Despite the fact that the concept/entity known in English-speaking countries as a trust does not exist in Roman-law nations such as Switzerland, the Swiss will still arrange one for you. They will handle it in one of two ways, either through their Liechtenstein connections using that principality's form of trust, the *anstalt,* or send the request to their U.S. attorneys to establish a U.S./English form and have it administered through their offshore facilities in the Bahamas or Caymans. This is a service provided only by the major banks and a handful of smaller ones. But it does have an advantage in privacy. Once a banking relationship is gained in Switzerland, it is simply one more confidential service of which you can avail yourself, either by direct communication to Switzerland or by a visit to the bank's offshore branch or subsidiary.

As noted previously, to establish a trust in a foreign country one must have a U.S. attorney handle the American legal aspects first, and preferably one with full familiarity with the laws of the second country. Once begun, a local foreign attorney can carry the matter to conclusion. Because of the double legal fees and the variety of circumstances into which your trust may fit, it is difficult to estimate the cost factor. But if lines of communication to your Swiss bank are good, direct inquiry, including details of your trust needs, will bring the required information. Note again that Swiss bank branches in the Bahamas or Caymans are now most reluctant to undertake foreign trust work for Americans because of the changes in U.S. tax laws.

The final important service we are considering in this book, the "companies" service, is also readily available through your Swiss bank, and again may involve any of the havens in which they operate. Here, there is no general concern about dealing with Americans, and advice on the establishment of a company will be readily forthcoming, with costs attached. A Swiss banker pointed out to me that there is even a market for existing but dormant companies in Zurich, including Liechtenstein-registered entities. His small bank estimated the cost of establishing a Liechtenstein corporation at about SFr. 4,000, but at the time of my visit one was "available" for about SFr. 2,500. Minimum nameplate operations of the corporation would run about SFr. 4,000 per year, he estimated. In general, costs of establishment and annual operation of a small firm should follow those guidelines noted in the earlier chapters on the respective havens, even if initially arranged through your Swiss bank.

INVESTMENTS

There should be no doubt about the interest of the Swiss banks in securities portfolio management. One has only to observe the window displays along Zurich's Bahnhofstrasse or in bank branches throughout the country to see Swiss banks' interest in securities management. Quotations and latest prices of all issues trading that day on the Zurich Bourse plus 50 major New York Stock Exchange issues seem to be the minimum available by closed circuit television displays for passersby. The most elaborate reminder of Swiss banks' role in the international securities markets is at the head office of Swiss Credit Bank on the Paradeplatz in Zurich. Visible from any of a half-dozen large windows at the corner of the Bahnhofstrasse is an eight-paneled revolving stock price board stretching nearly to the ceiling. It contains four closed circuit TV displays rolling stock prices upward, a series of electric quotation panels with latest prices and net changes on a full range of Swiss and U.S. shares, plus 16 clocks showing times for each major time zone in the world. It serves as a monument to the interest of Swiss banks in international investments.

Swiss banks are among the world's most internationally minded investment managers, following some 15 stock markets from Tokyo and Hong Kong to London and New York. Their success in this pursuit, or lack of it, is not published by any of the banks, however. The only clues we have to results come from the mutual funds run by the larger banks. As Tables 10–4 to 10–7 (pages 202–5) show, the performance records of most funds, other than those specializing in gold or real estate, have been little better than those of their

American counterparts. The Swiss banks' available funds, specializing both geographically and by type of securities, is very broad (see page 199).

A positive factor in the personal portfolio management arena surfaces in management fees the banks will charge to "run" your portfolio. Most Swiss banks do not charge a management fee per se, contrary to U.S. practice. There is a significant word of caution necessary here, however. True to form with many fees and charges at Swiss banks, the small items and individual fees for various services can add to a greater total than the single set fee, usually 0.5 percent, charged by U.S. securities management organizations. The most common Swiss bank management conditions are revealed by Swiss Bank Corporation procedures.

The bank indicates it will not accept a managed account of less than SFr. 1,000,000, and that for this size portfolio they will charge SFr. 2,500 per year (2.5 per mil of value) for "full management." In addition, they will be paid for brokerage fees, since banks in Switzerland are brokers as well as advisers. On top of these charges will be a securities custodial fee which amounts to 1.25 per mil of value annually, per stock held. If the shares are held at a correspondent bank or subsidiary of the Swiss bank in New York, the charge is $6.50 per 100 shares held. In general however, the charges amount to less than those for a managed account in the United States. Quite clearly, these charges can rapidly add up, thus the insistence upon the relatively high minimum portfolio size. By "full management," Swiss Bank Corporation means review of the account as needed and issuance of quarterly written reports on the progress of the account.

However, Swiss Bank Corporation will accept a portfolio of securities from you down to around SFr. 100,000, for management on a "nonfee" basis. Such nonfee accounts receive infrequent review, perhaps monthly, and will not include quarterly written reports. Any reports or actions required by the client on such accounts are charged according to the amount of work involved, whether it be for a written progress report or establishment of a Liechtenstein trust. These nonfee accounts are still subject to the custodial fee for securities safekeeping, as well as brokerage charges as incurred.

The other major banks as well as the private banks have varying minimum managed account sizes. Union Bank indicates it prefers SFr. 500,000 minimum for full management, while Swiss Credit Bank says it has no minimum per se, if the account is given on a full discretionary basis. Again, they will not charge a separate fee for management but will levy individual fees plus brokerage and safekeeping charges depending upon the communication needs of the client. Most private banks look to the level above SFr. 500,000 as minimum portfolio size.

The physical form in which your securities may be held can vary considerably depending upon the country of domicile of the company whose shares you have purchased. Swiss shares are *bearer* shares, and will be registered in the name of the bank through which you purchase them and then endorsed in blank. This form may also be used for any of the 70 U.S. stocks listed on the Zurich Bourse. Where American corporate shares are purchased, other than those listed in Zurich, they are registered in your name, but may be held physically at your Swiss bank's subsidiary in New York, or may be registered in that subsidiary's nominee name and held there at your discretion. If you wish your U.S. shares registered in your name, even if listed on the Zurich Bourse, they will be bought and sold through the U.S. market. When this is done by your Swiss bank you will pay extra for the privilege. The additional charge results from the required payment of U.S. brokerage commissions by the bank, plus their charge of normal Swiss brokerage on top. While this latter charge is not large, amounting to 1 percent of value on stocks trading under SFr. 150 per share and 0.625 percent on stocks above this price, plus SFr. 1.15 per mil of value in taxes, it simply adds to your costs of doing business. Unless you have a total portfolio managed by one of the Swiss banks at their discretion, it makes better sense to order purchase and sale of individual American stocks through your American broker, in order to save the Swiss brokerage fee.

A final fact about which you should be aware when considering portfolio management by a Swiss bank is that they manage an enormous number of investment programs. In order to be able to keep their fees as low as they are (subject to change, of course), they do not believe in adding managers for your convenience. As a result, each portfolio manager handles a large number of accounts. As many as 1,000 accounts may be run by a single person, although the bulk of these may be essentially inactive accounts. One private bank in Geneva manages "several thousand" accounts, but has only 15 persons actually doing the managing. Personal attention, unless you ask for it, is a rare commodity at most Swiss banks. Exceptions are at the very small banks, including some of the private banks. And this is one aspect of small bank services which they attempt to promote. Foreign Commerce Bank's Geneva manager told me in 1974, "We have few enough accounts that we can get to know them all personally." He estimated about 50 accounts per manager. The belief hadn't changed by 1977. Cambio & Valorenbank's Zurich manager said then, "Our investment trading operation has just five persons handling everything. A client can call one of us and have his orders acted upon personally and directly. This is an advantage in quick executions. And we'll call the confirmation by phone, even to the United States, without charge."

If this personalized service is an important aspect of investment management to you, then you must consider the smaller banks. But don't overlook the possibility of using a smaller branch of a major bank instead.

This is not to suggest that you won't be treated warmly by a major bank branch at which you have your securities portfolio, especially if it is of healthy size. You may expect a personal conversation with your manager during a trip to

Switzerland, and he will be available for telephone consultation very readily, so long as the practice is not overused. If it is, you will be charged for it.

The major Swiss banks and a few of the private banks have established stock brokerage affiliates in the United States to facilitate their trades in the American market. This also makes the capture of brokerage commissions that much more lucrative for them where both Swiss and American rates are charged. For reference, Union Bank of Switzerland owns Swiss-American Corporation, New York, members of the NASD and the Pacific Stock Exchange. Swiss Bank Corporation owns Basle Securities Corporation, New York, members of NASD. Swiss Credit Bank owns a portion of SoGen, New York, with four other European banks and indirectly owns a 17 percent interest in the American firm of White, Weld, Inc., New York, who are members of the New York Stock Exchange. In addition, the bank holds a 40 percent interest in White, Weld Finance Corp. in Europe. Julius Bär & Co. owns Bär Securities of New York, members of the Midwest and PBW Exchanges.

INVESTMENT FUNDS

For those of us with something under the normal $100,000-"plus" required to obtain a managed securities portfolio at a Swiss bank, the major banks and a handful of the private ones have long provided their own mutual funds. The oldest date to the 1930s. As with stock brokerage functions, Swiss (and most other European) banks are permitted to sell, manage, and advise on their own mutual funds, where U.S. banks are not. Where the American banks went through the trauma of having their investment activities stripped from them by the Glass Steagal Act of 1933, with certain exceptions such as trust management, the European banks did not. Thus the availability of their mutual funds, and revenue from stock brokerage.

The Swiss bank fund business is sizable, if still tiny compared with the giant U.S. fund industry. The 1976 fiscal year-end fund assets of the Big Three banks totaled under $4 billion at an exchange rate of 2.5 francs per dollar.

Swiss bank funds are available for purchase with relatively small acquisition charges, the maximum of which are around a 4 percent spread between bid and offer. Swiss bank fund shares are issued somewhat differently than American mutual funds, in that they are often quoted on the Zurich Bourse in the open market, but have special share issues offered by the banks as well. These bank issues are a constant offering. They are, however, made on a net price basis where the Bourse prices require adding of commissions. A comparison of recent pricing structure for a few of Union Bank's funds will give you an idea of how prices vary between the bank and the open market.

Bond-Invest, their international bond fund, was available for SFr. 74 per share, from the bank, net. The same day's price on the Bourse was SFr. 72.50 plus commission and tax. Fonsa, the Swiss securities fund, was offered at SFr. 89.50 by the bank, net, and at SFr. 88 plus commission on the Bourse. A far larger spread was seen in Safit, the South African fund on that day. It was offered at SFr. 370.50 by the bank, but available at SFr. 352 on the Bourse. Obviously, it can pay to do a little shopping when considering acquisition of a Swiss bank fund.

Most Swiss funds are available with no minimum size purchase requirements through your Swiss bank, providing you have a current account there. When purchased through the Bourse, a minimum 100-share purchase is usually required. Here your bank will act as agent for you just as with any stock purchase. Regular investment plan purchases can be arranged and dividends/capital gains can be automatically reinvested. Sale of fund shares can be made on the open market or directly to the fund management at the fund's managing bank.

Dividends paid by funds investing less than 80 percent of

their funds outside Switzerland are subject to the 35 percent Swiss withholding tax. Those which are 80 percent or more invested outside the country are not subject to the tax.

In perusing Tables 10–4 to 10–7 (investment fund performance), you will notice a large number of real estate funds, and that their results, especially those managed by Union Bank, have been among the best. Some deal outside of Switzerland, but each bank has one or more which hold Swiss real estate exclusively. These vehicles are the only direct way foreigners can purchase Swiss real estate, and in my opinion offer an interesting play in this valuable commodity. They are available under the same terms as securities funds, that is, either directly from the bank or in the open market, usually with a 3–4 percent spread between bid and offer. However, an important caveat should be observed. Offering a liquid vehicle such as a fund in a fundamentally illiquid asset, real estate, can present redemption problems in a sharply declining market. In fact, most funds have a provision permitting the managers to postpone redemption for up to one year. The properties are usually valued only once a year, based on direct appraisal, which is an arbitrary series of decisions. This means there is nothing to prevent the share price from declining well below appraised book value either before or after such an appraisal. This did occur in the 1974–75 bear market. Be advised it could happen at any time.

STOCK EXCHANGES

The Zurich Bourse is the point of focus for the Swiss securities industry, although there are bourses in Geneva and Basle as well. The Zurich Bourse dates to 1744 and features trading in some 70 American stocks, 192 Swiss and other foreign issues, and 1,540 separate bonds. However, the market is very thin by U.S. standards. Large block trades are a rarity and even small blocks are often difficult to execute. The market is dwarfed by the size of the banks dealing in it. The

TABLE 10–4
Swiss Bank Corporation mutual funds

Fund	*Year founded*	*Total assets at financial year-end (in SFr. millions)*		*Price per share at financial year-end (in SFr.)*					*1976 cash dividend per share (in SFr.)*
				1972	*1973*	*1974*	*1975*	*1976*	
America-Valor (USA, Canada)	1974	25.6	(March 31)	—	—	—	393.09	463.94	11.50
Japan Portfolio (Japan)	1972	45.2	(Sept. 30)	502.29	406.60	304.13	346.31	370.72	9.00
Swissvalor (Switzerland)	1957	123.0	(May 31)	280.22	265.41	203.87	189.28	204.59	7.80
Intervalor (growth fund, Europe, overseas)	1969	86.8	(April 30)	102.99	95.35	75.04	61.86	64.77	2.10
Intercontinental Trust income fund, Europe, overseas	1939	61.5	(Aug. 31)	394.38	318.26	237.51	246.53	262.39	12.20
Universal Fund (balanced fund, Europe, overseas)	1960	93.6	(Dec. 31)	136.72	103.08	68.59	88.61	93.72	3.40
Universal Bond Selection	1970	1200.7	(Sept. 30)	113.94	94.67	76.40	78.06	80.57	5.65

TABLE 10–5
Real estate investment funds*

Fund	*Year founded*	*Total assets at financial year-end 1976 (in SFr. millions)*		*Price per share at financial year end (in SFr.)*					*Cash dividend per share, 1976 (gross, in SFr.)* †
				1972	*1973*	*1974*	*1975*	*1976*	
Interswiss	1954	366.8	(Dec. 31)	1,248.00	1,175.00	1,060.00	1,220.00	1,335.00	54.00
Swissimmobil									
Neue Serie	1949	541.5	(Dec. 31)	2,400.00	2,130.00	1,800.00	1,965.00	2,140.00	92.00
Swissimmobil 1961	1961	261.8	(Dec. 31)	1,125.00	1,170.00	960.00	1,075.00	1,080.00	45.00
Swissimmobil Serie D	1938	87.3	(Dec. 31)	4,100.00	3,950.00	3,020.00	3,350.00	3,510.00	115.00
Canada Immobil	1954	39.2	(June 30)	1,000.00	1,050.00	840.00	700.00	665.00	37.00‡

* Management: Société Internationale de Placements, Basle. Depository Banks: Credit Suisse, Zurich, and Swiss Bank Corporation, Basle.
†Subject to 35 percent Swiss withholding tax.
‡ No Swiss withholding tax deduction for unit holders domiciled outside Switzerland with bank declaration.

TABLE 10–6
Credit Suisse mutual funds

Fund	Year founded	*Total assets at financial year-end 1976 (in SFr. millions)*		*Price per share at financial year-end (in SFr.)*					*Cash dividend per share, 1976 (in SFr.)*
				1972	*1973*	*1974*	*1975*	*1976*	
Credit Suisse Fonds—Bonds (international bonds)	1970	1,289.5	(Oct. 31)	109.25	95.75	74.00	73.25	74.25	4.70
Credit Suisse Fonds—International (international shares)	1970	211.9	(Oct. 31)	115.25	96.00	62.25	67.50	65.75	1.90
"Actions Suisses" (Swiss securities)	1949	118.6	(April 30)	2,950.00	2,900.00	2,525.00	235.00*	251.00	8.00
Ussec (U.S. securities)	1951	60.0	(Aug. 31)	1,166.00	861.00	590.00	653.00	656.00	16.00
Canasec (Canadian securities)	1952	53.4	(May 31)	999.00	816.00	707.00	542.00	563.00	18.00
Europa-Valor (European securities)	1959	46.9	(April 30)	171.75	171.75	135.50	131.50	127.75	5.00
Energie-Valor (Energy-related securities)	1961	33.2	(May 31)	118.00	106.50	83.50	82.00	80.25	2.20

* Split 1:10 (October 1974).

TABLE 10–7
Union Bank of Switzerland mutual funds

	Year founded	Total assets Dec. 31, 1976 (in U.S.$ millions)	Price per share (in U.S.$) December 31					Last cash dividend per share (in U.S.$)
			1972	1973	1974	1975	1976	
Amca (U.S. and Canadian stocks)	1938	152.7	19.75	15.86	10.87	13.17	14.19	0.40
Bond-invest (International bonds)	1969	1047.1	28.57	27.48	27.08	27.86	31.14	1.83
Canac (Canadian stocks)	1955	31.5	44.81	42.96	30.04	33.21	33.69	1.23
Convert-invest (international convertible bonds)	1973	43.2	—	30.41	26.58	29.68	32.67	1.43
Denac (retail trade, food processing industries stocks)	1961	6.3	30.89	25.40	20.36	27.29	28.79	0.76
Espac (Spanish stocks)	1961	5.2	70.67	86.99	97.43	95.99	75.15	3.27
Eurit (European stocks)	1959	25.4	44.42	40.95	36.76	45.23	45.13	1.64
Fonsa (Swiss stocks)	1949	192.2	32.88	31.56	26.68	33.21	37.98	1.21
Francit (French stocks)	1959	5.3	29.30	29.56	22.33	31.87	24.91	1.12
Germac (German stocks)	1963	11.8	35.13	33.41	36.56	41.98	42.07	1.36
Globinvest (international stocks)	1968	103.2	28.77	24.79	20.16	24.81	26.96	0.77
Helvetinvest (Swiss fixed-income securities)	1971	52.6	27.31	29.93	35.22	36.87	42.72	2.25
Itac (Italian stocks)	1958	1.5	59.40	57.43	45.65	41.60	31.86	1.61
Pacific-invest (Pacific area stocks)	1969	39.7	34.74	24.48	20.55	28.82	33.29	0.85
Rometac-invest (raw material and energy stocks)	1972	22.3	133.78	143.80	115.42	122.33	130.08	3.11
Safit (South African stocks)	1948	37.0	64.04	88.38	118.38	84.73	49.83	5.56
Sima (Swiss real estate)	1950	519.5	43.22	53.12	68.38	66.41	71.06	3.23
Swissreal Series A (Swiss real estate) *	1960	16.0	34.87	39.11	37.15	44.27	52.48	2.28
Swissreal Series B (Swiss real estate) *	1962	27.6	29.04	31.87	30.83	37.02	43.50	1.97

* Prices on the Zurich Stock Exchange.

investment fund assets of Swiss banks exceed the Bourse's share capitalization by nearly six times.

GOLD AND PRECIOUS METALS

The first introduction many Americans had to Swiss banks occurred prior to gold ownership legalization. They bought their illegal gold through Zurich or Geneva in a frenetic atmosphere. Now the process is quite routine.

The Big Three Swiss banks have established the world's largest volume gold market both in spot and forward (futures) contracts. Zurich gold pool dealers are principals in the market. That is, they buy and sell for their own account and risk, with long or short positions as they see fit. The normal unit of sale is known as the "standard" bar of 400 troy ounces, at least 995 parts pure. When one obtains a Zurich quote on bullion, it is for this bar or larger quantities. For smaller sizes, say down to the one kilogram bar (32.15 troy ounces), you can expect to pay a premium over the standard bar price. This will vary from bank to bank, but a good rule of thumb is now 5–10 percent. Prior to U.S. gold legalization, estimates of 15 percent premiums were common. All the banks have gold counters where units as small as 10-gram bars may be purchased at daily changing prices. Premiums are built into these prices, so that as with anything we buy in small unit sizes, they will be more expensive than the standard unit.

Swiss banks will store gold bullion for you with no precise minimum requirement as to size lot. Their charge is 0.125 percent of value of gold stored, per year. However, another good rule of thumb for requesting safekeeping of bullion is, if you can carry it, don't ask your bank to store it. Swiss bankers will suggest you rent a safe-deposit box for storage of anything less than a 400-ounce standard bar, but will probably store down to one kilo bars if you are not planning to be in Switzerland.

Another point about gold spot purchases: In ordering gold from your Swiss bank, don't plan to buy odd amounts. Place orders for kilo bars and not odd-ounce sizes. Swiss gold does not come in 15-ounce or 50-ounce units, or in any in between except 32.15 troy ounces, one kilogram. Orders should be placed in kilogram units, and their small tola bars ignored in long-distance gold purchases.

Spot gold may be purchased on margin, as may silver, with varying percentage margins depending upon market conditions and bank. Thirty percent has been a common level for new accounts at the Big Three in recent years. Here, interest will be charged quarterly on the debit balance, usually in Swiss francs at the prevailing Swiss domestic interest rate. As the purchase is thus valued in Swiss francs, you will have both the gold price and the franc/dollar exchange rate to watch, assuming you'll take your profit or loss in dollars ultimately.

The gold futures market is a specialized side of the precious metals business at Swiss banks, but most of them will deal in it readily, again with varying margin (or more properly, security deposit) requirements. The standard forward (futures) contact, with maturities up to one year, is for ten kilos or 321.5 ounces. Again, a common level for security deposit on the contract is 30 percent for new business. However, the interest charges are calculated differently for futures than for spot. The security deposit at 30 percent is charged against the spot price with the prevailing Eurodollar interest rate charged for the full duration of the contract. For example, at a $150 per ounce price, 30 percent = $45/oz. security deposit. If Eurodollars were available at 6 percent and the contract was for one year, interest would be $9/oz. purchased. The total deposited would then be $54/oz., or $17,361 for a standard ten-kilo contract under the above terms.

One important point to note when dealing in gold at Swiss banks is that they usually act as principals, not agents, as do U.S. banks or brokerage firms. This means there will be no commission charges, per se, on Swiss gold. Their profit, other than interest charges, comes through the spread between bid and offer in the market itself. At any moment of the day there will be a retail spot price for Swiss gold, and it is upon this figure that all spot and forward purchases will be based. Spreads between bid and offer are generally $0.50 to $1.00 per ounce except in extremely fast-moving markets.

The above-noted margin or security deposits are very flexible, as I've indicated. Moreover, they can be modified by customer relationship. The banks' philosophy behind both capital and margin minimums, since they are not set by the central bank as in the United States, is to discourage speculation by those who cannot afford it. Once you have demonstrated sufficient capital depth through your relationship with a bank, your margin level could well be as much as ten percentage points less than the new account requirements I've discussed.

Currency futures contracts are calculated in the same manner as gold futures, with interest denominated in the currency borrowed at prevailing Eurocurrency rates, and charged quarterly. You should think in terms of a 20 percent margin guideline.

Swiss banks also deal in the whole panoply of metals, including silver (standard contract of 5,000 oz.), platinum, paladium, and so forth. Direct inquiries for terms are the order of the day.

PRIVATE BANKS

While dealing with the subject of investments, we must note the important role that the private Swiss banks play in securities portfolio management. The most significant part of this role has often been considered that of the unlimited liability of the bank partners in standing behind their portfolio management.

"The Swiss private banks," explained one private banker,

"have always had unlimited liability. This means the definition of such banks has required a partnership. And I believe this in turn has led clients to believe we might be more cautious with their funds."

The private banks were the forerunners of modern Swiss banking, establishing their operations even before the turn of the 19th century. This has led to their reputation of deep tradition, conservative methods, and for those now in operation, a belief that they are run by people of personal wealth and substance. Yet proof of this reputation is difficult to come by.

The private banks are not required to publish annual balance sheets as are the public banks. They do business in small, externally austere buildings, marked only with obscure brass plaques stating their presence. They are not permitted to solicit client business in any direct way. They discourage portfolios being brought to them under the substantial size of $250,000, although, as one bank partner remarked, "for close friends, we might take $100,000 or even $50,000." Friendship and references are the principal means through which the private bankers obtain their new clients. They represent the ultimate in privacy in a nation where privacy is both a legal and habitual watchword.

Some private bankers believed this was all about to be torn asunder when the largest in their midst incorporated. On January 1, 1975, Julius Bär & Co. of Zurich became a limited company, discarding the partnership mantle it had worn since 1895. While Bär officials explain the move as purely pragmatic, involving such mundane considerations as their heir's succession, social security taxes, and modern banking methodology, other private bankers weren't so sure.

"It could start a trend which can only end in all of us being forced into limited company status," observed another private banker with a frown. "A great tradition may be lost."

Bär partner Hans Bär agreed that a trend toward limited liability status will be forthcoming in the private banking group. "But it will be a matter of their seeing the significance of the tax legislation which went into effect in 1974, and its increased personal and partnership liabilities for social security taxes."

Over and above the ostensible reasons which mark the emergence of Julius Bär & Co. as a limited company bank (although it will still be closely held by the Bär family), are the more obvious considerations of protection of personal assets in the current era of wide swings in securities values, other major bank losses in foreign exchange, and perhaps most likely, the future need for capital to continue growth. Whatever the ultimate outcome, there has been no rush to incorporate, as yet.

All this notwithstanding, what can private banks do for you?

They will provide all the special services that go with asset management: accounting, special reports, tax return information, and personal consultations—if you have the portfolio size and contacts to be properly introduced to them. They dote on personal service.

"A client can visit our highest level officers, and always meet with the same people," offers partner Pierre Keller of Geneva's Lombard Odier. "Typically this means a partner, his assistant, and his secretary. We like to see our clients regularly, or at least correspond regularly with distant accounts."

I asked Mr. Keller what he would most like Americans to know about private banks in Switzerland. "We in the private banking group," he said, "attempt to be very professional, high-quality managers of securities portfolios. We would hope to stand up to any leading professional managers in comparison. This and personal attention to client requirements are our most important assets."

Perhaps behind this is the importance of the client relationship itself. From the initial question, "Who gave you the name of our bank?" asked by private bankers of persons requesting their services, to their conservative reputation and professional services with close client attention, it is the formation of a *proper* relationship with affluent clients that the private bankers desire most.

"It is said," offered one private bank partner, "that a banker is often a confessor to his client. Over the years, there is built up a tremendous mutual confidence between the two."

That is the sort of relationship private bankers would like you to believe in before sending your funds to them. When you do, be certain the funds are sizable as well.

SWISS BANKS' BEST SERVICE?

Your first visit to a major Swiss city will likely bring you face to face with one of the numerous electronic timepieces posted as sentinels outside jewelers' shops or banks. Most of these marvels tick off not only hours, minutes, and seconds, but tenths of a second as well. If your reaction to these Olympic-style timing devices is similar to mine, you'll wonder why passersby on a busy street need such precision. Sharp eyes can only recognize three or four tenths per second and then become glassy after five seconds.

Practicality isn't the point, of course. Those electronic hair splitters are positioned to demonstrate the watch seller's *capability;* he has a toy which cuts time into pieces virtually too small to see. Think of what else he might be capable.

The exposition of the fast electronic timepieces is similar in a real sense to the Swiss banks' multicurrency checkbooks. They both impress with their capability. Their usefulness is up to you. The banks want you to be aware that they deal in *any* currency; the jewelers, that precision is their hallmark.

For most people, the multicurrency checkbook, where you write on the blank check whatever currency you wish to use to pay a bill or invoice, will be far more useful than a rare timing clock or watch. In fact, an American resident of Switzerland throughout the 60s, who was intimately involved with Investors Overseas Services of Geneva, believes Swiss banks' multicurrency of checkbook is the *only* true advantage of Swiss accounts over other banks. Wherever you rank it, the any-money checkbook is a bright idea for anyone who travels or does business abroad, or who might in the future. And, it can be just as useful in the United States. A dollar check, no matter on which bank it is written, will probably be acceptable with proper identification. Only the collection time is different.

The multicurrency check function is simple. By writing a check in any currency you select, and without regard to the currency you hold in your Swiss account, you have at your disposal a truly international currency, and one which will be accepted anywhere a check is accepted. Paying a hotel bill in London? Write "£" on your Swiss multicurrency checkbook, pay the hotel directly in their currency, and avoid the usually barnwide spread that hotels offer in currency exchange. When the check arrives for payment, your Swiss bank will exchange funds from your account, no matter what currency the account is held in. Your account remains in its original denomination. And since the check will be paid by your Swiss bank as written in any currency, it is as simple to write as your U.S. bank's check.

This multicurrency checkbook is eminently useful in business as well. You receive credit for payment at the time the check is accepted by your foreign supplier or seller of services, since it is denominated in his own currency and will in turn be accepted directly by his bank. There should be no waiting for collection on his part.

The principal disadvantage—in fact, the only one I can think of, aside from letting the payee know that you have a Swiss account—is that the exchange rate between account funds and the foreign currency check is not determined until the check reaches your Swiss bank. This could be as long as one or two weeks from the date of presentation for a bill in any city outside Switzerland. If the exchange rate between the denomination of the bill and the denomination of your account in Switzerland moves against you during the check clearing period, you will lose something as a cost of convenience. On the other hand, if one had kept a Swiss account in Swiss francs over the past several years, the rate changes against most currencies would have had the effect of providing a discount on your bill or invoice, a pleasant dividend.

Thus, the Swiss have offered a device in the multicurrency checkbook which both advertises their capabilities in international currency handling and dispels the myth that Swiss francs aren't useful to anyone but those persons going to Switzerland. While there is certainly no guarantee that the dollar/franc rate will continue to benefit holders of francs in the future, if you have already made a decision to hold Swiss francs for appreciation potential the multicurrency checkbook will provide you with a useful tool while you're waiting. Besides, you can switch your account denomination to any other currency you wish without affecting your multicurrency check-writing capability.

A NUMBERS RACKET

I have left the subject of the Swiss banks' most infamous commodity for last in this chapter for the simple reason that I know of no other impractical idea about which more fuss has been made both inside and outside Switzerland. The "numbered account" is, with rare exceptions, a waste of both time and money. Attempting to establish one can set your relationship with a Swiss banker on entirely the wrong footing and will require a good deal of effort on your part.

Nicholas Bär put the matter bluntly "I consider the whole fuss over numbered accounts to have been launched by people who can't think. In computerized times all accounts are numbered. Since there is no legal difference between regular and numbered accounts, why should you want one?"

Bär has identified the first misconception about numbered

accounts: in Switzerland, since all accounts have numbers assigned to them, the famous phrase "numbered account" refers only to those which have the connection separated between the owner of the account and the number. Regular accounts do not. This is accomplished by holding "numbered account" records in number only when they are handled by regular employees of the bank. The bank's vault or minimum-access locked files contain the names corresponding to the numbers.

Still, some persons must have access to the connecting papers. The customer's man who opens the account will obviously know the tie. So will some back-office person and the secretary responsible for correspondence between the bank and the numbered account holder, unless it is always given in person. And the bank manager will have access to the name-number association record if he so desires. Compared with regular accounts, where any employee having to deal with the account, from the investment department on securities trades, to bullion or foreign exchange clerks and interest recording staff, can see the name on any account, the limitation to a few persons handling numbered account records is sharp. But it is not a fail-proof concept. This limited access only offers a degree of improved protection against inadvertent remarks or accepted bribes.

The active myths about the numbered account are still numerous, if gradually declining. The purest of these myths is that they are the only accounts afforded the full protection of the secrecy laws. Of course, we have already stated that all Swiss accounts have precisely the same legal safeguards, numbered or not. Correspondingly, violations of criminal statutes in Switzerland will pry open both numbered and regular accounts with equal ease.

The press made a good deal of fuss about the alleged numbered account into which Edith Irving deposited the McGraw-Hill funds, claiming that it was a "super-secret" account. There is no such thing. Moreover, Swiss Credit Bank later announced that the account was a regular account, not a "numbered" account at all. And the bank insists that it would have handled the matter of information about either a numbered or regular account in the Irving case in precisely the same manner.

The idea that numbered accounts are widely used in intelligence-gathering activities to wash informational money payoffs and other nefarious activities was probably true at one time. Intelligence services have used numbered accounts in the past, but such use has almost certainly lessened. Spies dislike nothing more than publicity, which they have certainly received in Switzerland. With the availability of several other bank secrecy havens in the world, few self respecting spies any longer need the difficulty of opening numbered accounts in the land of the yodel. What is more, regular accounts held by paper (but legally established) corporations serve the purpose just as well. Thus, much of that intelligence-gathering money which has not left Switzerland is probably buried under corporate facades in regular accounts.

The same conditions apply to Mafia/underworld money. The plausibility of past reportage of the Mafia/underworld use of numbered accounts has made the concept virtually irrefutable. But equally irrefutable is the high degree of probability that most such funds have journeyed away from the light of publicity, however shrouded by secrecy it might have remained for a time. On too many occasions the time period has been only temporary; and a temporary cover isn't worth the risk. What is more, any such illegal underworld funds almost certainly had to be placed in Switzerland without the complicity of any major Swiss bank. Now with all the fame gained by such potential uses of Swiss banks, the bankers have become both more aware and more diligent in ferreting out the simple masks used to cover these funds. Why should the underworld undertake the difficult in Switzerland when the simple will suffice elsewhere—say in Lebanon, Mexico, or Hong Kong?

Both the spy and Mafia uses of Swiss banks are likely, at best, overblown in their extent. The reality of use probably lies somewhere toward the minimal end of the scale, with just one certainty in the entire matter: no one can know the full reality, not even the Swiss bankers. We have only probabilities.

"Banks which must depend upon customer confidence for their business, cannot act fraudulently for long," offers Swiss Credit Bank's Dr. Mast. "The interest of honesty in dealing with customers is primary. A bad account, a shady customer, simply cost too much. Look at the cost of the Irving case." (Reportedly, it was upward of $100,000 in direct expenses for the banks involved.)

In addition to these myths, pure or diluted, there is the naïve belief in some quarters that one can open a numbered or regular account with equal ease. Not so. Partly because of the infamy which now surrounds numbered accounts, partly for legal reasons, Swiss bankers become suspicious when being asked by Americans to open these accounts.

"We are very reluctant for Americans," one major bank customer's man explained to me, "because Americans are required to declare existence of their foreign accounts to the IRS. Therefore, we must wonder why they want the most protected of secret accounts?" There may be reasons, he implied, but the modest request to open one will still be met with suspicion. This skepticism progresses to questions of those wishing a numbered account. They will always be asked in person; numbered accounts cannot be opened by mail in the practice of most banks. The apparently innocuous inquiry as to whether one will accept correspondence at home or business is another key for the Swiss banker. A negative reply for either address, or even a demurral, will raise further doubts about the legitimacy of the account. Why would one not want to receive unmarked Swiss letters at his most useful address?

"We will definitely refuse the account if we are concerned

about its reality," offered a banker, "and we will either refuse it outright, or set a very substantial minimum on it. One we are quite certain cannot be met." These numbered account minimums are usually left vague until other questions have been answered. As a result, one may hear amounts ranging from as low as $25,000 to that stated publicly by a "Big Three" bank at $100,000. The Swiss know that those prospective numbered account users who truly want the account will ante up. Only competition from smaller banks keeps the minimum size within reason. Some would say even that "reason" is a substantial deterrent to a numbered account. They're catching on.

Since numbered accounts must be opened in person only, the prospect will be asked to produce a passport identification and register the account in that name alone unless accompanied by others joining the account, also in person and with passports in hand. Most banks will not accept numbered accounts from corporations any longer, a function of dislike of the anonymity they afford, nor will they accept any "dummy" or anonymous names. I have yet to find a bank making an exception to the anonymous name prohibition, although I have been told that some small banks will.

Over and above these inquiries and roadblocks is the matter of references. With numbered accounts they are *de rigueur* at most banks unless you are already known to them. The reference matter requires a bit of verbal juggling on the part of the Swiss bankers, and in some cases references may be checked only for existence, not for direct inquiry about a prospective account holder. But of one thing you may be certain: Your Swiss banker cannot tell your reference his real reason for inquiry. To say that the inquiry is being made for the purpose of your opening a Swiss bank account would be an obvious admission that you were seeking one and prima facie evidence that one could exist. This is a potential violation of the bank secrecy laws, something fervently avoided. Instead, the inquiry to your reference may come as an alleged information request from a prospective business associate or a Swiss exporting firm wishing to extend you credit, but not for the purpose of opening a bank account.

If the foregoing hurdles haven't deterred all prospective numbered account holders, a final inconvenience can be added. Persons traveling outside the United States, as we've seen, are required to declare whether they are carrying $5,000 or more in cash on any one trip. There is nothing illegal about carrying the funds, but they must be declared. Since numbered account deposit minimums are substantially above this level, if the purpose of opening the account is maximum secrecy several trips would have to be made to avoid the traveler's identification to the U.S. Treasury. This transfer can be accomplished more readily by bank draft directly to the Swiss bank after formalities have been attended to on a personal visit, but the U.S. Bank Secrecy Act requires domestic bank notification to the Treasury of all transactions involving $10,000 or more. Thus, the multiple payment inconvenience is still left, if privacy is to be maximized. Even then, a record of all payments over $100 is kept on file at your bank, a product of the same act. That desire for privacy through a numbered account in Switzerland has taken on the aspect of being surrounded by a barbed wire fence. Funny, that seems to be what both the Swiss and the U.S. Congress had in mind.

What are the advantages of the numbered account? For nonresidents of Switzerland they are miniscule. As we have seen, the obvious one, increased secrecy protection, is both a sometime matter and a relative one at that. Increased secrecy does not come from increased legal protection, but only prevention of multiple-person access to bank records. This access can only be circumvented by specific information ferreting about a specific account, or bribes of connected employees. Formal legal proceedings undertaken from the United States, even under the new Mutual Assistance Treaty, require equal concurrence of a Swiss court for either regular or numbered accounts. Thus, the question is one of whether it is likely that anyone, including those attached to a U.S. government agency, would go to bribery efforts over your account. If so, the numbered account might be useful. If not, why bother?

There can be some advantage in holding a numbered account for inheritance purposes, but again, this same advantage applies to the regular account. Since there is no inheritance tax applied in Switzerland, someone wishing to draw on joint account funds held under individual signature rights could do so upon the death of one party without probate of the funds. But this would require the omission of such funds in U.S. reports required for estate purposes, a clear violation of U.S. tax laws.

Since these deterrents would seem to turn away all but the most ardent criminals or those persons with some other compelling reason to snare a numbered account, we can reveal that which most curiosity seekers will never see elsewhere. This is what a numbered account looks like:

430 879 XQ3

That's it, at least at one large bank. Two sets of three numbers followed by a combination of three letters or numbers. But this number varies from bank to bank. It can be any combination, or just numbers.

This is the way the issue of the numbered account stands. But, like other aspects of Swiss bank secrecy, it is under pressure for change, perhaps the most of all, as it symbolizes Swiss secrecy more than any other function.

"We could have done away with these because of automation," observes Alfred Matter, Central Director of Swiss Bank Corporation's Zurich branch. "They are not set by law. But now we have a new aspect: terrorists have come to us in Basle with names of customers asking for ransom." He adds,"Then too, there is the common market harmonization of the tax system. I would expect pressure from this source to be great to do away with the numbered account. In the longer prospect, I would think there would be some changes."

And yet, as anachronistic as numbered accounts may be, it is difficult to think of Swiss banks without them.

Whatever your feelings about numbered accounts at this juncture, you will probably agree that Swiss banks at least attempt to be one-stop financial shopping centers. At this I believe they succeed quite admirably. You should also, at this point, have a good idea of whether they will be useful to you in your financial planning needs. If a Swiss bank is, in concept, useful in your circumstances, an obvious decision is now in order: which bank?

chapter 11

TAKING ACTION

THE ACTUAL PROCESS of opening a Swiss bank account in order to avail yourself of the bank's bevy of services is simple, once a few decisions have been made, including how much money you'll deposit, the currency in which it will be held, and whether a savings type or current account will be most useful as openers. Since we have already dealt with the pre-opening aspect of those decisions, clearly the question of which bank to select is next on the agenda. And it is at this point that the expectations you have for use of a Swiss bank may limit your choices. What is more, you may go to great detail in analysis of potential banks, or you may follow a few simple steps and arrive at an equally useful answer, in my opinion.

For openers I recommend a personal visit to the Zurich or Geneva main offices of each of the Big Three major banks plus Bank Leu. In Geneva you will be dealing with a branch office, albeit a large one, just as Swiss Bank Corp.'s office in Zurich is a branch of its Basle headquarters. Selection of Zurich or Geneva for a first visit is suggested both for the scope of bank operations there and for your convenience. In Zurich, all four major banks, as well as Swiss Volksbank, are within a few hundred yards of each other on or adjacent to the Bahnhofstrasse.

My contacts at these banks won'd do you much good unless you're opening a sizable account, something over $100,000, as they're difficult-to-reach senior officers. One excellent exception occurs at Bank Leu, where Dr. Joseph Buschor, a friendly Vice Director whom I've met, will try to discuss your needs personally. His bank is the oldest (1755) of the public banks, and fifth largest in the country. Buschor has indicated his bank's interest in dealing with Americans, and points out certain advantages which may be pertinent: (1) a current account minimum of just $125; (2) their stated intention to give more personalized service than the other major banks; (3) their acceptance of a minimum securities portfolio or investment fund of $30,000, upon which they will advise provided you make the buy-sell decisions; (4) their importance as a gold dealer, having participated directly in the IMF gold auctions, coupled with a notable expertise and an inventory of old gold coins; (5) their in-house travel agency (also found at most of the other major banks) ; (6) their lack of branches in the United States which might be subject to financial "hostage" inclinations of the U.S. Treasury; and (7) their subsidiary in the Bahamas.

At the other major banks, an inquiry about new account information will bring you a visit with a junior officer who can readily explain all their services, minimums, and so on, and provide you with a large volume of literature. On request, if you evidence investment cash or portfolio worth upward of $100,000, he will probably provide an appointment with an investment manager specializing in your area of interest, be it gold, stocks and bonds, currencies, and so on. Other detailed queries will be answered by qualified persons if the junior officer is unable to do so. These queries should include your asking for the best method of communicating with the bank about (1) administrative details of your account, (2) your account balance, and (3) investment confirmations and performance. What you are looking for is assurance you will always have a name of an English-speaking person with whom you can talk by phone, if necessary, or write to.

Upon obtaining this information, their reading matter (designed to impress), and your feelings about the banks' suitability to your circumstances, you've covered the first important step in selecting a Swiss bank.

The second step is far simpler. Make mental note of the fact that these four banks survived the most recent postwar recession, went through World War II camped on the borders of both Italy and Germany, and weathered the Great Depression when they lost nearly 50 percent of their assets. (Union Bank, as previously noted, was reorganized into a new bank, but without loss to depositors. It has grown to become the nation's largest.) Whatever catastrophe may threaten your funds in the next 50 years you will have a most reasonable chance of surviving it with your assets in a major Swiss bank. If it doesn't withstand the financial storms, you may be sure few smaller banks will.

An interesting example of Swiss bank solidarity and cooperation was seen in April 1977, when the problem of anticipated losses by Swiss Credit Bank ($16.5 billion in assets) arose in its Chiasso branch. The details of how the losses occurred are unimportant, except to note that a Liechtenstein Anstalt was involved, but they were sufficiently grave to cause three of the branch's officers to be jailed pending investigation. The loss was estimated to be as high as $870 million by the Chiasso prosecutor handling the case. Despite Swiss Credit Bank's assurances that it had reserves far greater than any possible losses, the other two of the Big Three joined the Swiss National Bank in offering a standby credit of $1.2 billion to SCB. It was promptly rejected as unnecessary.

The intriguing aspect of this mutual aid offer is the introduction of the Swiss National Bank into the picture. A potential risk to the country's third largest bank was deemed consequential enough to muster the credit of the *nation* as well as the other major banks. Do you have any doubt that similar action would be taken under circumstances of a financial panic? Could you say the same about any of the smaller banks, such as those which have been allowed to collapse over the past decade? (See page 226.)

THE PROBLEM OF "LIQUIDITY"

The above method of detemining a bank's safety is certainly imprecise. You are relying on history and reputation in a country which has made much of both, but not looking at specific figures or other details. In addition to holding important personal conversations with your would-be bankers, I believe this is the most practical second step in determining safety. I would certainly not waste time calculating so-called liquidity ratios or other external financial measures. *In theory,* a liquidity ratio may be useful, but only under certain specific conditions. None of these would likely exist in a financial panic.

While more than one author has promoted the liquidity measure as important in determining a depositor's chance of surviving a run on a Swiss bank, practical circumstances suggest otherwise. Specifically, a liquidity measure does not give a real and useful indication of whether the last depositor in line to demand his or her money would get paid after all other depositors had demanded and received theirs during some type of panic. Second, liquidity ratios invariably lead users to the smaller closely-held banks, and history has proved them as a group to be the riskiest.

As a basis for discussion, let's take author Harry Browne's definition of liquidity—the ratio, expressed as a percentage, of claims on a given bank which can be presented without notice, but that can be covered by the bank's cash equivalent or "quick" assets. This means that if all depositors (potential claimants without notice) could be paid on the day they demanded funds there would be a 100 percent or greater liquidity ratio by the Browne formula. So *in theory* it is perfectly valid. But I said earlier that *practical circumstances* make such calculations useless in finding out whether the last man in line would get paid. The reason is time.

In the first instance, time from the date of the last balance sheet upon which the liquidity percentage was calculated to the day of the panic is critical. Since the major banks issue balance sheets quarterly and the majority of smaller banks do so semiannually, we have a time horizon of from one day to six months, depending upon the bank, during which something can happen to change that liquidity ratio. Since the only times when a full run on a bank is likely to occur are those of financial distress or when a bank is suspected of going under—times when things are bound to change fast—to expect that the 100 percent liquidity XYZ Bank had even a few weeks previous would remain valid, is to expect the very rarest of happenings. And that is to put it mildly. What about that most common of excuses, a "delay" in issuing a balance sheet?

What could happen to change the quick asset coverage of unexpected depositor demands if the bank is 100 percent liquid on its last balance sheet? Several things could occur, either singly or together, but all before you became worried enough to get in line for your money. Take one simple example: Suppose the owning group of industrialists of a small bank discovered difficulties in their manufacturing business and found it necessary to temporarily remove all but a small amount of their large deposits and at the same time to borrow twice as much on a long-term note secured by a mortgage on foreign plants? A seemingly sound deal, since of course they are the bank's owners. Now if we assign a value to these asset/liability changes we see the problem that, in reality, several Swiss banks have faced in the past few years. If the bank had 100 percent liquidity before the withdrawal and loan, and deposits drawn were equal to one eighth of the bank's short-term liabilities, and the assets drawn down in cash were twice that (under our example), or one fourth of the cash assets, the bank would be temporarily one eighth less than 100 percent liquid. If a "run" hit the bank before it was able to replace the liquid assets, or—more likely in a deteriorating financial situation—other new loan demand or financial market declines were absorbing cash assets more quickly than the bank could bring semiliquid assets to liquidity, some depositors simply couldn't be paid.

True, this is hypothetical. But consider two points about it: (1) few depositors could be aware of such developments prior to the "run," and (2) this set of circumstances could most likely occur in a small privately controlled bank rather than a large public one for the simple reason that the public bank would not have a private group of owners, and would be unlikely to have any deposit of sufficient size to obtain an eighth (or even a sixteenth) of the bank's assets in cash.

Some might say this couldn't happen in a small bank either. The board or the lending officers or someone would prevent it. But of course it could happen. The owners could engage in some falsification or other skullduggery, or they could simply rely on their power as owners and insist on the action.

Would they be so foolish? That depends upon the owners. In fact, several important cases of bank failure happened in Switzerland between 1964 and the present under just such circumstances. Two Swiss banks within the financial empire of one Julio Munoz collapsed under the weight of loans to his operating companies in 1963–64: Banque Genevois d'Epargne et de Credit, and Schweizerische Spar und Kreditbank. In 1967 the small, $7 million-asset Bank Germann closed its doors "in the interest of our clients" after the death of its founder Walter Germann under peculiar circumstances. It is generally believed, although not proved, that he and clients bled the bank after running into trouble with "hot" money deals. And the Arab Commercial Bank of Geneva closed for a decade in the mid-60s over asset ownership disputes involving Algerian Nationalist funds and Mohammed Khider. Indeed, nonpublic banks can and have collapsed under the tutelage of their owners. True, we don't have pre-collapse balance sheets to compare their liquidity ratios. We don't need them. If you understand the nature of bank assets and liabilities and the fact that a 100 percent liquidity balance sheet would not likely be published and valid on the day of a financial panic, you have most of what you need to know about liquidity ratios.

However, we can go a bit further. We can take two examples from 1976: Bankag Zurich, and Weiss Credit Trade and Investment Bank of Lugano. The former had the intriguing distinction of possessing a 130.9 percent liquidity ratio, according to author Harry Browne, on December 31, 1974. In fact, it ranked eighth on Browne's list of the 25 most liquid banks.[1] (None of the five largest Swiss banks was on this list.)

But, with utter disregard for Browne's ranking, Bankag, Zurich, collapsed in November 1976, also ignoring a better than 100 percent liquidity ratio, according to Browne's formula, on December 31, 1975. The announcement of its formal liquidation came in August 1977 when it was also revealed the bank had suffered losses of $12 million on assets of $9.9 million!

"The important thing about banks is the *quality* of their assets, not someone's definition of liquidity," says Swiss Credit Bank's Dr. Hans Mast. "We know some of these smaller banks which Browne has recommended have held highly speculative investment positions. For us, this formula is completely crazy."

Of course, Swiss Credit Bank, while the third largest and

---

[1] Harry Browne, *Harry Browne's Complete Guide to Swiss Banks* (New York: McGraw-Hill Book Co., 1976), p. 56.

oldest of the Swiss public banks, ranks low on Browne's list: 35.53 percent liquidity.[2] But it was large enough to acquire the sound remaining assets of our second example of 1976 failures, Weiss Credit Trade and Investment Bank. Admittedly, Weiss Credit had only an 80.36 percent liquidity ratio on December 31, 1975, before being taken over by Swiss Credit Bank. But the point remains, Bankag's 100 percent plus ratio and Weiss Credit's 80.36 percent ratio meant nothing to the later viability of the banks. Moreover, Swiss Credit Bank was able to absorb Weiss Credit and Chiasso branch drains and remain fully viable.

There is a further point to the usefulness of liquidity ratios: the second time factor, or how long it takes you to get in line for payment. Do you suppose that upon hearing about financial difficulties at your bank in Switzerland, your letter or cable demanding your funds will be acted upon in time? Possibly, but if the bank is experiencing a run, you'll get yours only if the bank is 100 percent liquid (or sufficiently liquid to pay off all depositors demanding funds) when your communication reaches them. And if the bank is truly in difficulty, your communication, even by phone, will not likely be treated the same way as a demand from someone there in person. It is simply too easy for the bank to blame nonpayment of a foreign demand on a computer, paperwork, or even the mail. Let's face it, a U.S. depositor would have a difficult time getting in the payment line at a Swiss bank in trouble, except by good fortune. That's the same chance you'd have if you never heard of a liquidity ratio.

If any further belief remains about the validity of a liquidity ratio in determining a bank's viability, the comments of a respected U.S. banker should put the matter to rest. Dr. Eugene Conatser, economist and vice president for planning at the Bank of America put it this way. "Analyzing

---

[2] Ibid., p. 59.

the liquidity position of a commercial bank beginning with some ratio of assets and liabilities according to maturity may be an interesting starting point, but is certainly not the end of the analysis," he explained. "A bank requires liquid assets in those situations where it is unable to avoid a reduction in deposits or other liabilities. In such situations, the maturity structure of assets is not a good indicator of potential cash flow." Most tellingly, he continued, "asset maturity as a first approximation is just as likely to give false hope as true security. In fact, no single ratio can give any useful information. Unless one is a highly sophisticated financial analyst, reading foreign bank statements is no more than an interesting pastime."

So much for liquidity ratios. If it is safety you want, deal only with the major banks, or accept some unknown risk in dealing with a smaller private bank, recognizing that if it has survived as long as the majors, under the same management, that risk is probably reduced. And, if at all possible, interview your prospective banker to give you an adequate feel that his concepts of doing business mesh with yours. Finally, if it is private and personal attention you want from your Swiss (or any other foreign banker), investigate dealing with one of the smaller branches of a major, public bank.

THE SIZE PROBLEM

The negative interest charge noted in Chapter 10 raised, perforce, the question of account size. It has also answered it in part: *maximum* size for savings accounts. But what about the minimums? Do they exist?

In very real terms, yes for both savings and current accounts. They are a simple function of individual bank rules, a handful of which are quite straightforward. The majority of the rules are not. They are highly flexible, especially at the major banks. The smaller banks usually establish minimums and publicly quote them out of their own best interests. They can and usually do require higher minimums than the major banks, especially when dealing with Americans, to provide more personalized service, they say.

Most people are of the opinion that they need a good deal of money to open a Swiss bank account. "They must be for the Big Boys," is a typical observation. This is not necessarily so.

The only practical rule of thumb for account size at Swiss banks is that the more funds you have, the more services you will be able to make use of and the more valuable the banks will be. Like a financial department store, a Swiss bank becomes more significant in your total financial plans as the number of products which you can use, grows. This concept does not exclude the average person with a few dollars to invest or place on deposit. It simply means that he or she will be tapping only a small portion of what Swiss banks have to offer, and that this situation must be compared with the inconvenience of doing so.

But the major Swiss banks, including the Big Three and the Cantonal Banks, will accept small deposits. It just pains them to do so. A senior official of a Big Three bank explained:

> It is terrible that we can't help the small man as much as we'd like. They need help in protection against inflation as much, probably more, than big investors. But how could we handle 10,000 new accounts for a few hundred dollars each? Staff costs alone would kill us. And yet, we have always offered our services to the smaller account, so we must continue.

Even more straightforward was the observation of another major banker. "We will take the small accounts because we feel we have to. But please don't encourage them. They cost us money."

Another banker raised the same points but upped the ante.

"We are in a delicate position now. We don't want every Peter and Mary in America sending a few thousand dollars to us. But we have always accepted any size account when it was given to us. Now we are getting too many. But how can we discourage them?"

The fact is that the major Swiss banks will accept accounts as small as $100 now, and even took $50 accounts a few years ago. The real question should be, for what reason do you want to put $100 in a Swiss bank? If it is only a token of total resources, don't bother a Swiss bank until you have sufficient funds handy to avail yourself of well more than a current account deposit. If it is the last $100 you have, don't send it to Switzerland—at recent inflation rates you'll need it here tomorrow for necessities. Even $1,000 is not considered important at Swiss banks, which are used to dealing in hundreds of thousands, as the Clifford Irving case revealed during my research on that subject.

Having obtained the details of the Irving hoax from a few bankers and several published reports, I wanted to verify them with the principal bank involved, Swiss Credit Bank. Dr. Hans Mast of that bank agreed to have his legal department look into the facts and verify what I had written. A short time later, I received a series of written comments on the facts, one of which caught my immediate attention. Where I had described the $50,000 which Mrs. Irving had deposited as "obviously a sizable account," the bank made the observation, "actually accounts of that size are rather frequent even for private persons." Obviously a big fish in the Swiss bank pond must have more weight to it, or so they would have us believe.

One can utilize any of nearly half the services available at a major Swiss bank for less than $5,000 per account. Something over $25,000 will permit use of several services at once or the lower end of the consequential category. But less than $2,000 will certainly get one in the door. And SFr. 1,000 will still secure a checkbook.

SOME DETAILS

A handful of specialized circumstances must be dealt with when holding a Swiss account, or even inquiring about one. Since they will cost you something in cash, time or both, they are worth noting.

The least expensive form of communication with Switzerland, the airmail letter, is also inordinately slow, despite the fact you can hop a plane and be there in one day. From the U.S. West Coast, allow five to seven days, and three to five from the East, assuming no special delays. Airmail requires $.32 postage per half ounce weight. A check sent airmail should take between two and three weeks to clear your U.S. account after your Swiss bank receives it, and can take longer. Up to six weeks isn't unusual. The process is a bit faster when a check is written on the Swiss account for deposit here, but not much.

Cable charges run in the $3 to $6 range for a standard length, depending upon the type sent, while telephone charges to Zurich are $6.75 for a three-minute station call from anywhere in the United States, and $12 person to person.

Time works against a caller from the United States, as well. When it is a convenient 10 A.M. for your Swiss banker, it is 2 A.M. in San Francisco and 5 A.M. in New York. At 10 A.M. in Chicago it is 4 P.M. in Switzerland, allowing only a one- to two-hour time window to reach your banker and conduct business, office to office. All calls from the United States should be placed in our morning to reach a Swiss banker at his office, and on the West Coast they must be placed before 9 A.M. So much for the convenience of personal communication.

Other costs of doing business with Swiss bankers are bothersome too. While those banks usually levy no monthly service charge on checking accounts, contrary to most banks' practice here, that holds true only until you do something with the account . . . such as transact business. Then you are charged a modest fee for almost everything. There is a charge to collect a check from a foreign bank, a charge for conversion to a different currency (that is, from dollars to Swiss francs), and several types of "handling charges." The holders of accounts at the ill-fated UCB, Basle, for example, while unable to do anything with their accounts for over a year, were charged a handling fee when the accounts were freed. The Swiss are paid for everything in one form or another.

Check writing, per se, costs you nothing at most Swiss banks. However, since the Swiss don't use checks as frequently as Americans (their local transactions are usually in cash), they name these accounts "current accounts" and require a minimum balance to issue checks as noted above. Granted, many U.S. banks levy similar charges for their international efforts; we rarely see them in an average domestic account. But with frequent activity in your Swiss account they can add up quickly. It is wise to ask a Swiss bank for a list of such charges when requesting information about opening an account.

Deposit guarantees

There is no such thing as deposit insurance on Swiss bank accounts, again contrary to practice in the United States where individual accounts are insured up to $40,000 by the Federal Deposit Insurance Corporation. (Never mind that the FDIC only has cash on hand for such insurance to the extent of less than 1 percent of the value of accounts insured.) The Swiss don't go through even that formality. In fact, it would be quite against their nature. One must presume the integrity and honesty of every bank. To do less would suggest some doubt about their tradition of stability and frugality, and even open their privacy to question. More than any insurance law, the Swiss bankers rarely allow any deposit to go unprotected as to its integrity. No Swiss bank has failed, including those that closed during the Depression, and left its accounts less than fully paid unless there was criminal fraud involved. And such instances have been at small banks. At UCB, Basle, depositors were paid off to the penny, and with interest where appropriate, by parent Western Bancorporation of Los Angeles, undoubtedly with more than gentle prodding by the Swiss banking authorities. The fact that depositors were without the use of their funds for a year does not alter the fact that they were paid in full in Swiss bankers' minds. Besides, it was an American-run bank, they say, with just a hint of, "what else could you expect?"

Swiss bankers operate, as does all of Swiss industry, on an informal collective guidance system, as we saw with Swiss Credit Bank, Chiasso. The Swiss might well charge a service or handling fee for protection in the event of a collapse, and major banks would attempt to support a closing bank where no evidence of fraud existed. Where a bank is run by a foreign entity, even though it must be Swiss controlled, there could be some conceivable leniency in delay of payment. Nothing is certain in this world. But few things are more likely than a Swiss banker's belief in protection of reputation, integrity, and ethics. Thus, the lack of deposit insurance should not really be considered a negative for Swiss accounts, given the above caveats.

TECHNICALITIES

The following are frequent detailed queries and answers which arise in holding a Swiss account.

Q: Can a Swiss account be opened in more than one name, and what are the inheritance ramifications of this?

A: Yes, a Swiss bank account can be opened by a husband and wife or other persons who are legally associated. However, as with any bank account in Switzerland or abroad, including the numbered accounts, signature rights are important. If there are individual signature rights on the account, any of the account owners may withdraw funds at any time upon presentation of the single signature. This may be advantageous in the event that either party in a joint account dies, in which case funds may be utilized or the account acted upon by the surviving party without any bank delays or Swiss government restrictions. In this regard it may be important to note that there are no inheritance taxes for nonresidents in Switzerland.

Q: Are commissions to purchase securities through Swiss banks higher or lower than the cost of buying directly in their country of origin?

A: Securities transaction commissions can be either higher or lower, depending upon the circumstances. They are higher by about half if the security is not issued by a Swiss company nor listed on a Swiss exchange. They are lower by about the same cash amount if the security is of Swiss origin or dually listed in its country of issue and on a Swiss exchange and purchased on the Swiss exchange.

Q: If a gain is made on securities bought through a Swiss bank is there a tax on the gain in Switzerland?

A: The only tax payable on returns obtained from securities in Switzerland is the 35 percent withholding tax on dividends or interest paid by the company issuing the security. There is no capital gain tax in Switzerland. However, the U.S. capital gain tax is applicable for U.S. citizens even though the securities are bought and sold in Switzerland.

Q: What are the advantages of a certificate of deposit compared with a regular deposit account in Switzerland?

A: Principally negotiability. A CD may be sold through a bank to a third party carrying its original rate of interest, where a normal deposit account is not a negotiable instrument. (This is also true in the United States.) In addition, CDs may be obtained through a Swiss bank via fiduciary deposits in the Eurocurrency market, sometimes for smaller amounts than the normal minimums of $25,000, thus yielding both high interest and negotiability. For example, June 25, 1977, bid rates for three-month Euromarket deposits were 5⅞ percent for dollars, ⅝ percent for Swiss francs, 4 percent for Deutsche marks.

Q: Are Swiss banks required to hold large liquid deposits as reserves against total deposits as a means of protecting account holders?

A: Yes, not only as a means of protecting depositors but to aid in halting the inflow of capital by making it less attractive for the banks to use. Cash liquidity requirements are approximately 15 percent of total deposits. This has two components. The First Liquidity, which must either be held by the bank concerned or deposited with the National Bank and which must be available on one day's notice, amounts to half of the cash requirement. The Second Liquidity, the other half of the requirement, can be deposited with any bank but must be available on 30 days' notice. In addition, 57 percent of all new current accounts, since 1972, have to be placed as reserves with the National Bank, although they can be counted against the liquidity requirements as well.

PAPERWORK

Account forms are simple at most Swiss banks. They will follow the format of Figure 11–1 for current and savings accounts with little variation. The forms will be sent upon your request, along with signature cards and general conditions.

You may also request a checkbook in any currency you wish; the major trading currencies are available. A checkbook which has no currency indicated can be obtained, allowing you to write checks in any money, irrespective of that held in your account.

Note at the bottom of the sample form that you must designate the method by which funds are being transferred to your bank. Maximum privacy will require a statement "in person," and your delivery of a cashier's check for under $5,000 per visit.

Once the current account has been opened, you will receive a letter similar to the following in confirmation:

Dear Sir (s),
We are pleased to confirm herewith having opened in your name on our books a (name of currency) current account at the following conditions:

Interest: None bonified on credit balances (or stating interest payable on savings accounts)

Turnover Commission: 1/20 of 1% per six months on the larger side of the ledger incl. balance. Items resulting from bullion, foreign exchange and stock exchange transactions effected through our intermediary being exempt.

The minimum charges are:
the equivalent of SFr. 5—up to a turnover of SFr. 10,000—the equivalent of SFr. 10—for a turnover exceeding SFr. 10,000— (incl. balance)

This account is subject to the general conditions printed overleaf. The number assigned to the above account is __________, which may, however, only be utilized in conjunction with the name of the account holder. Transfers in your favour must be payable to your name plus indication of the above punch-card number.

As acceptance of these terms, please sign and return the attached duplicate copy of this present letter.

Very truly yours,
YOUR SWISS BANK

FIGURE 11-1 A sample account form

Gentlemen:

I wish to open the following account(s) with your bank:

☐ Current (checking) account in ☐ Swiss francs ☐ U.S. dollars ☐ ____________

☐ Time deposit for _____ months in ☐ Swiss francs ☐ U.S. dollars ☐ ____________

☐ Cash deposit account

☐ Savings account

☐ Investment Savings account

Full name: Mr./Ms. ____________

Address: ____________

Nationality: ____________ Date of birth: ____________

Country of domicile: ____________

I wish to confer power of attorney on the following person(s):

1. Full name: Mr./Ms. ____________

   Nationality: ____________ Date of birth: ____________

2. Full name: Mr./Ms. ____________

   Nationality ____________ Date of birth ____________

All correspondence is to be ☐ sent to the following address ☐ retained by the bank

Name: ____________

Street: ____________

City & postal code: ____________

Country ____________

☐ I enclose check for ____________

☐ I instructed (name of bank) ____________

☐ to transfer the amount of ____________ to you in my favour.

____________ (place & date) ____________ (signature)

Thereafter, usually at six-month intervals, you will receive a statement indicating the transactions in your account for the period covered. It will be similar to that shown in Figure 11–2. The numbers included are for example only.

In addition, the statement will have totals for numbers of entries and the number of days the account has been held during the period covered by the statement. Statements are generally sent airmail and always, as is the case with any communications from a Swiss bank, without return address. The only indication of their origin will be the Swiss city postmark and "Helvetia" on the stamp or imprinted postage. If Swiss bank accounts are to be private, the Swiss believe they should be private from the postal employee as well as anyone else. (Despite IRS efforts to glean information from the imprints.)

The multitude of variables in attractiveness of Swiss bank accounts, and especially their recent changes, form a balance

FIGURE 11–2

(Bank name)

(City in which account resides)

Please examine this statement of
your account and report any discrepancies
to us within four weeks.

Kontokorrent per
Compte courant au
Current account as per (date)

(Account name)

Konte Compte Account
No:
123.456.07A

Wahrung
Monnaie
Currency
Franken

Datum Date	Test Texte Particulars	Val	SOLL DEBIT	HABEN CREDIT	Saldo Solde Balance
25 09 75	TRSF	18		11 459.55	11 459.55

scale for each person considering their use. I would doubt that the balance between pluses and minuses would be the same for any two people or families. But if you wish to "hide" money quite legally, Switzerland must be one of the leading places to consider. Of course, very personal requirements such as travel or residence plans, retirement, or children's schooling, may quickly tip the balance one way or the other. If those factors involve Europe, they may readily make a Swiss account a practical necessity since they reintroduce the deposit convenience factor.

Equally important, political and economic events of the next few years could compound your money-protective fears and alter today's balance of considerations. But it is likely to be in the profit-making potential of Swiss banks that the majority of your weighting will take place. Then, the greater your availability of funds and the greater your investment sophistication, the more Swiss banks will become attractive for a portion of your funds.

HAVEN ACTION

With the details of opening a Swiss bank account fully spelled out, we now return to the important matter of the specific steps to take in utilizing a tax haven, per se, perhaps in addition to the Swiss account. Following is a specific check list for haven action, the initial steps of which should be undertaken well before a firm decision to use a haven is made.

1. Spell out your objectives in detail. Before discussing your ideas and those in this book with an international tax attorney, make a detailed list of the goals you wish to reach through use of a haven. These might include, re trusts: keep some funds in a hard currency, acquire foreign property, provide for heirs/others with regard to present property/assets, have discretion over control of those assets until death; re companies: develop sales potential for *x*

product in countries *a, b, c;* seek foreign business partners, place royalty income from overseas/domestic sources in foreign company, and so on. You should be prepared to discuss with your international tax attorney the reasons why you wish to accomplish these objectives, and the reasons should go deeper than simply saving taxes. For example, the first three reasons given re trusts above, can be accomplished in the United States. You'll need a sound reason why they should be done offshore to justify the expense and time required.

2. From the information provided herein and from any other sources you may have developed, list which tax havens could be used to accomplish the objectives in (1) above. Due to the similarity of laws in many havens, this list will likely include several havens. Now, go over the list and reduce it as far as possible through use of the Tax Haven Comparison Table found on p. 42. Certain of these factors may weigh more heavily than others in your personal circumstances and beliefs. Don't forget to consider the havens listed in Chapter 7, The Missing. Certain of these may be more appropriate than those listed in our comparison.

3. Specify the assets available for use under your objectives, both now and for the expected future. It will be helpful to break down the asset availability by rough time periods, for example, immediate, 6 to 12 months, two to three years, five years, or more. This will be of use to your tax advisor in planning haven development under your objectives.

4. Determine the costs you would be prepared to stand to accomplish your goals. Note the incorporation and trust establishment fees specified in this book, and keep in mind that legal and tax advisory fees can easily run well into four figures, sometimes five. Therefore, initial use assets should exceed $100,000 to prevent the start-up costs from absorbing excessive principal. My rule of thumb is that total start-up costs should run no more than 5 percent of initial assets deployed.

5. You are now ready to begin your first consultation with an international tax adviser. Your local tax adviser or attorney should be able to refer you to someone well versed in this field.[1]

6. Your first discussion with an international tax lawyer should center on the viability of the objectives you have determined and the list of havens which you believe might be most useful for their attainment. In this regard, the most recent developments in U.S. tax law and in local haven law should be at the top of the agenda. Local haven laws change quite rapidly, and while these changes are not usually monumental in the long established havens, they can have a bearing on the suitability of a given haven for your objectives. The tax attorney will likely be up-to-date on any changes, plus changes in U.S. tax rulings and court cases. Become familiar with them and develop your haven use plan in light of them.

7. As you may have noted in the previous pages, I believe in direct visits to the foreign country in which you wish to do business. While this can be avoided on the advice of your international tax lawyer as being unnecessary in your circumstances, a far better feel for the undertakings can be secured through a personal visit. Moreover, you will require the services of a local haven attorney in establishing an entity in your chosen haven. A trip to the locale will give you an opportunity to personally discuss your plans and objectives with him, plus any bank, trust company, or accountant you may require. Your tax lawyer should be able to make the appropriate referrals.

---

[1] The author maintains a preplanning service for tax haven use, where for a few hours' time-expense, a plan ready for legal implementation plus referral to a respected international tax attorney can be obtained. Address correspondence to:

Robert Kinsman
International Tax Planning
P.O. Box 881
San Rafael, CA 94902

Contacts

Some people wish to do their own direct contact work in any place of potential business, and may want to do so prior to contacting an international tax attorney or other foreign financial planner. For these reasons, we have compiled the following list of reputable financial institutions in the havens we have visited. Again, a personal visit is most desirable, although correspondence addressed to the managing director of the institution should be answered in due course.

The Bahamas

Bahamas International Trust Company
Post Office Box N7768
Nassau, Bahamas
Phone: (809) 322–1161

Wobaco Trust Limited
Post Office Box N9100
Nassau, Bahamas
Phone: (809) 322–7411

RoyWest Banking Corporation, Ltd.
Post Office Box N4889
Nassau, Bahamas
Phone: (809) 322–4500

The Cayman Islands

Cayman International Trust Company, Ltd.
Post Office Box 500
Grand Cayman
British West Indies
Phone: 9–4277

World Banking & Trust Corporation (Cayman), Ltd.
Post Office Box 1092
Grand Cayman
British West Indies

Swiss Bank and Trust Corporation, Ltd.
Post Office Box 852

Grand Cayman
British West Indies
Phone: 9–4231

The Channel Islands

Barclaytrust International, Ltd.
Post Office Box 82, Barclaytrust House
39–41 Broad St.
St. Helier, Jersey
Channel Islands
Phone: 0534 73741

Wobaco Trust (Jersey) Ltd.
11 The Esplanade, P.O. Box 120
St. Helier, Jersey
Channel Islands

Liechtenstein

The General Trust Corporation, Ltd.
Vaduz, Liechtenstein

The invisible hand

We have stressed throughout this book that the prospective user of foreign tax havens should become familiar with (to the degree possible) and pay attention to pertinent aspects of the U.S. Internal Revenue Code and the appropriate rulings and cases affecting the type of entity being considered. To prevent memory slips on this point, the Internal Revenue Service requires that several information tax returns be filed when one is involved with foreign entities. The following list identifies the most important as of September 1977.

Form	*Covering*	*Who must file*	*When required*
4683	Foreign bank accounts	Anyone with financial interest in or signature authority over a foreign bank account	Annually
3520	Foreign trusts	Person (s) who create a foreign trust or transfer assets thereto	90 days after creation or transfer
957	Foreign personal holding companies; general corporate information	U.S. persons acting as officers, directors, or shareholders of a foreign personal holding company	Annually
958	Foreign personal holding companies; company financial information	Same as 957	Annually
959	Any foreign corporation	U.S. persons acting as officers, directors, or shareholders of any foreign corporation	90 days after subscription of corporate shares
3646	Controlled foreign corporations	U.S. persons who own 10 percent or more of a controlled foreign corporation	Annually
2592	Controlled foreign corporation; financial information and dealings with controlling shareholder	Any U.S. person who controls more than 50 percent of voting stock of a controlled foreign corporation	Annually

chapter 12

MERE CANT

> *Over and over again courts have said that there is nothing sinister in so arranging one's affairs as to keep taxes as low as possible. Everybody does so, rich or poor, and all do right, for nobody owes any public duty to pay more than the law demands: taxes are enforced exactions, not voluntary contributions. To demand more in the name of morals is mere cant.*
>
> JUDGE LEARNED HAND

THE FOREGOING is reprinted here because it is simply the *raison d'être* for this book. It makes clear that there is a distinction between tax evasion and tax avoidance. The former is illegal. *Tax avoidance* is legal and it is indeed mere cant to asperse efforts to pay the minimum tax allowed by law.

I have stressed that there is every reason to resist, within the law, the three pressures discussed in Chapter 1: inflation, the "equality in poverty" bias of our liberal politicians, and the invasions of privacy by federal and state officialdom. We must understand that the Bank Secrecy Act and the Tax Reform Acts of 1969 and 1976 are as serious in their personal economic consequences as steady inflation, the collapse of the dollar, and high unemployment. Real financial risks exist when these political and sociological factors are at work. We must protect our financial freedom by using every opportunity the law permits. If you can avoid taxes and retain your financial freedom by applying what you have learned in this book do so.

As a preparation for dealing with the complexities of our tax laws as applied to tax havens, we have observed the enormous complexities of our whole tax code. The portions applicable to haven use are only in certain areas more devious than what could be termed the *involution mean* of the overall code. We have seen the necessity of some familiarity with this ravaging monster on two levels. The first level is at the preplanning stage where one can determine whether haven use is possible or potentially important before incurring sizable professional fees. To accomplish this is the purpose of this book. The second level is to become aware of the pitfalls into which tax haven users can fall, not the least of which are the costs of U.S. tax code and foreign law complexities transmitted through the need for two attorneys, probably a fair amount of travel and research time/expense, and varying amounts of soul searching, depending upon the reader.

We have journeyed to four havens in search of legal caches through the eyes of three common potential haven users, touching on both the diverse options open (or closed) to them, and the havens' local flavors. And, we have brought the important low-tax nation of Switzerland under the microscope for the prominent role its banks can play in fending off two of the three dangers to financial freedom, as well as their position as doorstep to the havens themselves.

There will be, undoubtedly, some readers who feel a

twinge of guilt (albeit fleeting) at contemplating the tax-free accumulation of wealth in secret. To those twinges of guilt I would inquire, where stands our total freedom in the absence of financial freedom?

BIBLIOGRAPHY

COUNTING PERIODICALS, it is possible that international taxation has been the subject of more written opinion and comment than any other topic on the international scene except travel. Langer's book, for example, devotes 60 pages to reference materials. However, there are only a handful of fundamental books covering the broad range of tax havens world-wide. They are noted here alphabetically for additional reading on the subject.

Diamond, D. B., and Diamond, Walter H. *Tax Havens of the World.* Matthew Bender & Co., Inc., 235 E. 45th St., New York, N.Y. 10017. The basic edition, published in 1974, is updated periodically (loose-leaf). Contains individual chapters on more than 20 havens.

Grundy, Milton. *Grundy's Tax Havens,* Bodley Head Ltd., and HFL, 9 Bow St., London, WC2, England, 1974, 160 p. Grundy has edited this volume which contains chapters on some 15 havens, principally written by local trust companies.

Langer, Marshall J. *How to Use Foreign Tax Havens.* Practising Law Institute, 810 Seventh Avenue, New York, N.Y., 10019, 1975, 254 p. Prior to the Tax Reform

Act of 1976, the definitive work on tax havens for Americans.

Spitz, Barry. *Tax Havens Encyclopedia.* Butterworth & Co., 88 Kinsway, London, WC2B 6AB. Edited by Spitz and written by attorneys in some 20 havens, this is a loose-leaf service which is continually updated. Its price of £40 includes all current additions.

In addition to the above extensive surveys, some periodicals and newsletters feature updates of current developments in the havens and international taxation in general.

International Tax Report, Institute for International Research, Ltd., 30 E. 42d St., New York, N.Y. 10017. Approximately 8 pp. published biweekly.

Foreign Tax and Trade Winds, Walter H. Diamond, Matthew Bender & Co., Inc., 235 E. 45th St., New York, N.Y. 10017, a monthly newsletter supplement to three loose-leaf volumes.

Financial Times Tax Newsletter, Bracken House, Cannon Street, London EC4, England, a monthly survey of tax developments around the world.

Basic Data on The Economy of ______, and *Establishing A Business In ______,* Overseas Business Reports, U.S. Department of Commerce; Superintendent of Documents, Government Printing Office, Washington, D.C. 20402. Periodically updated reports on several important foreign nations.

Foreign Tax Law Bi-Weekly Bulletin, Foreign Tax Law Association, Inc., P.O. Box 2187, Ormond Beach, Florida 32074. Current tax changes in all nations.

INDEX

U

V–Z